FIBONACCI SEQUENCE

A NOVEL

J. MICHAEL STEPHENS

To order additional copies of this book, contact:
Xlibris Corporation
1-888-795-4274
www.Xlibris.com
Orders@Xlibris.com
27037

DEDICATION

"In life we shall find many people that are great, and some that are good, but very few people that are both great and good."

Charles Caleb Colton

This novel is dedicated to Delmer Cummins, Ina Cummins, Harold Hudson, Bonnie Byron Beard and Tina Beard. Five people I was blessed with in my life who, were and are, both great and good.

INTRODUCTION

FACT: Fibonacci Sequence {fee-boh-nah'-chee}—A Fibonacci sequence is one in which each term is the sum of the two terms immediately preceding it. It is named for its discoverer, Leonardo Fibonacci (LEONARDO PISANO). The numbers may also be referred to as Fibonacci numbers. Fibonacci sequences have proven useful in number theory, geometry, the theory of continued fractions, and genetics.

One industrious young computer programmer in Dallas applied the Fibonacci theorem in creating an analytic solution to cryptographic systems. As the majority of the computer mainframes and networks throughout the world are protected using the Data Encryption Standard (DES) developed by IBM in 1976, the young programmer now had the "key" required to access any mainframe system he chose.

FIBONACCI SEQUENCE

July 27, 2005

Clay Peterson, a young computer programmer, worked on his computer at home in Dallas, Texas. He had successfully accessed the mainframe computer system in major Swiss and Canadian banks. He was able to enter the system by developing a revolutionary method of cryptanalysis. Clay now attempted to recreate one of the accounts that he discovered while searching through the data stored within the banks' computer systems.

SAC Brian Whitfield was in a staff meeting at the Hoover Building in Washington. The associate director of the FBI informed him, along with the other FBI special-agents-in-charge, that the DEA was involved in a major assault upon the drug cartel in Colombia.

Alberto Rojas, leader of the Medellin drug cartel, discovered that ten million dollars was missing from a cartel bank account in Switzerland. He ordered his people to locate those who were responsible for the disappearance of the money.

Special-Agent-in-Charge Brian Wilcox and Alberto Rojas would both begin their search for the young computer programmer in Dallas. One wanted him for what he had. The other wanted him for what he had done.

Neither of these men would have ever known the name "Clay Peterson" had it not been for THE FIBONACCI SEQUENCE.

CHAPTER ONE

ARTICLE 1

July 24, 2005, 2:35 p.m.
Comp-Link Corporate Headquarters, Irving, Texas

Clay Peterson sat in his cubicle, holding a cold cup of coffee, staring at his computer monitor. His eyes were focused on the screen. However, his thoughts were elsewhere. Clay's mind was far from the confines of his small cubicle in Dallas. At the moment, he was imagining himself on a beautiful palm tree-covered, sparsely populated island. He dreamed of living where the sun always shined and the ocean was the same light blue as the cloudless Caribbean sky. It looked as though it ended only when it reached the horizon. The sunsets were a fiery, breath-taking, and intense visual display filled with soft orange, yellow, pink, and vermillion hues. Of course there was a woman. Oh yes, there was a stunningly beautiful scantily clad young woman on his arm watching the sunsets with him each evening. Clay would embrace her, and she him, and give her a passionate kiss as the sun disappeared until the morning. Then they would begin their daily ritual of making love under the moonlight with the gentle and soothing sound of the waves breaking on the beach in the background.

This was Clay Peterson's fantasy. In reality, Clay was a twenty-five-year-old computer nerd living in Dallas, Texas. Without realizing it, he looked and dressed the part to perfection. He stood just over six feet one inch in height, weighed 175 pounds, wore dark-rimmed glasses with thick lenses, and tied his shoulder-length black hair back in a ponytail. He dressed in a manner which would suggest that he did not know how to iron and that he was color blind or did not care if his clothes were color coordinated. Clay was employed by Comp-Link, a Dallas-based computer software development firm specializing in the development of networking software. He had been with the company since graduating from college with a computer science degree three years prior. He loved his work, and excelled at his job as a lead programmer. His job was all that he had, however. Clay was an introvert, avoiding social situations and functions of any kind. He did not date, even though despite his dress women found him to be attractive. He was not gay, and he was not a virgin. His eighteen-year-old babysitter had seen to that when he was just fourteen. Clay liked women, admired and appreciated their beauty. However, he was cursed when an opportunity to have a conversation with one presented itself. He had one true passion, one true love, and only one hobby: his computer.

The sound of his name being spoken interrupted Clay's thoughts of the beach and his stunningly beautiful partner.

"Clay? Clay, are you all right?" the female voice asked.

Clay was startled and sat up quickly in his reclined chair. While leaning forward, he spilled the cup of cold coffee in his lap.

"Lisa!" Clay said in surprise as he stood with coffee stains covering the crotch of his pants.

"I'm sorry, Clay . . . I . . . I didn't mean to startle you," Lisa said.

"No . . . no, you didn't . . . startle me. I . . . was just thinking about the PASCAL algorithm problem I'm trying to resolve with the data-storage specifications for the new payroll software project," Clay said while trying to look even a little dignified as he stood in front of her.

Lisa Tinsley worked in the distribution department of Comp-Link. She was twenty-four years of age. Clay thought that she was a stunning sight to behold, as did all the male employees at Comp-Link. He had been discreetly watching her since she joined the company three months ago. Lisa was a petite woman with a sculptured figure. She had long silky fair hair, striking blue eyes, and a bubbly outgoing personality. She loved sports of all kinds. Lisa spoke of her abilities as a tennis player and golfer, and she enjoyed watching and attending contact sports like football and hockey. She was single. However, unlike Clay, her social calendar was full more often than not. Every single male in the building had taken a shot at asking her out, but she always had a prior engagement. Clay knew all about her. He had accessed her personnel file from his home computer the first day he saw her.

"Can I talk to you for a minute?" Lisa asked.

"Uh . . . Sure . . . Yeah, come on in and sit . . . down," Clay said as he looked around his cluttered cubicle, realizing that there was no place for her to sit.

Clay walked nervously to a chair that had a stack of files and analysis reports on it. He picked up the stack of papers and started toward a corner of the cubicle. He tripped over his briefcase lying in the middle of the floor and the papers went flying across the floor as he fell. He jumped up quickly, slipping on the loose documents under his feet as he attempted to stand.

"Are you okay?" Lisa asked trying to hold back a smile.

Clay could feel his face flushing with embarrassment as he stood fumbling his hands between his pants pockets and his hips.

"Yeah, it happens to me all the time."

Lisa sat in the chair Clay had prepared for her. Clay walked around his desk and sat in his chair. He watched intently as Lisa crossed her legs. He quickly moved his eyes from her thighs to her eyes when she spoke.

"Clay, I want to move into sales. A position is opening in August and I want to apply for it."

"Oh . . . Lisa, you would be really great in sales. Really."

"Thank you, but I need to have a working knowledge of the software we develop. I know how to package it. I know how we distribute it and I have a reasonably good understanding of our marketing strategy. Now I need to formulate an understanding of how we develop it and how it works in the field before I can knowledgeably sell it."

Clay looked at her supple red lips and blue eyes as she spoke, hearing only half of what she said. He was daydreaming about his ocean and sunsets again. This time he was with Lisa on the beach.

"Do you understand what I mean?" Lisa asked.

Clay shook his head as if to wake himself. "Sure . . . Yes . . . I mean you should have an understanding of the development process and application if you are going to be in sales. But why are you telling me?"

"I want you to teach me."

"Teach you? You want me to teach you?" Clay said in surprise.

"Well, yes. I can't think of anyone better qualified to teach me. You design the software, and you could be a great deal of help to me in learning development and application."

"You want me . . . to teach you," Clay said more to himself than to Lisa.

"Dumb idea, huh?"

"No . . . Oh no, I would be happy to teach you. Really, I would be more than happy," Clay said quickly.

"Great! What are you doing tonight?"

"Tonight?" Clay said, again in surprise.

"Yes, I thought that if you weren't busy we could get together and start."

"Start?"

"Yes, you could start teaching me tonight. Is that all right?"

"Well yeah, it's all right with me. Do you want me to teach you here in my cubicle?"

"No, I don't want anyone to know what I'm doing. Do you have a computer and programs at your house?"

"No . . . I mean yes I do, but you don't want to come to my house."

"Why? I don't mind."

"Well, I live by myself. My house is a wreck. Really, it's a total wreck. All I do is sleep and work there, and I don't really spend much time cleaning up."

"Clay, I lived with four brothers when I was growing up. I can assure you that I've seen everything. It won't bother me."

Clay thought for a moment. If he could get off a little early, he could go home and clean the living room and kitchen. Those were the only rooms she would be seeing. Oh, and he would have to clean the bathroom as well. He knew he did not have to worry about her seeing any of the bedrooms. That would be another daydream.

"Okay . . . we'll do it at my house . . . I mean I'll teach you tonight . . . I mean why don't you come over about seven?"

"Seven sounds good. Where do you live?"

"Twenty-three seventeen West Sage. It's not far off the LBJ near North Park Mall."

"I live close to the mall too. I'll give you a call before I come over. Don't eat anything before I get there. I'll bring a pizza and some beer with me if that's okay."

"Sure . . . pizza and beer are the main staples in my diet."

"Good then, it's a date," Lisa said as she stood and walked to the cubicle exit.

"Okay . . . it's a date," Clay responded, not believing he had just spoken those words to Lisa.

Lisa stopped before leaving the cubicle and turned to Clay. "You're in the book, right?"

"The book?"

"The phone book. I can get your number out of the phone book?"

"Oh yes, the book. I'm in the book. Under Clay Peterson," Clay responded.

"Okay," Lisa said with a slight frown and grin on her face.

After she left his cubicle, Clay sat and thought about what he had just experienced. "Under Clay Peterson. You idiot. Why didn't you just say yes?" he said to himself.

Clay Peterson's house was in a quiet new middle-class Dallas neighborhood. Clay leased the house under a lease-purchase agreement he had negotiated with the builder six months ago. It was a three-bedroom two-car garage 2200-square-foot brick home. The lot had a large fenced backyard without trees. Clay could have qualified to purchase the house with the money he had in savings along with his thirty-four-thousand-dollar annual salary at Compu-Link. Buying, however, prompted a sensation of permanency, and Clay was not ready to sink any roots in his life at twenty-five. He wanted to remain mobile, free of any long-term personal or financial commitments until absolutely necessary. His measure was marriage, and he did not believe that he would be faced with that decision for some time, if ever.

Clay pulled his 1972 red Volkswagen Beetle into the driveway and pressed the garage door opener. As the door reached the top of the opening, he drove the car into the garage. He got out of his car and opened the door leading from the garage into the laundry room. The laundry room was piled high with clothes. He could not distinguish clean from dirty anymore. Clay waded through the clothes that blocked his path, using his briefcase to knock piles down and out of his way. Once he had walked the gauntlet, he entered the kitchen. It was a disturbing sight. Fast-food packaging was stacked high on the cabinets, table, and chairs. He grabbed a trash bag out of one of the cabinet drawers and began moving around the kitchen, throwing the fast-food containers, boxes, cups, sacks, and in some cases dried food, into the bag. To his surprise, the kitchen did not take very long to straighten up. It didn't look half bad with all the trash out of the way.

He moved from the kitchen to the den and from the den to his office. After he had straightened up the office area, he went to the guests' bathroom. It was in quite good shape because no one had ever used it. Clay could not remember the last time he had even been in there. He made sure that the toilet paper holder had a fresh roll of paper and that there was a fresh bar of soap at the sink.

When he finished with the bathroom, he closed all of the bedroom doors. He then walked through the house another time to make sure that nothing had been missed. As he walked through the kitchen, he noticed a stench in the air. He thought that it must be left over from the moldy food he had just thrown in the trash. He panicked because he knew he did not have any room freshener. Why, he thought, would he have ever had the need to buy a room freshener? No one ever came to see him. He finally found a spray can under his bathroom sink. Clay read the label. It was a can of athlete's foot spray he had purchased several months ago when he experienced itchy feet. He sprayed a sample into the air and put his face in the mist as the spray dissipated.

"Smells okay to me," he said as he left his bathroom with the spray can.

Clay walked through the house confidently spraying the foot medication. When he finished, he stood in the kitchen with a look of satisfaction. The phone rang interrupting him.

"Hello."

"Clay, it's me Lisa. Listen, I've ordered the pizza and I'm ready to come over if it's okay."

Clay looked at his watch and saw that it was only 5:45. He had not taken a shower or changed clothes, but he was not about to tell her no.

"Sure, come on over. Do you know how to get here?"

"We only live a couple of blocks from each other. I live in the Castle Rock apartments on Commerce across from the mall, and Sage is just south of here."

"I know where you live. Yeah, that's right. Just drive south on Commerce and turn left on Sage. I'll be here."

"Thanks, I'll see you in a bit."

Clay was in a panic again, this time over the way he looked. He did not want her to see him in the same clothes he had worn to work. He dashed to the laundry room and began sifting through the stacks of clothes. He found an old pair of Levis, smelled it for any odor, and finding none, placed it over his shoulder. He continued his search, now for a relatively clean shirt. He found a T-shirt imprinted with "Women Love Computer Hacks Because They Know How to Fax with a Modem." He looked at the shirt for a moment, shook his head, and threw it back in the pile. He finally found a white T-shirt with the USC Trojan emblem on it. It was clean and surprisingly free from wrinkles. Clay had attended the University of Michigan and had no idea where the Trojan T-shirt came from.

He ran back to his bedroom and changed quickly into his casual clothes. He went to his bathroom and looked at himself in the mirror. Clay's hair was looking good with the ponytail neatly combed, and he was proud of his T-shirt-and-jeans combination. He wondered how he smelled, however. He looked around the bathroom and under the sink without finding cologne of any kind. Then he spied the can of foot spray he had used earlier, sitting on the counter. He thought for a moment then sprayed each armpit with the foot deodorant. Clay walked back into his bedroom and began a search for a pair of tennis shoes he knew was buried under the books and clothes that covered his floor. He found the shoes and sat on his bed to put them on. When he finished, he sat for a moment to catch his breath. Then he heard the door bell.

Clay jumped off his bed and dashed down the hall. As he turned toward the door, he remembered that his bedroom door was open. He abruptly turned and ran back to his room, closed the door then ran back to the front door. He stood for a moment to compose himself then opened it.

Lisa stood in front of him holding a pizza box and a sack containing a six-pack of beer. She was wearing a tank top that left little to the imagination regarding the size of her breasts and the firmness of her nipples. She had on a pair of cutoff blue-jean shorts, and wore tennis shoes with half socks. Her hair was tied back in a ponytail, exposing every beautiful feature of her face. Clay stood in awe of her.

"Sorry I'm so early."

"It's okay. Really, it's . . . okay," Clay said as he continued to stand in the doorway.

There was an uncomfortable silence as Lisa stood holding the food and drinks while Clay looked at her.

"Can . . . I come in?" Lisa asked.

"Oh, I'm sorry. Please come in, and let me take that for you," Clay said as he took the pizza and beer.

Lisa walked into the house with Clay following her. She walked into the living room and sat on the couch. Clay again stood watching her while he held the pizza and beer.

"Clay, I think you might want to put the beer in the fridge before it gets too warm."

"Yeah, the beer. Right."

Clay took the pizza and beer to the kitchen. As he was putting the beer in the refrigerator, Lisa spoke to him.

"I think you have a nice house, Clay."

"Thanks, I like it. It's comfortable for me anyway."

"You keep it clean. I thought you said it was a wreck. It even smells almost antiseptic."

Clay thought for a moment before answering. "Thanks, it's a new kind of air freshener my mom sent me. I'm glad you like it."

Clay prepared a plate of pizza for each of them, placed napkins on the plates, held two beers, and took the dinner into the living room to Lisa.

"Hey, thanks. I would have fixed my plate."

"That's okay. I was glad to do it. You cooked so I serve. Would you like some music?"

"No thanks. Why don't you start telling me how you do what you do for the company?" Lisa asked.

Clay had just taken a bite of pizza. He chewed the mouthful of food and thought about what she had asked and how he would explain his job to her. He still had half a mouthful of food when he began to speak. "Well, it's kind of complicated and then again it's not to me. See, computer programming, which is what I do, can be broken down into five stages: requirements definition, design specification, coding, testing, and maintenance. The requirements stage involves quantifying the necessary operation to be performed by the program. In the design specification stage, directions are programmed for meeting the requirements by quantifying the processing steps and the data-storage structures in greater detail. Coding is the stage in which the design is turned into steps expressed in a chosen programming language. Testing is the stage in which the program is verified as being correct with respect to the requirements and design specification. After we have tested the program and found it to be correct, we release it to you, or rather your department. The final stage is maintenance. During this stage, enhancements and corrections are made. The maintenance stage takes the most time and is usually the most expensive phase of the programming process."

Clay paused to take another bite of his pizza. Lisa too was eating as she listened to Clay describe what it was that he did. She did not fully understand it; however, she felt as though she had a preliminary grasp.

"Okay, so give me an example of what happens in the requirements definition stage," Lisa asked.

"Well, take a sophisticated accounts payable system. Customer requirements specify approximately how many purchase orders or invoices are going to be processed and the reports that they will generate. We then decide how the information managed by the computer will be stored. That would be the requirements stage on that kind of project."

"God, how long have you been doing this?" Lisa asked.

"If you include college time, I've been programming full time for about five years. But that doesn't include my hacker time."

"Hacker time?"

Clay paused in the middle of taking a bite of pizza as if he thought he had said something wrong. He finished his bite, and with the food muffling his words, he spoke. "Yeah, hacker . . . you know, I fool around on the computer trying to break mainframe codes and languages. I've been doing it since I was ten."

Lisa looked surprised at this. She was also fascinated by the notion.

"You mean you get into some other company's mainframe and access records?"

"Well . . . yeah."

"Like what companies?"

Clay was a bit uncomfortable. He did not know if Lisa approved or disapproved of what he was telling her and he thought he should expound on the subject before he went any further.

"I don't want you to think that I break into their systems and steal or get information or anything like that. I just do it to see if I can get in."

"No, I didn't think that. I just can't believe that you or anyone else can access another computer mainframe."

"It's really not that hard. It takes a lot of time to break the code, but once you do that you're in."

"Can you show me?"

Clay thought for a moment. Then he realized that in order to show her, they would have to be sitting very close to one another. Clay didn't see any problem with that. "Sure, let's go into my office."

Clay led Lisa into his office, which was actually supposed to be the formal living room. He set a chair next to his chair at the computer. Lisa sat in the chair he positioned for her and Clay took his seat. The computer monitor was on with the screen saver showing a multitude of flying toilets. He entered his code and the screen changed to show many files. Each file was the name of a company or organization. The files included the names of three major airlines, twelve banks, the Credit Bureau, U.S. Treasury, Pentagon, and the Department of Motor Vehicles.

Clay looked at Lisa for a moment while she gazed at the monitor. His pulse was racing as he looked at her.

"God, she is beautiful," he thought.

"Are these the systems you have accessed? Oh . . . my . . . god, you accessed the U.S. Treasury and the Pentagon?"

Clay returned his attention to the screen. "Yeah. And here is the list of other systems I've been working on."

Clay typed once again on the keyboard and a second list of files appeared. This list of files listed another airline, the Royal Bank of Canada, and the Dallas Chamber of Commerce.

"What did you do when you accessed the Treasury and Pentagon systems?"

"What do you mean?"

"I mean did you look around, or alter anything? Could you alter anything?" Lisa asked.

"Yeah, I could have but I didn't. Once I've accessed a system the challenge is over, as far as I'm concerned. The challenge to me is getting in."

"You can access the mainframe computer of the Department of Motor Vehicles?"

"Well . . . Yeah," Clay said proudly.

"Can you look me up and see what my driving record is?"

"Sure," Clay replied.

Clay used the mouse to move the cursor to the DMV file. He clicked the mouse and the screen went blank for a moment. Then, Texas Department of Motor Vehicles appeared in bold black letters across the monitor. Clay then entered a sixteen-digit code, and after a moment, a list of files appeared. He selected Records, and the screen again changed. Now the monitor displayed DMV Driving Records. Below the title were the prompt categories. He had a selection of MOVING VIOLATIONS, PARKING, STOLEN PROPERTY, WARRANTS or ALL OF THE ABOVE. Clay selected All of the Above.

The screen changed again. It was the information screen which requested personal information on the subject of the inquiry.

"Okay, give me your social security number," Clay requested.

"Four-four-eight-seven-seven-zero-seven-seven-five."

Clay entered the nine numbers into the computer and pressed Enter. He sat back in his chair and waited for Lisa's driving record to appear on the screen. While he waited, he once again looked at her. He imagined what it would be like to be with her. And he wondered why he was so intimidated by her appearance. He wasn't intimidated by her mind or her personality. He was only intimidated by the fact that she was so beautiful. And Lisa was extraordinarily beautiful.

"There it is!" Lisa shouted.

"What?" Clay said startled.

"My record, my driving record is right there."

Clay began scrolling down the screen.

"Let's see what it says. No wants or warrant, that's good. No stolen vehicle reports, that's good. No parking tickets, that's good. Tickets . . . Whoa . . . You do have tickets. One, two, three, four, five. Five speeding tickets. Four of them are ten miles over. Those go to your insurance company. Man, Lisa, one more and you lose your license, don't you?"

"Yes. But the last two weren't really my fault. I went through a construction zone on the highway going fifty-five. The speed limit was forty-five. I couldn't talk the guy out of it. I even told him that I was in a hurry to get home because I had just started and needed something for it."

"Started?"

"My period."

"Oh . . . god, I'd have let you go."

"It usually always works, but this guy was an asshole," Lisa said as she returned her attention to the screen.

"Now can you change the record once you're in?"

"Yeah, but I've never done it."

"Why?"

"I don't know; it just doesn't seem right. I don't access the system to change it. I don't think I could do that. Besides, I could end up in jail for doing it."

"Well, show me one that you're working on."

Clay closed the DMV file and pulled up the screen that showed the saved files he was attempting to access.

"How about the Royal Bank of Canada?" Clay asked.

"Good."

Clay moved his cursor to the file and clicked. The screen was filled with letter and number combinations. Lisa did not have a clue what it was she was looking at. As Clay scrolled down the page, the number and letter combinations were complicated by the addition of symbols and fonts that Lisa did not recognize.

"What is all that stuff?"

"It's computer language. Computers are programmed with precise notations called programming languages. Some are basic and others are very difficult. This one is PASCAL. It's a more complicated one."

"How do you know what it all means?"

"It's like learning any other kind of language, only this one consists of formulas instead of words. The formulas are really commands and I use them to establish the data-storage structure of the system and access code."

"How long have you been working on this one?"

"I guess about six months now. But I almost have it, I think. Once I determined that they used PASCAL instead of COBAL, I was pretty much on my way to accessing the system."

"How much longer will it take?"

"I haven't worked on it for a couple of weeks. I could be in any time now. All I have to do is break their security access code."

ARTICLE 2

July 24, 2005, 6:50 p.m.
The Estate of Alberto Rojas, Medellin, Colombia

One man stood and five men sat around a white marble conference table in the plush surroundings of Alberto Rojas's massive mountaintop estate. These six men were leaders of the most sophisticated, powerful, wealthy, and violent criminal organization in the world: the Medellin cartel. Each member of the cartel controlled a segment of the enormously profitable drug production and distribution organization. They were feared by their own government, as well as those who worked for them and those who apposed them. They did not consider themselves criminals; rather, they believed they were businessmen. And by all accounts, they were correct. Their drug production and manufacturing business grossed tens of billions of dollars annually for the cartel. Their methods of production and distribution were as secret as they were sophisticated. Their human resources policy was very simple: Those who work for them and are successful, receive handsome rewards; those who fail or cross them, die.

Jose Santiago, Roberto Diego, Ricardo Sanchez, Pedro Bevearo, and Joseffe Pinilla were seated around the table. Alberto Rojas stood at the head of the table addressing the group.

"My brothers, we have had a very good year so far. Profits are up, production is up, and the Americans do not seem to be as interested in our operation as they were last year. I believe this is largely due to the idea and efforts of our brother,

Ricardo Sanchez, who sits here before us. He suggested some time ago that we begin shipping decoy loads of product into the United States. We have been allowing the Americans the opportunity to find substantial quantities of our product. We have in fact provided them with anonymous tips regarding location, times, and quantities of shipments. To date, they have confiscated approximately two hundred million dollars of our product. While they were kept busy confiscating these decoy shipments, we were able to successfully ship, distribute, and sell $1,650,000,000 worth of product. And we are only seven months into the year. We are ahead of projections by one third."

Rojas walked around the table and placed his hands on Ricardo Sanchez.

"Join me in applauding Ricardo's efforts in behalf of our organization gentlemen," Rojas said.

As the men began clapping, Rojas moved away from Sanchez. He pulled a gun from his back, put it to Sanchez's head, and pulled the trigger. The muffled blast of the gun sent blood, bone fragments, and brain matter flying across the white marble table. Sanchez's lifeless body slumped over and his head hit the table with a slap, sounding like a wet sponge falling on a tile floor. The blood continued to flow on top of the blood-spattered white marble from the gaping head wound inflicted by Rojas.

Rojas walked back to the head of the table and once again spoke to the cartel leaders. "A terrible tragedy, my brothers. However, we cannot tolerate dishonesty among our employees or within this leadership body. Sanchez was a good man. Ah . . . but he was a greedy man as well. I do not condemn greed. However, I condemn stealing and betraying in order to satisfy it. Our friend and brother, Ricardo Sanchez, was lying to us. He was lying to all of us! The Americans, in truth, only confiscated $123,000,000 worth of our product. The balance went to Sanchez's own network of people. He stole from our organization. He has a bank account in Switzerland, a fucking bank account in Switzerland, with over seventy-five million dollars of our money in it!

"Those who were involved with him in this deceit will pay. They will pay with their lives and with their very souls. They knew that their actions were against the interests of our organization. They were concerned only with their personal interests and agenda. We will make them pay, and they will be examples of what this organization does to those who would betray it."

Rojas walked back to Sanchez's chair. Sanchez's body was still slumped on the table and his head still seeped blood. Rojas reached over the body, grabbed the bloody hair on top of Sanchez's head, and jerked it up for all to see. As Sanchez's head jerked back, a large portion of his brain slipped out of the hole in his forehead and now lay upon his unrecognizable face.

"This man was our friend! This man was also a traitor, a liar, and a pig! Individually we are nothing! Together we rule an empire, an empire that is wealthier than most countries, my brothers. Look at him . . . look at his face . . . remember what you see. This is our destiny should we decide that our personal interests are more important than those of the cartel. He had no true face in life, now he has no face in death."

Rojas once again let the head fall to the table. He walked back to his chair at the head of the table as the eyes of the other members were fixed on him. He wiped the blood of Sanchez from his hand with a cloth as he spoke. "Why don't we continue our discussions on the veranda, gentlemen? I believe my chef has prepared an excellent dessert for us this evening."

ARTICLE 3

July 24, 2005, 8:45 p.m.
Clay Peterson's House, Dallas, Texas

Clay was standing with Lisa at the open front door of his home. They had concluded a long evening of discussion regarding Clay's work at the office and the work he did at home. Lisa seemed truly fascinated by Clay's abilities and computer prowess. He was not the guy she thought he was. He wasn't "nerdy"; he was very shy and sensitive. The more time she spent with him, the less she thought of him as a nerdy computer wizard. She actually liked this susceptible, reticent, introverted man. It was a refreshing change for her to be around a guy like this. Lisa had thought they didn't exist anymore.

As the two stood in the doorway, Lisa was the first to speak. "Do you think we could do this again soon?"

"Any time. It would be my pleasure. Really," Clay said coyly.

"Thank you, Clay. I really appreciate all you taught me tonight. I think it will be a big help to me when I interview for the job."

"Well you know, there is a lot more to it than what we talked about tonight. We should probably get together again while everything is still fresh in your mind."

"I'm not busy tomorrow night," Lisa hinted.

"What a coincidence, neither am I."

"Same time?"

"Same time. Only this time I buy dinner."

"Great, I'll see you tomorrow at the office then. Good night," Lisa said giving him a wide smile.

"Good night, sleep tight," Clay said as he watched her stroll down the walk to her car.

Clay watched as she got into her car, started it, and began to drive away. He waved to her as she left. When Lisa was gone, he closed the front door and spoke to himself. "Sleep tight? What the hell kind of thing was that to say. Dammit, man, you should have just kept your mouth shut!" he said as he went back into his office.

As he entered the room, he could still smell Lisa's perfume. He went to the chair at the computer and sat for a moment recounting the evening with her. Clay thought that the evening had gone well. He hadn't really fumbled over his own words; he didn't spill anything on himself, or more importantly, Lisa. He could only recall two stupid comments the entire evening. All in all he considered it a success.

He interrupted his thoughts of Lisa and turned his attention back to the computer. The screen was still showing the Royal Canadian Bank access codes he had assimilated in trying to breach their security system. To Clay, the most difficult part of accessing any system was determining the language used in formatting or structuring it. He had already determined that the Royal Canadian Bank system was written in PASCAL rather than COBAL, as he had first assumed. Now all he had to do was enter the system using PASCAL algorithm and gain access.

"Okay, RCB, let's see how smart you are," Clay said as he looked at the monitor and began typing on his keyboard.

With only a few keystrokes, he had entered the bank's computer system. Now he had only to break the code that would allow him to access it. He paused for a moment to think about his next course of action. He decided on his strategy, started typing, then abruptly stopped.

"Nah, that would be too simple. They wouldn't have a CASE on their access system. What the hell."

He began typing again in an attempt to pull up the CASE (Computer-Aided Software Engineering) program. This program automates various phases of computer programming. In some cases, it automatically rewrites a computer program whenever a change is made that may affect numerous other parts of the same program. Clay was hoping that the CASE program would be attached to the access system, thereby allowing him to see what, if any, changes to the system had been made recently. If it worked, the CASE program history may provide him with the access code if the code itself had been changed. The access codes were sometimes encrypted, but this did not stop Clay. He had a solution for that situation if it presented itself.

He finished typing and waited for the computer to digest the information he had requested. Moments later, the computer responded with a tone and the CASE program history was in front of him on the screen.

"Yes! God, I love this game," Clay exclaimed.

He began scrolling down the screen and found an activity and a date. The activity was ENTRY ALGORITHM, the date JULY 15, 2005. He looked at the date and entry for a moment. He decided that, based on his previous success in accessing banking systems, they typically would alter their access codes on the first and fifteenth of each month. He highlighted the entry and date with his cursor, and pressed Enter. The information regarding the entry was then shown on the screen. It was exactly what Clay had hoped it would be. The access code had been changed on July 15, 2005, from R*007{HPT}C*533{YUX}B*006 to TBC(2485)<LCP***(9090)>rcb. Clay believed that he had the access code for the system.

"All right! Now let's see if you work," he said to the monitor.

Clay exited the CASE file and reestablished the main system file. He keyed in the access code he had found in

CASE and pressed Enter on his keyboard. The computer began processing and the screen remained unchanged. Clay started to think that he would get the typical first read out: Access Denied—Invalid Access Code. He stood from his chair to go to the kitchen and get a beer, when the computer beeped once again. Clay turned to look at his monitor. He couldn't believe what he saw. It had never happened the first time he tried. He looked at the words on his monitor and spoke out loud.

"ROYAL BANK OF CANADA OPERATING SYSTEM [Accessed]," Clay read with confidence.

ARTICLE 4

Alberto Rojas was forty-six years of age and controlled 65 percent of the Medellin cartel empire. He came from very humble beginnings and had been brought up in the violent and unpredictable world of drugs. He started working in a cocaine production camp when he was eight years old. By the time he was twelve, he was already a seasoned veteran at producing and smuggling drugs. When he was seventeen, he watched as his mother and sister were killed in a government raid on their encampment in the Central Cordillera. It was rumored that one of the drug lords had given up the drug encampment to the Colombian government to ease U.S. pressure on the government regarding their inability to control the drug trade in their country. Alberto vowed revenge against the government and against the drug lord suspected of being a traitor to his own people. He was twenty-two before he was able fulfill his promise of revenge against the drug lord.

His name was Antonio Vaschez. He was a member in the then fledgling Colombian drug organization that called themselves the Medellin cartel. Vaschez was one of seven men in the cartel in the early seventies. He controlled roughly one-sixth of the production of cocaine at that time. Alberto Rojas was just beginning to make a name for himself in Medellin at the time. He had successfully completed a number of smuggling missions for each of the cartel members except Vaschez. Most liked Alberto as they thought him mature beyond his years in terms of his business acumen and logic. Most of all, they trusted him. Trust in Colombia is a rarity.

Vaschez asked to meet with Rojas one afternoon in the middle of May. He told him they had some business to discuss. He said he had a proposition. Rojas agreed to meet on the condition that Vaschez and he met alone. The meeting took place in a clearing on the outskirts of Bogota. Rojas arrived first in his Jeep and waited patiently for Vaschez to arrive. Moments later, Vaschez drove up alone in his Range Rover. Vaschez got out of his car and walked up to Rojas.

"Thank you for meeting me, Alberto. I trust that the drive was not too difficult."

"It was fine. What did you want to see me about? You mentioned a proposition," Rojas replied.

"Yes, I have a proposition for you. And I would like you to consider it an opportunity as well."

"I'm listening."

Vaschez studied this young man in front of him for a moment. He had heard that he was a brave young man; a man that had displayed his loyalty to those he worked for on many occasions, in many different ways.

"I want you to work for me," Vaschez told him.

"Doing what?"

"I have heard many good things about you, Alberto Rojas. I have heard you are loyal and can be trusted. Those are attributes that are scarce in Colombia these days."

"Not if you know where to look."

"Exactly. That is why you are here. I want you to work for me as my protégé. As you may or may not be aware, I have no sons, only one daughter. I am of the age to begin looking for someone I can trust my business to. I would like to give you the opportunity to work for me and grow my business with me."

"Grow your business? Where would you propose to grow your business?"

"Right here, my boy. There are those in the organization who, I think, don't look to the future as I do. They grow weaker each day and they have no one to work with them, no one that they trust with their business."

"So you would take them out?" Rojas asked.

"You put it so harshly, my boy. But yes, I will take them out. And when I do, I will control the majority of the cartel. If things work out between you and me, that means that someday you will control the cartel."

"I don't think so, Mr. Vaschez," Rojas said. He pulled a gun from his back, and pointed it at Vaschez.

"What do you think you're doing?" Vaschez asked.

"It is called justice, Vaschez, poetic justice. You betrayed your people once. My mother and sister lost their lives; they were murdered because of you. Now you say you will betray the cartel; you will go to war against those who are your brothers. I am going to see that you betray no one ever again."

Rojas pointed the gun at Vaschez's leg and shot him in the kneecap. Vaschez fell to the ground screaming in pain. Rojas walked to the back of his Jeep and retrieved a machete. He walked to Vaschez who was attempting to crawl to his vehicle. Rojas stood over him feeling no remorse or sorrow for the wounded man. With tears in his eyes he spoke to Vaschez. "I swore on my mother's and sister's souls that some day I would have your head. Now I fulfill my vow to them."

With that, Rojas lifted the sharp machete high over his head and struck Vaschez behind the head at the base of his skull. The severed head hit the ground with a *thud*. Blood spurted wildly from the headless body quivering on the ground. Rojas rolled the head over so he could look into Vaschez's eyes which remained open. Rojas showed no emotion as he stared at the head. Sanchez's mouth still moved as if to attempt to speak. The eyes too moved from side to side uncontrollably. Then nothing. A blank stare and stillness.

Rojas drove back to Medellin with Vaschez's head and presented it to the other members of the cartel, explaining what had happened and what Vaschez had planned for them. Rojas was rewarded for his loyalty. The cartel gave him a portion of Vaschez's holdings and a seat on the cartel. That was the beginning of Alberto Rojas's rise to power within the cartel. Over the next twenty-four years, he slowly and quietly acquired additional holdings in production and distribution of Colombian drugs. He was now the most powerful man in the Medellin cartel.

The number had been quickly and brutally reduced to five. All of the men were now sitting on the tiled outdoor veranda of the Rojas villa. The hour was very late and all of them were tired. However, Rojas had business to discuss.

"We must deal with those who worked with Sanchez in the United States. They are cowards and they will die like pigs. I swear it on my mother's soul!" Rojas shouted.

"How did you get your information, Alberto? How did you find out about Sanchez's activities?" Jose Santiago asked.

"Hulio told me," replied Rojas.

"His son? His own son?" Pedro Bevearo said in surprise.

"You are surprised, Pedro?" Rojas asked.

"Yes. I am surprised. What Sanchez did was very wrong and he paid for it with his life as is our law. But we should have found out about this internally. We should not have to rely on having a man's children to dishonor their father for us to find out about things like this."

"I agree with Pedro. This speaks to our internal security. We need to look at our procedures, the people we have entrusted with much responsibility, and the methods used in tracking our product. This is a problem much deeper than just Sanchez, Alberto," Pinilla said.

"Pedro, my friend. You are disturbed about the fact that Ricardo's son told me of his father's treachery. I am not. I would expect nothing less from my son than to tell one of you if I were betraying your trust. That is how I have raised my children. That is how Ricardo Sanchez raised his son. Somewhere along the line, Ricardo forgot. He forgot about his obligations and commitment to each of us. He forgot the meaning of trust and of loyalty. He forgot about these values he had given his son, and it killed him. Hulio did not dishonor his father by telling us about his activities. I believe the opposite. Hulio honored his father, and in the process proved himself to be the better man.

"Hulio Sanchez will now take his father's place among us. He is the beginning of this organization's future. And I am proud of him. He possesses the values of this cartel. He will be a good leader one day.

"And you, Joseffe, you believe this problem to be much larger than just Sanchez. If that is the case, then we are in trouble. I look at my staff and those who have great responsibility within my operation, and my heart is satisfied. I put those people in those positions. If I begin to distrust them now, then I am in truth distrusting myself. They are all committed to me. They are all loyal to me. And, my friend, they are all afraid of me. They know I will kill them and their families if they betray me. If your people do not hold you in this regard, then I believe that the blame lies with you and you alone; and you have reason for concern."

"I do have trust in my people. They too are afraid of me, and they also fear everyone who sits at this table with me. Fear is not the problem, Alberto. Greed and want are. Combined, they blind fear," Joseffe said.

"Then you tell me what the solution is, Joseffe. You tell me," Rojas ordered.

"I do not have the solution, Alberto. I only voice the concern that I believe all of us here have."

"Is this true, my brothers? Do all of you hold these concerns about your own organizations?" Rojas asked.

Some of the men looked down at the table. Still others continued to look directly at Rojas. None responded to his question.

"Perhaps the problem then lies with you, Joseffe. Perhaps you have grown weak and have lost the faith of your own people," Rojas prodded.

"I am not weak! I am as strong as you are, Alberto, as strong as you! I will not play your little game of words. I have given my opinion and your disrespect for my opinion is not appreciated. Is this not a forum for discussion? Is this your leadership manner? You insult me, insult my people, and my business simply because I have an opinion and a concern? You can go straight to hell, Alberto Rojas! I am tired now and I am leaving."

With that, Joseffe Pinilla jerked away from the table and stormed off the veranda into the house. The four remaining members of the cartel sat and looked at one another for a moment.

Roberto Diego, the senior member of the group, spoke first. "This disturbs me. We should not be fighting among ourselves. Joseffe is upset. He and Ricardo were very close. I am sure that Sanchez's betrayal hurt him more than his death did. He will calm down. He will be all right. I respect you, Alberto. You have proven to all of us that you are a wise man; however, you should go to Joseffe and make peace."

"Joseffe acts like a child. He will calm down; and when he does, he will come to me. I am not the one who needs to make peace. He will come to me!" Rojas said.

"And if he doesn't?" Pedro Bevearo asked.

"He will, Pedro. He will," Rojas replied.

"What are we going to do about Sanchez's people in America?" Bevearo asked.

"Hulio is going to take care of that for us. He is setting up another decoy shipment. When it arrives, they will be in for the surprise of their miserable lives."

"And what about the money? The seventy-seven million?" Diego asked.

"We will have it wired to our BVI joint account. It will be disbursed equally between us within the week. The money is not my main concern, Diego; nor do I believe it should be yours. I intend to find all of those who were working for Sanchez and I am going to kill them. I am going to kill them all."

ARTICLE 5

July 24, 2005, 11:30 p.m.
Hoover Building, Washington, D.C.

Special-Agent-in-Charge Brian Whitfield was sitting at his desk reviewing a case file. Whitfield had been with the FBI for twenty-four years, ten of which as an SAC. He had made plans to retire in December, which would conclude a very distinguished career with the bureau. He joined in 1970, a time when racism was still an issue within the bureau. He was black and proud of his heritage. He never made his race an issue, nor did anyone else within the bureau. Brian was a brilliant man. He let his performance speak for his capabilities. Brian was respected by his peers and well liked by FBI supervisors. He loved his work and excelled at it.

He had been married for twenty-three years to the same beautiful woman. Her name was Marlene. They had three children, all girls. The oldest was twenty-one and lived in North Carolina with her boyfriend. Brian did not like him; however, he kept his feelings to himself. He knew that the guy would screw up eventually and Carrie would dump him. His middle daughter, Rachelle, was a mischievous nineteen-year-old and a freshman in college. She attended Bethany College, a well-respected small private liberal arts institution in West Virginia. She wanted to be a television journalist and the school offered an excellent program. She had the personality, intelligence, and looks to succeed in that business, Brian thought. She just needed to stay focused on her career goal instead of guys. His youngest daughter, Tanya, was sixteen. He had been through that age twice before and still did not know how to handle it. With every girl the problems seemed greater and their animosity toward him and his wife seemed to grow stronger. He loved his youngest daughter; however, he hated her opinionated age group. All in all, Brian Whitfield was a good father, a good husband, a good provider, and an excellent FBI agent.

Brian was working late that evening, reviewing a case he had been investigating for the past year. He was special-agent-in-charge of the bureau's telecommunications fraud division. His responsibilities were broad, and in fact changed every day due to the technological advances in the communications field. The case file was thick with background documentation, case history, and a suspect profile. He was reviewing the suspect profile when another agent approached his desk, holding a document in his hand.

"Brian? Christ, man, you're working kinda late, aren't you?" Agent Beck asked.

"No rest for the wicked, Beck, you know that."

"I got a fax for you. It came in on the priority line so I thought I would bring it up to your wicked self." Agent Beck handed the facsimile to Brian.

"You're a charmer, Beck. 'Preciate it," Brian said as he took the document.

"No problem. You keep the midnight oil burning, I'm going home to my wife and bed. Not necessarily in that order you understand. Then again given your age and all of that grey hair, you probably don't," Beck said jokingly.

Brian looked at him for a moment, leaned back in his chair, and smiled as he spoke. "Son, I was getting it up and in while you were still jerkin' off to *I Dream of Jeanie*. I'm not the man around here with the 'minute man' reputation. If you know what I mean."

Beck shook his head and laughed at Brian's comment as he walked out of the office. Brian sat back up in his chair, massaged his tired eyes for a moment, then began reading the facsimile Beck had given him. The facsimile was from one of his field agents. The subject was the case he had been reviewing that evening and investigating for six months. They had identified a suspect in the investigation; however, they needed proof. Brian decided that the only way to obtain the evidence needed for prosecution was to place a field agent undercover in the suspect's operation. Their efforts in this regard had been successful. The document Brian held read simply as follows:

EYES FACSIMILE

TO: SAC Whitfield   July 24, 2005
FROM: Special Agent Hendrix   Re:#952213

Made contact with target. Subject (s) plan is still unclear. Follow-up in two days.

Hendrix

CHAPTER TWO

ARTICLE 6

Clay was frantically moving about the kitchen. He would periodically walk to the oven and peer in the window at the baked chicken. He had selected chicken because he believed it would be very difficult to screw it up, and it didn't take long to cook. He would walk from the oven to the stove and lift the lids off the pots of boiling vegetables. Then he would go to the table and rearrange silverware, glasses, and napkins he had moments earlier positioned. Clay was a nervous wreck. He hadn't had a woman in his house for dinner since . . . well, he had never had a woman over for dinner. He had never cooked for a woman. He rarely cooked for himself. He hoped and prayed that he did not poison Lisa with his confection. Clay was looking into the oven once again when he heard a knock at the door. He quickly surveyed the kitchen to make sure that it at least looked like he knew what he was doing then he went to the door. He opened it to find Lisa standing there, and again her appearance left him speechless. She wore a Dallas Cowboy's T-shirt, again with no bra, tucked into her cutoff blue-jean shorts. The cutoff jeans were shorter than those of the evening before and had two slits up either side exposing a small portion of Lisa's hip. She again wore tennis shoes with half socks and her hair was tied back in a ponytail. Clay thought she was absolutely stunning and incredibly sexy as she stood in front of him.

"Hi, I'm early again," Lisa said happily.

Clay stood and admired her for a moment, not really hearing her comment. He then realized he was allowing her to remain outside in the early evening heat, and spoke. "It's okay . . . come on in."

Lisa walked past Clay in the doorway and Clay stood holding the door open, watching her legs and rear as she walked down the foyer to the living room.

"God, she looks good," he thought.

Clay closed the door after Lisa disappeared into the living room. He walked quickly after her. Lisa was in the kitchen looking into the oven when Clay walked in.

"Smells great, but you didn't have to go to all this trouble."

"It was no trouble. I like to cook and I don't get many opportunities to do it. I usually order out or go somewhere to eat."

"I do too. When I left home to go to college the first thing I missed, besides my own bed, was my mom's cooking. She was one of those moms that cooked for every meal. My dad was a meat-and-potatoes kind a guy so we ate meat and potatoes most of the time."

Clay moved around the kitchen pretending he knew what he was doing during their conversation. "Where did you grow up?" he asked.

"All over, really. I was born in Kingsport, Tennessee; moved to Phoenix when I was eight; moved to Vegas when I was sixteen; and Oklahoma to go to college."

"Christ, was your dad in the army or something?"

"Worse, he was a corporate executive. Just when he settled into a job, he would either get laid off due to management headcount reductions, transferred, or a headhunter would call with a better opportunity."

"Where'd you go to college?"

"OU."

"Really. I went to the University of Michigan. I didn't move around a lot when I was a kid, and I didn't stray far from home when I went to college."

"Where did you grow up?"

"In Cheboygan, Michigan. It's a great city that sits at the peak of the state between Lake Huron and Lake Michigan. I lived there until I went to Michigan State in East Lansing."

Clay walked to the oven, opened the door, and pulled the casserole dish out to inspect the entrée.

"It really smells good, Clay. I'm starved," Lisa said.

"I don't know how it will taste, but it's done . . . I think." Clay took the chicken to the counter and transferred it to the serving plate. "I thought we could just smorgasbord it, if it's all right. Just grab a plate off the table and get what you want."

"Sounds great," Lisa said.

The pair served themselves, sat together at the table, and began eating. Clay watched intently as Lisa cut her chicken breast and took her first bite. He continued to watch anxiously as she chewed and swallowed.

"It's good, Clay. In fact, it's excellent."

Clay gave a sigh of relief. "Good, I'm glad you like it," Clay said, realizing then that he had forgotten the wine. "Would you like some Chardonnay? I have it chilling in the fridge," Clay asked.

"That sounds perfect."

Clay got up and went to the refrigerator to retrieve the wine. He opened the bottle and walked back to Lisa. He poured her glass of wine, noticeably shaking from nerves. Lisa said nothing while he finished and returned to his chair. He poured himself a glass and began eating again.

"Clay, do you mind if I ask you a personal question?"

Clay looked at her anxiously. "No, I don't mind," he said with a mouth full of food.

"You don't date much, do you?"

Clay choked on the food he was attempting to swallow upon hearing the question. He regained his composure, took a sip of wine, wiped his mouth then answered.

"It's that obvious?"

"Well . . . I just notice that you are really nervous around me. I was just wondering if it was me or if you don't spend a lot of time with women."

"It's you," Clay said without thinking. "I mean it's not you . . . it's . . . I don't spend time with women. I mean I'm not gay or anything. I just don't get the opportunity to spend time with women."

"Don't you go out? Don't you meet women when you go out?"

"Not really. I go out to movies and to eat, but I'm not really into going to bars. I read somewhere that a good place to meet women was the supermarket. Specifically in the produce section because it gave the impression that you were a health nut or something. It didn't work for me. And frankly I got sick of fruit and vegetables."

Lisa laughed at Clay's comment. She studied him for a moment then asked him another question. "Do I make you nervous?"

Clay thought for a moment. He did not know how to answer this question. If he told her the truth, that she did make him nervous, she might think him a spineless nerd. If he said she didn't, she might be offended and she would know he was lying. "What the hell, I'll be honest with her," he thought.

"You scare me to death," he said quietly without looking at her.

Lisa looked at him with compassion and concern. "Why?"

Clay did not look at her; he found his courage in the chicken lying on his plate. He could not look at her while he spoke for fear of alienating her with his answer. "Lisa . . . you are the most beautiful girl I have ever been around. When I'm near you I can't think right. I have a feeling in my stomach, a feeling that I can't really describe." He paused and looked up from his plate and into her bright sparkling blue eyes. "It's like a nervous feeling, but it's not. It's like the feeling you get when you're on a roller coaster and speeding down the first big hill. Or like the feeling you get riding in a car and you go over a small hill at high speed. I shake. I can't control it and I don't know how to control it."

Clay looked into her eyes as he spoke. She sat listening to him with a serious and yet companionate look. Clay continued. "You know . . . You're like the cheerleader in high school and college that I would watch but never had the courage to speak to. You're like a fantasy, only you're real and sitting at my table with me. I guess I'm really nervous around you because I don't want to do anything to screw up the time I get to spend around you."

Clay looked back at his half-eaten chicken breast. Lisa sat and looked at him. She smiled slightly as she watched him. Then she spoke. "I think you are the sweetest guy I've ever met, Clay Peterson," she said as Clay raised his head to look at her again.

"Thanks," he said sadly.

"What? You don't like it that I think you're sweet?"

"No, it's not that. It's just that I have always been the 'sweet' guy, ya know? The guy that was a perfect 'really good' friend. It gets really old being sweet, let me tell you. Just once, it would be nice to be the boyfriend kinda guy, or the bad guy who's appealing. You know what I mean?"

"I think you're sweet in a sexy kind of way, Clay."

Clay looked at her in surprise. His pulse was racing as he spoke. "Really? A sexy kind of way?"

"Yep, and I think you're attractive too," Lisa said with a smile.

Clay was visibly embarrassed. His face was red and his palms were sweating profusely. He could feel himself shaking again, only this time due to excitement rather than nerves.

"You are a real guy, Clay. You're not plastic. You don't try to be something that you're not. You're honest, cute, and sensitive, and you are very intelligent. I'm surprised that some woman hasn't grabbed you yet."

"Lisa . . . would you ever . . . I mean could you maybe consider . . . like going out with me maybe, or something?"

"Sure. I'd love to go out with you."

"Really! I . . . I . . . mean . . . uh . . . great. That sounds great. When?"

"Let's go out tomorrow night. Let's go see a movie together."

"Great. Yeah, that's really great."

Clay was beside himself with excitement. He was having difficulty holding in his true feelings. There was a moment of uncomfortable silence at the table. Then Lisa spoke again. "How are you coming with your Royal Bank code?"

"Royal Bank?" Clay asked.

"Yeah, the Royal Bank of Canada code you were working on last night."

"Oh, right. I broke it and accessed the system."

"You're kidding. Just like that, you broke the code and got into their system?"

"Yes. You want to see?"

"Can I?"

"Sure, come on. We'll check out the financial stability of the Royal Bank of Canada together."

Clay and Lisa got up from the kitchen table and went back into Clay's office. Clay pulled Lisa's chair close to his before she sat. He then sat at the computer and keyed in the file for the Royal Bank of Canada. The system screen appeared and he entered the code he had written on a notepad sitting next to his mouse. They waited together as the computer began processing the code then the computer tone notified them that they had accessed the bank's operating system. The screen in front of them showed specific

categories and files which were available for their review and/
or access.

"There it is, we're in," Clay said feeling very proud of
himself.

"God, I can't believe this. Now if you wanted to you could
change things in the system, like bank balances and stuff like
that?"

"Sure, but I just look. I don't ever alter anything once
I've accessed a system. Let's look at the saving accounts."

Clay moved the cursor to the Savings Account icon and
clicked the mouse once. There was a long pause. Then the
Savings Account screen appeared.

"Okay, now give me a name, any name," Clay said.

"Like Smith or Jones or something?"

"No, I like to use celebrity names. You know? Okay, here,
I always start with this one."

Clay began typing on the computer as Lisa watched the
screen intently.

Crawford, Cindy

"Cindy Crawford? Why Cindy Crawford?" Lisa asked in
surprise.

"Why not?" Clay said with a sheepish smile.

The computer began searching for account information
on Cindy Crawford. Moments later the screen read NO
INFORMATION ON FILE.

"Okay, here . . . here, I have one. Ask for Harrison Ford,"
Lisa said.

"Okay. Harrison Ford."

Clay again requested account information on Harrison
Ford and the response from the computer was the same. Both
of them sat and thought for a moment. Then, Clay had an
idea. "Let's try wealthy," he said.

"Wealthy?"

"Yeah, who is the wealthiest person you know of?"

"Okay, try Ross Perot."

"Ross Perot," Clay said in approval of the choice.

He requested information on Ross Perot's accounts and again the computer indicated that there was no information available. They sat again for a moment thinking of more names. Lisa was first to speak.

"How about Conrad Douglas?"

"The billionaire that just died? That's a good one. Let's see if he's in here."

Clay asked for the information on D. Conrad Douglas and again waited for the computer to search. This time, the screen changed and there in front of them was the account history of Conrad Douglas. Lisa and Clay looked at one another then returned their attention back to the screen.

"It's his savings account. Well, it says Trading Account, but I'm sure that it's a savings account," Clay said.

"My god, look at the balance. That's the balance as of today. Is that right? How is it possible for anyone to have $854,000,000 in a savings account?"

"Trading account," Clay corrected.

"Whatever. How could one person have that much money in an account?"

"Well, he was a multibillionaire. He had to keep all that money somewhere. But look at the deposits. Every month for the past twelve months was the same. Every month he deposited $71,166,666. The same amount every month. That's weird, don't you think?"

"Yeah, it's weird. And look at the beginning balance. He started with ten million dollars. Not a bad way to open a savings account."

"Trading account," Clay corrected again.

"Whatever."

"No, I don't think that this is a regular savings account. He didn't have any withdrawals. He opened the account a little over a year ago and each monthly deposit was the same. I'm curious."

"Well, you be curious, I have to get going," Lisa said.

"Get going? Why . . . I mean, where?"

"I have to go run some errands tonight if we're going out tomorrow night."

"That's right, we're going out. We have a . . . a date."

Lisa stood and started walking to the front door.

"That's right, we have a date. You want to pick me up around seven tomorrow night?"

"I'll be there. What's your apartment number?"

"Twenty-one twelve, it's on the second floor of the first building as you enter the complex off Commerce."

"Great, twenty-one twelve. Got it," Clay said as they reached the front door.

Clay stood at the door with both hands in his pockets. There was an uncomfortable silence. He did not know whether to shake her hand, give her a hug, or shove his tongue down her throat. He wanted to attempt all three, but just stood there instead.

"I had a really good time, Clay, and your dinner was excellent. You're a gourmet with chicken," Lisa said with a wide smile.

"I'm glad you liked it. And Lisa, I really . . . I mean, I—"

Lisa did not allow him to finish the sentence. She stood on her toes and gave him a very soft, very tender kiss on the lips. As she drew away from him, Clay stood with his eyes closed and lips puckered for a moment. He opened his eyes and found Lisa smiling at him again.

"You're so cute, Clay," Lisa said with a laugh.

She turned, opened the door, and started down the sidewalk to her car. She looked back halfway down the walk to see Clay standing in the doorway watching her. Clay was on cloud nine. He was still savoring the kiss he had received. As she drove off, he slowly closed the door then walked back into his office. He sat in his chair and looked at the computer, still thinking about Lisa.

"God, she is something," Clay said out loud.

He continued thinking about Lisa until the computer sounded a tone interrupting his thoughts. He watched the screen which was still showing the Douglas Trading Account activity. As he watched the screen, another log entry was being made by the bank.

Wire#0013-72595-006743214-8789-2212-85736825 . . . . $71,166,666.00

"Jesus. How could he be making deposits, the guy is dead," Clay exclaimed.

He continued to watch the screen for any additional activity. When nothing more happened, he studied the wire transaction he had just witnessed. He had educated himself over the years as he accessed banking systems and knew how a wire code was structured. He knew that the wire code was a language not unlike a computer language. The first four digits identified the transaction number. The second set of numbers detailed the date of the transaction. The next nine numbers were the originating account. The next four numbers identified the originating bank code. The next set of four numbers identified the receiving bank. The final nine numbers identified the account destination of the wired funds. Clay studied the numbers for a moment then spoke to himself again.

"Well, Mr. Douglas, wherever you are, I don't know what your 'trading account' is all about but I bet I can find out."

ARTICLE 7

July 25, 2005, 11:30 p.m.
E Dock, Port of Miami; Miami, Florida

The full moon gleaned off the still late-night water. The docks were deserted; the ships free from the loading and unloading activities which would begin again early the following morning. Three vehicles sat empty in front of the *E* dock shipping warehouse. The warehouse was packed tightly with cargo that had arrived that day from Buenaventura, Colombia, and now awaited customs inspection. The ship, *Apaporis II*, which had transported the cargo, was secured to the dock in front of the warehouse.

In one dimly lit corner through the maze of crates and boxes inside the warehouse, five men were having a meeting. Hulio Sanchez stood before the others, speaking in a low deliberate tone. The four men that surrounded him were his father's loyal followers in the United States. Juan Martinez, Jose Gonzalas, Miguel Santiago, and Roberto Bonitez were young and impressionable. They were all extended members of the Sanchez family, and all would have given their lives for Ricardo Sanchez.

"Rojas found out about our operation, my father is dead. Rojas killed him with his own hand. He does not know that I am the one who convinced my father to take control of his own destiny, to go his own path. Rojas believes I know nothing of this operation, and he instructed me to kill all of those involved with my father... all of you."

"We are all dead men!" Juan Martinez said in a panic.

"We are not. We must remain calm about this situation. We must not overreact. I find myself in a unique position with Rojas now. He killed my father because he believed he betrayed the cartel. He also believes that my father betrayed me as well. He is going to give me my father's position within the cartel. He told me that I am the beginning of the future and will be his protégé."

"What about us, Hulio? Does he know about us?" Jose Gonzalez asked.

"No, my friend, he knows nothing about you. He knows nothing about any of you, which will work to our advantage."

"And the money?" Gonzalez asked.

"He does know about the money. He will take it and divide it among the cartel members. But listen carefully to me, my friends. Do not lose sight of what we are doing or of our goal. The money is nothing compared to what we will have in the future. My role in the cartel is nothing compared to the power we will have. My father's death and the trust Rojas now bestows upon me will work to our advantage. I will make it so! My father will not have died for nothing."

"How does this give us the advantage, Hulio? He will take our money; we will be left with nothing. We can not fight him. Our organization is still small compared to his. We are beaten before we even begin to fight," Martinez said.

"There are many ways to fight a war, Juan. When your enemy is greater in strength and number, you do not let him know that he is in a battle until it is too late and you are in a position to win. How do we do this against the cartel? We divide them internally. Together they are a strong force. Divided, their resources are weakened and they will be looking for alliances to strengthen their own positions."

"How do we divide them? They are loyal to one another and they will not easily be separated," Miguel Santiago said.

"Rojas was close to my father, Miguel. They were like brothers. Yet this bond was broken because Rojas believed my father betrayed him. We must strike at the very foundation of the cartel if they are to be separated. There are no written contracts between the members. Their relationship is based on trust and honor. We will destroy the things they hold so dear and when we do, they will become weak and vulnerable. That is when we will strike. That is when we will take control."

"And if we fail?" Santiago asked.

"Then we will die, my friend. Does that bother you? We were all prepared to die for my father while he was alive, as he had been prepared to die for us if necessary. He died for us. Rojas knows nothing of our operation; he knows nothing about any of us. We owe that to my father. I am still prepared to die for my father. But before I die I will have my revenge on the cartel. I will kill those who killed Ricardo Sanchez and they will know why they die!"

Hulio surveyed the men who stood around him. Some looked at the floor in thought, while others looked with concern at Hulio. Hulio's eyes met those of Roberto Bonitez who had said nothing. They stared at each other for a moment until Hulio spoke to him. "Roberto, you've said nothing."

"There is nothing to say. Ricardo is dead. He was killed by Rojas. Rojas must pay. We have wasted enough time with questions and concerns about ourselves. I don't care about the money. I don't care about the power. A man I loved, a man we all loved, is dead! Rojas will pay, if I have to kill him with my own hands, he will pay!" Bonitez shouted.

The men were quiet. Hulio looked at each of them as Bonitez's words had a chance to sink in. Then his words once again broke the silence.

"We will seek revenge against Rojas and the cartel. We will be successful. And my father's name will be remembered. Rojas is correct; I represent the future of the cartel as he perceives it. You are the future cartel as I perceive it."

Hulio looked at Bonitez. "Did you bring them, Roberto?"

"Yes, they are in a crate in front of the building."

"How many?"

"Three, as you asked."

"When is the ship to sail?"

"It will leave in the morning before customs gets here to inspect this shipment. It will arrive in Tumaco in three days. We will have the cargo delivered to you in Medellin on the afternoon of the twenty-eighth."

"I want them alive. They must be alive."

"They will be alive. A bit hungry and thirsty, but they will be alive."

ARTICLE 8

Clay returned from the kitchen where he had poured himself another cup of coffee. As he sat back at his computer, the CASE analysis of D. Conrad Douglas's trading account appeared on the screen before him. Clay studied the information.

On June 15, 1994, Douglas opened the account with a deposit of ten million dollars. The account showed no activity until July 25, 1994. At that time, a deposit of $71,166,666 was wired into the account. The wire codes were the same he had witnessed earlier that evening, except for the transaction number which was #0001. As he reviewed the entire account history of thirteen deposits, all in the same amount, he made mental note of the fact that all of the wire codes were the same.

Clay reaccessed the main menu within the RBC system and moved his cursor to Wires. He highlighted the category and pressed Enter. A new category screen appeared. Clay surveyed the screen, highlighted ORIGINATOR and once again pressed Enter. He waited for a moment until the screen changed again. This time the screen displayed Originator Code:***. Clay looked at the code he had noted from the wire information in the Douglas account and entered the originating bank code. The computer paused for a moment while digesting the information. Clay sat back in his chair and waited. The screen changed again. This time the screen displayed Swiss World Bank.

Clay sat up in his chair and studied the screen for a moment. He assumed that because RBC and the Swiss bank communicated with each other, as evidenced by the wire he had witnessed earlier in the evening, the bank systems were the same. If not, they were compatible, which ruled out the Swiss system being COBAL based. This made his task a bit easier because PASCAL systems would not communicate with COBAL-based systems. If what he was about to attempt worked, he would not have to break the Swiss bank's code. The RCB system would allow him access.

He reaccessed the main operating system at RCB. Then he reversed the wire instructions, configuring the wire code so that RCB was the originating bank and the Swiss bank was the receiving bank. He waited for the computer to accept his instructions. A split window then appeared on the monitor. On half of the screen was the RCB prompt window requesting information regarding the account from which funds were to be withdrawn and wired. On the other half of the screen, the Swiss bank was requesting the destination account information. Clay used his Enter key to attempt to scroll through the information categories. It did not work. He tried to move the cursor with his mouse, but that did not work either. He looked down at his keyboard and thought for a moment. Then he tried the Tab key. When he pressed it, the cursor moved to the next information line.

Clay scrolled through the RCB screen using the Tab key. When he finished with the first half of the screen, the cursor moved into Swiss bank information. He scrolled down to the Destination Account line and entered the nine-digit code from his notes. He then moved the cursor to the PROCESS box located at the bottom of the screen and pressed Enter on his keyboard. Clay watched the screen intently, waiting for the computer's response.

When screen display changed, Clay shouted, "Yes! Damn, Peterson, you're pretty good at this."

He studied the screen intently. He had before him Douglas's Swiss account information. As he studied the account activity history, he was puzzled. In lieu of an opening balance, there was a number. Then the activity history began.

SWB ACCOUNT #006743214

DATE	TRANSACTION	TYPE	AUTHORIZATION	BALANCE
06-15-94	#273567			
07-24-94	P.O. # 273567	PBN	SWB-RCB-27652	71166666
07-25-94	P.O. # 273567	PBN	SWB-RCB-27652	-71166666
08-24-94	P.O. # 273567	PBN	SWB-RCB-27652	71166666
08-25-94	P.O. # 273567	PBN	SWB-RCB-27652	-71166666
09-24-94	P.O. # 273567	PBN	SWB-RCB-27652	71166666
09-25-94	P.O. # 273567	PBN	SWB-RCB-27652	-71166666
10-24-94	P.O. # 273567	PBN	SWB-RCB-27652	71166666
10-25-94	P.O. # 273567	PBN	SWB-RCB-27652	-71166666
11-24-94	P.O. # 273567	PBN	SWB-RCB-27652	71166666
11-25-94	P.O. # 273567	PBN	SWB-RCB-27652	-71166666
12-26-94	P.O. # 273567	PBN	SWB-RCB-27652	71166666
12-27-94	P.O. # 273567	PBN	SWB-RCB-27652	-71166666
01-24-95	P.O. # 273567	PBN	SWB-RCB-27652	71166666
01-25-95	P.O. # 273567	PBN	SWB-RCB-27652	-71166666
02-24-95	P.O. # 273567	PBN	SWB-RCB-27652	71166666
02-25-95	P.O. # 273567	PBN	SWB-RCB-27652	-71166666
03-24-95	P.O. # 273567	PBN	SWB-RCB-27652	71166666
03-25-95	P.O. # 273567	PBN	SWB-RCB-27652	-71166666
04-24-95	P.O. # 273567	PBN	SWB-RCB-27652	71166666
04-25-95	P.O. # 273567	PBN	SWB-RCB-27652	-71166666
05-24-95	P.O. # 273567	PBN	SWB-RCB-27652	71166666
05-25-95	P.O. # 273567	PBN	SWB-RCB-27652	-71166666
06-24-95	P.O. # 273567	PBN	SWB-RCB-27652	71166666
06-25-95	P.O. # 273567	PBN	SWB-RCB-27652	-71166666
07-24-94	P.O. # 273567	PBN	SWB-RCB-27652	71166666
07-25-95	P.O. # 273567	PBN	SWB-RCB-27652	-71166666

The opening balance number corresponded with the PO number which remained unchanged over the thirteen-month transaction history. Clay focused on the PO number. He believed it to be the key to the account structure. Because the Swiss system allowed him access through the RCB system, he assumed that the Swiss structure must be the same. He requested the CASE analysis on the Douglas Swiss account. Clay waited a moment for the computer to respond.

The computer screen flashed INVALID REQUEST moments later. Clay sat and looked at the flashing screen. He knew that there had to be a detailed history on each account entry. He studied the screen intently. Then he had an idea. He moved the cursor to the first number entry under the BALANCE heading. He pressed the Enter key and waited. The new display prompted another outburst from Clay.

"All right, user-friendly Swiss programmers. I like it . . . I do."

The new display reflected the specifics of the transaction that Clay had highlighted. The programmers had structured the system so that in lieu of running an entire account CASE analysis, one could review one transaction history at a time if desired. He studied the transaction history on the screen in front of him.

Date	Transaction	Type	Amount	Collateral Acct.
06-15-94	0001	Prime Bank Note P.O.#273567	100,000,000	2212285736825

Clay determined from the transaction history that the PO number in the account represented prime bank notes purchased or controlled by the purchase order. The purchase order bought or controlled one hundred million dollars in prime bank notes. The collateral account indicated was Douglas's RCB trading account which on June 16, 1994, had an opening balance of ten million dollars, exactly 10 percent of the prime bank note purchase order value. Clay studied the transaction history for a few more minutes. He made several notes on the pad which lay on his desk beside the computer. When he had completed his notes, he requested that the computer return to the account history screen. The computer obliged and Clay began probing the file information again. He focused on the account deposit and withdrawal activity. He knew that the ten million correlated to the one hundred million. But he could not figure out how the two numbers related to the withdrawal and deposit amounts. He thought for a moment then entered numbers into his calculator without any luck. He rubbed his tired eyes while he thought.

Clay decided to run a CASE analysis on the transaction again to see if he could get any additional information. He moved the cursor to the TYPE heading and pressed Enter. He waited. The computer responded with a tone and the screen changed. Clay read the words on the screen: SECURITY CODE REQUIRED. Clay studied the screen for a moment then looked at his watch which indicated that it was 1:30. He was tired, but he was too intrigued with the trading account to stop now. He began entering different number codes in an attempt to access the system.

Clay tried all of the codes he could find in the Douglas RCB and Swiss bank files. He attempted letter-number combinations. This process took quite a long time. After not having any luck with the base codes, he inserted the PASCAL language code disk he had used successfully in accessing other banking systems. The disk interacted with the bank's operating system in an attempt to break the security code. Again this failed. He even took a long shot with his COBAL code disk, and again the same computer response resulted: INVALID ENTRY CODE.

Clay looked at his watch once again. The time was now 3:45 a.m. He did not want to give up on this project, but he had to if he was going to be worth anything at the office that day. He sat and looked at the monitor. He couldn't imagine that the security code on a single transaction history could be that complicated.

"Christ, it's not like the Pentagon or U.S. Treasury, and I accessed their systems," Clay said out loud. An idea then struck him. He had been working on the code based on the fact that it was a business-oriented system—a system like any other with PASCAL-based logistics and security.

"What if the system had two levels? What if there was a primary operating data base for logging and storing information, and a secondary data base for information that the bank wanted to keep confidential for security cleared internal use? Not unlike the Pentagon or U.S. Treasury systems. A bit sophisticated for a bank, but then again, this was a Swiss institution and they prided themselves on secrecy and security," Clay thought.

"So now how to break your secondary security level codes?" Clay asked himself out loud.

He studied the screen as he thought about his strategy. Then he had an idea. Maybe the system's security was based on the same principle that the Pentagon and Treasury used. Perhaps the Swiss applied the same cryptological language and theorem. If so, he could break it and he knew it. Clay reached into the top right-hand desk drawer and retrieved his disk storage box. He flipped through the disks until he found the one he was looking for. The one he thought would break the Swiss World Bank security code. The disk was programmed to work interactively with the operating system, identifying and deciphering security codes. This file disk had taken Clay over one year to formulate. It was highly technical in its structure and content, based on a numbers theorem that had been incorporated in more sophisticated and security conscience computer operating systems.

The disk Clay selected was labeled with two words in capital letters: FIBONACCI SEQUENCE.

ARTICLE 9

July 26, 2005, 1:37 a.m.
Hoover Building, Washington, D.C.

The priority fax machine rang once then began receiving an incoming facsimile transmission. The document slowly emerged from the receiving end of the machine. It read as follows:

EYES FACSIMILE

| TO: | SAC Whitfield | July 26, 2005 |
| FROM: | Special Agent Hendrix | Re: Case# 95-2213 |

Movement expected within the next forty-eight hours. Should have evidence required for arrest and prosecution by then. Do not have a complete understanding of suspect's intentions at this time. Intend to play it out as initially planned. I will keep you advised.

Hendrix

CHAPTER THREE

ARTICLE 10

Alberto Rojas was standing on a beautifully manicured grass area just off the veranda. He was surveying the emerald green tree-covered valley below his mountaintop estate. Rojas held a driver in his hand and a bucket of golf balls was positioned a few feet from him. A man stood near the bucket with his hands behind him, waiting for Alberto's command. Rojas snapped his fingers and the man retrieved a fresh golf ball from the bucket and placed it on a tee below Rojas's feet. The man walked back to his place by the bucket of balls and Rojas positioned himself for his shot. Rojas moved his hips from side to side, adjusted his feet, looked at his hands, then looked into the valley, picturing his perfect drive. He drew the club back slowly, keeping his eyes fixed on the ball. Rojas shifted his weight, and with a mighty thrust, brought the club forward toward the ball. When he finished his swing, his position was perfect, with the club suspended above his left shoulder and his upper body and head facing forward. Rojas looked anxiously into the air in an attempt to locate the flight path of his ball. He did not see it. He turned to the guard standing next to the bucket of balls.

"Where'd it go?"

The guard sheepishly pointed to Rojas's feet. Rojas looked down and saw the ball still sitting on the tee. He glared at the ball for a moment then returned his attention to his guard. Rage was visible on Rojas's face as he brought the club back like a baseball bat, and without any provocation or warning, struck the guard on the side of the head. The club hit him just behind the ear with a *thud*. The guard collapsed. Rojas looked at him lying on the ground for a moment then cocked his head and raised his eyebrows as if he had a thought. He held the club up in front of him and began swinging it like a baseball bat. After three swings, he stopped. He studied the golf club for a moment then tossed it to where the guard lay unconscious and bleeding profusely.

"Baseball. I think I will take up baseball," he said to himself as he walked back to the house.

As Alberto walked onto the veranda, he was greeted by a male servant dressed in white and holding a cordless telephone. Rojas took the phone from the manservant and walked to the umbrella-covered table on the veranda to sit.

"Rojas," he answered.

"Alberto, this is Hulio."

"Hulio, my boy, where are you?"

"I'm still in Miami. I dealt with that problem we discussed last week. We have no more outside competition to worry about."

"Are you sure? You got them all?"

"I am sure, Alberto. I am bringing three back to you for your own interrogation as you requested. They are a stubborn group, very loyal. I don't think they will tell you anything that we don't already know."

"It is possible. On the other hand, when I am through with them we will be certain. When will you return, Hulio?"

"I will be back in Medillin late tomorrow afternoon. The live cargo will arrive the following afternoon."

"Come see me when you arrive. We will have dinner and celebrate together."

"Celebrate?"

"A new beginning, my boy. Your presence at the membership table marks a new beginning for all of us."

"There is still unfinished business regarding my father's activities that we must deal with, Alberto. Until that is done, I will not feel much like celebrating."

"What business do you speak of, Hulio?"

"The money. The seventy-seven million that rightfully belongs to the cartel."

"You gave me the information I need to transfer the money, Hulio. It isn't going anywhere. I told the members that it would be transferred to the BVI account this week and then disbursed. They know about it, and they are satisfied. Why do you worry about such things?"

"I will not feel that my name has been fully vindicated until the money is where it belongs: with the members of the cartel."

Rojas laughed. "You are a good man, Hulio. Your heart is in the right place; however, your impatience is a sign of your youth. It will be refreshing to work with you. You may in fact instill some of that youthful impatience and motivation into the others, even into me. I will deal with the money tomorrow and the transaction will be complete before you return. Then you can celebrate with me?"

"Yes, Alberto, then I will celebrate with you."

"All right, my boy, it will be done then. Have a safe return and I will see you late tomorrow afternoon," Rojas said.

He hung up the phone and smiled as he reflected on his conversation with Hulio. Rojas was excited about working with this young and aggressive man. He would teach him and mold him into a great leader of men. Hulio already had the unconditional commitment to the cartel. His father had done a good job with him in that regard, perhaps too good, which turned out to be unfortunate for Ricardo Sanchez. Rojas liked this boy and knew that he would be a positive addition to the cartel.

Rojas signaled to the manservant who had positioned himself outside of the glass door leading into the house. He stood awaiting Rojas's next command. When he saw Rojas raise his hand and wave him over, he immediately went to him. He stood in front of Rojas without speaking. The servants were not allowed to speak.

"Bring me my briefcase," Rojas ordered.

The manservant turned and quickly went into the house. Moments later he emerged carrying the briefcase Rojas had requested. He sat it next to his chair.

"On the table, you idiot!" Rojas shouted.

The man picked the briefcase up and gently placed it on the table and in front of Rojas. He took a step back from the table and waited additional instructions. Rojas gave the manservant a look of indignation and waved him away. The man gladly retreated back to his place in front of the glass doors.

Rojas opened his briefcase and flipped through the files until he found the one he was looking for. The file contained the information Hulio had given him detailing Ricardo's activities. Rojas opened the file and began looking through the documents it contained. There were two sets of detailed shipping inventory logs. One set indicated the product that Sanchez reported the Americans had seized. The second set was for his personal records and detailed the product that he had retained for his benefit. Rojas continued reading through the documents until he found the information he was looking for. He held the stapled set of documents in front of him. The heading on the cover page was Swiss World Bank Account. Rojas flipped through the pages until he found the page that reflected the bank's representation information. He looked down the page until he reached the category of Account Representative. Adjacent to the title was the name Felix Messner and a direct phone number. Rojas picked up the phone, pressed the power button, and dialed the number. After a short time, the phone was answered on the other end.

"Felix Messner," the male voice answered.

"Mr. Messner, this is Ricardo Sanchez," Rojas said.

"What can I do for you, Mr. Sanchez?"

"I would like to coordinate a wire transfer with you."

"Will you be wiring to us, or will this be a withdrawal?"

"A withdrawal."

"Very well, sir. Do you have your account information?"

"Yes, it is here in front of me."

"May I have your account number, please?"

"Yes, it is zero-zero-six-seven-four-three-two-one-six."

"All right, Mr. Sanchez, bear with me a moment while I enter that information for you."

Rojas waited for a moment while Felix entered the account number into his computer. When the account appeared on Felix's monitor, he spoke to Rojas again.

"Do you have a current balance, Mr. Sanchez?"

"Yes, $77,863,000," Rojas said as he read the number from the document he held.

"That is correct, Mr. Sanchez. How much would you like to withdraw from your account?"

"All of it."

"Are you closing your account with us, sir?"

"No, no, I have a business transaction working and need to show the funds on deposit in my British Virgin Island account for a time. I will be transferring the funds back in a few weeks."

"Well, Mr. Sanchez, we have many collateral programs that will allow you to show the liquidity strength that your transaction may require. And utilization of one of those programs would allow you to keep your funds safely in our institution while your transaction is completed. We work with BVI institutions quite often in this regard."

"I assume though, Mr. Messner, that your services in this regard do not come cheaply."

"Well, of course there is a fee; however, it is a small price to pay for peace of mind in a situation like this."

"I'll take my chances, Mr. Messner."

"I really wish—"

"Mr. Messner, if this is a matter that you can not or are unwilling to handle for me, I would like to speak with someone else," Rojas barked.

"Oh no, sir, I can handle it for you. I will be happy to handle it for you. I was simply making an effort to look after your best interests."

"I am fully capable of looking after my interests, Mr. Messner. The fact that I have over seventy-seven million in your bank should be evidence of that."

"Yes, sir, of course. In order to complete the transaction, I will simply need your BVI account information."

"The BVI bank code is seven-zero-seven-two, the account number is three-eight-six-five-five-one-four-two-nine."

"All right, Mr. Sanchez, I have all the information I need. I will begin the transaction immediately."

"No, Mr. Messner, not immediately. I would like you to schedule the transfer to take place tomorrow afternoon. I want you to wire the funds at five o'clock my time. Then you call me and let me know that it has been taken care of."

"There is a substantial time difference, Mr. Sanchez. I can schedule the transaction; however, I will not be here to call you when it takes place."

"Are you telling me that it will inconvenience you, Mr. Messner?"

Messner paused for a moment before answering, "No, Mr. Sanchez, I will be happy to call you when the funds have been wired."

"Thank you, Mr. Messner. I appreciate your cooperation and will remember it in the near future," Rojas said sarcastically.

"It is my—"

Rojas hung up the phone before Messner could finish his sentence. He looked at the document he held in his hand. To Rojas, it represented a chapter in the life of the cartel that he was looking forward to closing. It represented betrayal and deceit; and yet it represented a beginning as well.

ARTICLE 11

July 26, 2005, 1:30 p.m.
Hoover Building, Washington, D.C.

The fourth-floor conference room was filled with SACs, the bureau's divisional heads. This was their weekly staff meeting with Associate Director Stafford, the number-two man in the bureau. It was a weekly event that most loathed. The associate director was not a man who believed in complimenting good performance and acted as though he enjoyed chastising lack of performance. Stafford was a politician. And he was good at it. His job did not change with administrations. He could be an asshole to anyone or everyone if he chose, except of course to the director. And he usually was. He was an excellent administrator, however, and knew how to run the bureau. But then he should as he had been associate director for thirteen years and had been with the bureau for twenty-seven years total. The SACs were visiting among themselves when Associate Director Stafford entered the room accompanied by another man.

"Gentlemen, may I have your attention, please?"

The room was silent as Stafford walked to his chair at the head of the table. The man who accompanied Stafford took an empty seat on one side of the conference table.

"We will forgo the regular agenda. I would like to introduce Special Agent Randall Montgomery. Agent Montgomery is with the DEA. They are requesting our assistance in an investigation and I have committed our resources to them. He will brief us on not only the nature of the investigation, but on their needs as well. Pay close attention and be prepared to offer assistance in your areas of responsibility. Agent Montgomery, you may proceed," Stafford instructed.

"Thank you, Director Stafford. Gentlemen, as you know the United States has been assisting the Colombian government in their efforts to curtail the drug activity within their country. Our responsibility in that effort has been limited to tracking and intercepting drugs once they leave Colombian soil. We have been somewhat successful in these efforts. The president, in an agreement with the Colombian government, has expanded our responsibilities recently. The DEA will now play a more active role in the effort to stop the drugs at their source. We will be working with the Colombian government on Colombian soil to track down and destroy the drug operation there.

"As a result, our manpower and resources here in the United States will be depleted. We need your help in maintaining a strong presence on this end. We don't want to lose any ground against the smuggling efforts of the Colombian cartel."

Agent Montgomery began passing out booklets he had brought into the room with him. "These booklets contain information regarding the nature of our U.S. operation as it pertains to the Colombian drug smuggling operation.

"I have reviewed the booklets being passed out. There is a section in the book that is applicable to every person in this room. Read the whole thing. Understand it and understand that this is a priority, not just to the current administration, but also to the American people. And most of all, gentlemen, understand that I am making this a priority of the director's. So, review the information, work up a resources report and we will meet back here at eight o'clock tomorrow morning to coordinate. I assume that there aren't any questions, so let's get to work," Stafford said.

When the associate director left the conference room with Agent Montgomery, all of the agents stood and began filing out as well. Brian Whitfield was among them. As he moved toward the door, Special Agent Criswell spoke to him.

"What do you make of this, Brian?"

Brian looked up from the booklet to see Criswell standing in front of him. As they made their way to the door, they continued their conversation.

"Don't know. But you can bet your ass I'll have my report ready for Stafford tomorrow morning."

"Why the bureau? Why not the agency? They have the resources for something like this,"

"They may be involved. If they were, we wouldn't know about it. My guess is that they want us for the pub."

"Pub?"

"Yeah, you know. I'm sure that someone will make a big deal about this in the press. Politicians survive on kissing ass and good press. I'm sure they will want the American people to know that the FBI has joined forces with the DEA in the war on drugs. No matter what our role, they can play it up in the press. Makes everyone on the hill look like they know what they're doing."

Criswell laughed at Brian's comment as the two exited the conference room and went down the corridor to their separate offices. When Brian entered his office, he walked to his desk and sat in his chair. He reclined the chair and began reading the document he had been given in the staff meeting. He reviewed the table of contents in the hope that it was divided into categories of responsibility. To his surprise and delight, it was. He turned to the section on telecommunications and computers.

He read the information with interest as it detailed the DEA activities against the cartel from a telecommunications standpoint. They had successfully been monitoring telephone and computer modem activities for the past two years. They knew the identities of all the cartel members. They knew where they lived, who they called, and how sophisticated their communications network was. The DEA had been monitoring facsimile transmissions to and from Colombia and the United States. Brian was impressed with the job they had done. As he continued to read, he came to a section marked Objectives. This section dealt with the goals of the DEA as they related to telecommunications and computer activities. In order of priority, they read Banking Activities and Financial Records.

ARTICLE 12

July 26, 2005, 5:10 p.m.
Comp-Link Corporate Headquarters

Clay was in the process of packing his briefcase to leave. He surveyed the top of his desk to see if there was anything else he needed to take with him. A voice outside his cubicle interrupted him.

"Clay? Are you still there?" the familiar voice asked.

Clay looked up and saw Lisa. He looked at her and smiled. He could not hide the fact that he was totally and completely mesmerized by this girl. He just stood there, smiling and staring.

"Clay?"

"Yes, Lisa?" he said in a transcendental state.

"You are going to be so upset with me."

"Why would I be upset with you?" Clay asked in surprise.

"Our date," Lisa said with a grimace.

"You can't come," Clay said, his voice sounding pitiful as the words came out of his mouth.

"No, I can't. I forgot about a baby shower a friend of mine scheduled for tonight. I have to go. I promised her a couple of weeks ago that I would be there. She just called me a few minutes ago to see if I was coming. Are you okay with that?"

"Hell no, I'm not okay. Why would I be okay. That's the lamest excuse I've ever heard. Why don't you just come right out and tell me that you think I'm a jackass and you don't want to go out with me?" Clay thought. His response to her was toned down just a bit.

"Sure . . . Sure, I understand. Maybe some other time. Right?"

"Well, yeah. But would it be okay if I came over to see you after the shower? I mean if you're not busy?"

"After the shower? Sure, yeah, that would be great. I mean I'll look forward to seeing you. What time?" Clay said excitedly.

"I just need to make an appearance. She lives in Plano and it starts at 7:30. I'll stay about an hour then head your way if it's okay."

"It's okay," Clay said with a broad smile.

"Great then. I'll see you tonight," Lisa said. She smiled at Clay for a moment, gave him a wiggly finger wave goodbye, bounced up on her toe tips, and left his office.

Clay stood there for a moment and gave a rather heavy sigh. He was in love. He had to be, and it scared him to death.

Clay arrived home at a quarter to six. He walked into the house and made a quick survey of the rooms he knew Lisa would see again. He checked the guest bathroom, and all was in order. He thought that he kind of liked the house this way. It reminded him of his mom and the way she used to keep everything in its place.

He picked his briefcase off the kitchen table, took it into his office, and sat it beside his desk chair. As he rose from placing the briefcase, his arm bumped the chair, which then bumped the computer keyboard tray. The sudden movement prompted the computer to stop showing the screen saver and display the work in progress. Clay held the elbow he hit on the chair as he looked at the computer monitor. It displayed a blinking message: ACCESS GRANTED.

"Access granted?" Clay said out loud.

His mind had been so preoccupied with thoughts of Lisa, he had forgotten about the file he had been working on. Then, as he sat at the computer, he remembered. Before going to bed earlier that morning, he had inserted the Fibonacci Sequence disk into the computer. He had instructed the computer to search for the access code that would allow him to get into the portion of the Douglas account transaction history he wanted to review. Sometime between 3:45 a.m. and now, the disk had broken the code. He was in.

Clay pressed the Enter key on his keyboard. The monitor went completely blank for a few moments. Clay drew back from the computer with a look of concern on his face. He thought he had inadvertently erased the screen. He looked at the keyboard to make sure he had pressed the Enter key. He was sure he had. He didn't know what was wrong. Then the monitor displayed a new screen. Clay studied the jumbled mess displayed. It was a file, he knew that, but it was written in a language he had never seen before. It wasn't a computer language; it wasn't a foreign language; it was more like a code, a hieroglyphic code. The characters had to be words or have meaning because they were in blocks and separated at points. He had never seen anything like it before. He continued to study the screen.

Πυρχηασε ορδερ νυμβερ 0273567 ιν τηε αμουντ οφ 100,000,000 Μ Υ.Σ. δολλαρσ. Τψπε αχχουντ νυμβερ ΣΩΒ–8561–ΙΝΤ–7457. Χορρεσπονδινγ αχχουντ 212–285736825. Ιντερναλ αχχουντ ρεφερενχε 006743214. ΣΩΒ ΠΒΝ τσολυε 94,069,444.50 Υ.Σ. δολλαρσ. Τραδε γυαραντεε μινιμυμ τηρεε τιμεσ περ ωεεκ. Τερμ φιφτεεν μοντησ. Τερμινατιον δατε 9–25–95. Ρεσιδυαλ τρανσφερ ωιτηιν τωεντψ–φουρ ηουρσ αφτερ χομπλετιον οφ τραδε. Γυαραντεε μινιμυμ 3%.

After spending some time trying to decipher the symbols, he decided he would pick out a single set of symbols and try to focus his efforts on them. He looked through the paragraph in an attempt to see if he could locate any two sets which were alike. There were two sets of characters that were alike in the paragraph. He would concentrate on deciphering them and hoped that the result would be a complete understanding of the code. Clay highlighted the paragraph that appeared on his screen. With a few key strokes, he instructed his computer to print the highlighted text. The computer responded and the printer began printing the information. This process was time consuming. It took the printer twenty-five minutes to print a single paragraph. When it was through, however, he had an excellent printed draft of what appeared on the screen.

He now began to study the symbols further. The two groups he concentrated on were identical. 100,000,000M appeared in the first and third sentences. His thoughts were interrupted by a knock at his door. Clay looked at his watch and saw that it was 8:45.

"Christ, I've been working on this for over two hours. I'm not ready," he said under his breath.

Clay ran to the front door and found Lisa standing there when he opened it. She presented him with a bottle of wine and a smile.

"I'm early. The party was boring and lots of people showed up, so I kinda snuck out without being noticed."

"I'm glad you did. Come on in," Clay said.

As Lisa walked into the house, Clay began apologizing. "I don't have anything ready for you to eat, and I didn't have a chance to clean up. I've been working on the computer since I got home."

"It's okay, I'm not hungry and the house looks great. What were you working on?"

"A code. It's like nothing I've seen before. Like hieroglyphics or something."

"Really? Can I see?"

"Sure, you may even be able to help me with it."

The pair walked back into Clay's office and took their places at the computer desk. Clay picked up the paper on which he had copied the symbols and handed it to Lisa.

"Okay, this is what I'm trying to decipher. I thought that I had done the hard part. I accessed the Royal Bank system then I traced the Douglas trading account to an account in Switzerland. Then I accessed the Swiss system and got into his account there. I even broke a secondary level security system to get this information, and now I don't know what in the hell it means. It's not computer language; it's not mathematical formula; and from what I can see, it's not a foreign language. I'm stumped."

Lisa studied the paragraph of symbols for a moment. Then she smiled and spoke to Clay. "Ya know? All of the dorm rooms in college had a computer. We all had E-mail, okay?"

"Okay," Clay replied with a confused look on his face.

"Okay, so some of the girls roomed with real she-bitches. They would read their mail and tell everyone what was going on with them. So, you know what we did?"

"No, what?" Clay replied, without a clue where she was going with her story.

"We made up our own code. Well it really wasn't a code like in the army or anything, but it kept other people from knowing what was in our notes to each other."

"So what was your code?"

"We changed the font."

"The font?"

"Yeah, you know the way the letters are structured on the computer. We would use a different one every month. It was really cool. We had our own little language," Lisa said feeling proud of herself.

"I don't think that the Swiss World Bank would simply use a change of fonts in this system. It was very complicated to break the code to even access it. I had to use my Fibonacci Sequence disk to get it. It took five or six hours to do it."

"Fibo-what?"

"Fibonacci Sequence. It's like a numbers theorem. It was originally used in number theory, geometry, and even genetics.

Most codes or security systems built into computers are structured based on encrypted DES with sequenced numbers, mathematical formula, or cryptology sequences patterned to seem as though they are an unrelated phenomena when in fact there is a relationship. The Fibonacci Sequence correlates all of the possibilities and asserts that every finite zero-sum has a minimal value of mixed strategies that are allowed. After it analyzes a given system, it begins working through the code variations until the code is broken. It's that simple."

"Really, it's that simple? I don't have a clue what you just said. Where did you get this code-breaking Fibonacci thing?"

"I developed it. It took me a year to do it, but I developed it myself. I couldn't have accessed the Pentagon or Treasury systems without it. It was unusual to find it on a banking system. I wouldn't have thought to use it myself in programming a banking system."

"God, Clay, that's really incredible!" Lisa said.

"I guess it is pretty incredible when you think about it. But their systems probably have to meet more stringent—"

"No, I'm talking about this Fibonacci thing you developed. That's really incredible. You're like a real genius on the computer, Clay, a real genius," Lisa said with a smile.

"Well, thanks. I just spend a lot of time doing it. I don't think I'm any kind of genius or anything."

"I do. Now what do you think about my theory on breaking this code?" Lisa asked.

Clay knew that she did not have a clue about what she was talking about. A system as sophisticated as the Swiss World Bank would have used early Egyptian hieroglyphics or mathematical formulas or even a form of cryptology which was popular during World War II. They would not simply alter a font. He could not insult her though. He would not dare do anything that might hurt her. He looked at her blue eyes and the anticipation on her face.

"I think it might have merit. Let's try."

"Okay . . . okay, do you have Word Perfect?"

"Yes, why?" Clay asked.

"Can you get into it from where you are without messing everything up?"

"Yes."

Clay moved the cursor to the top right hand corner of the screen where an arrow was displayed. He clicked the mouse when the cursor was on top of the arrow and the old screen disappeared. Then he typed in some instructions on the keyboard, pressed Enter and sat back in his chair. The Word Perfect program then appeared on the screen.

"Okay, we're in Word Perfect," Clay said.

"Okay, now go to . . ." Lisa paused as she looked at the tool bar at the top of the screen. "Try Format."

Clay placed the cursor on Format and clicked the mouse. A list of options appeared.

"Okay, there it is, go to Font," Lisa said.

Clay moved the cursor to Font and again clicked twice on the mouse. A box appeared on the screen. The box had several sections. One section indicated the name of the font; another had a sample sentence which displayed the type of font selected; still another contained font size and formatting options. The two of them looked at the display for a moment before Lisa spoke.

"Okay, now we . . . no . . . that . . . this isn't a standard font, right? It's not like New Times Roman or Courier. It's something different; so we can pass the easy ones over."

"Okay, where do we start?" Clay asked.

"Go with the first one, Arial, and we'll work our way down the list. This is fun; it's like putting together a puzzle or something. It makes you use your brain."

"It's just like a puzzle. You're right. Okay, Arial, let's see your stuff," Clay said.

He highlighted the Arial font and they looked at the sample sentence screen. It wasn't a match. They then started down the list. There were 185 font types in his Word Perfect. This process could take them a while, he thought, but he really didn't care. She was next to him and she appeared to be having a good time.

They had been working on the font selections for a little over an hour. They were almost through with the font styles that began with the letter *C*. Clay was sitting at the computer and suddenly felt the urge to use the bathroom. He turned to Lisa who was studying the screen.

"I'm going to go fix something to drink, can I get you something?" he asked.

"A glass of ice water would be perfect," Lisa responded.

She looked at Clay in a thoughtful way. Then without warning leaned forward and kissed him gently on the lips. Clay's eyes widened in surprise.

"What was that for?" he asked.

"Just because," Lisa said with a smile.

"Well, feel free to express yourself in that manner whenever you need to."

"I will," Lisa said directly.

Clay cleared his throat, gave her a smile, and retreated to the bathroom. Lisa looked at the computer monitor with a frown on her face. She looked over her shoulder checking to see if Clay was anywhere to be seen. She moved into his chair and scrolled down to the next C-font style listed. The font style was CaslonOpnFce. She studied the sample sentence and it wasn't a match. She scrolled down the list to the next C font. It was CGTimes; she looked at the sample sentence and it was not a match either. Lisa scrolled the font list again, this time there were six Courier style fonts, and she knew that they wouldn't match. The next one on the list was called CyrillicA; she selected it and watched as the sample sentence changed. She looked at the screen then at the paper she held in her hand. Again she checked the screen and again she looked at the paper.

"Clay! Clay, you better come here and look at this!" Lisa shouted.

Clay was in the bathroom and when he heard Lisa shout he hurriedly tucked in his shirt and buttoned his jeans. He flushed the toilet, dashed out of the bathroom and back into his office where Lisa sat with a satisfied smile on her face. The smile turned to a wide grin when Lisa studied Clay's appearance.

"I think you forgot something, Clay," Lisa said attempting not to laugh.

Clay looked down and found that his shirt tail was protruding from his zipper. He had been in such a hurry to get to Lisa that he had forgotten to zip his pants. He turned away from her and quickly stuffed the shirttail in the hole and zipped his pants. When he turned around, Lisa was still smiling.

"God, that's embarrassing. I hate it when that happens," Clay said walking back to his desk chair.

"Has it happened before?"

"At my sister's wedding, at my high-school prom, at a football game I was attending in college. It happens to me all the time. Stuff like that always happens to me. I was born a klutz and I'll die one too."

"Well, you are a cute klutz, and you're a genius klutz as well. You broke the code."

"Broke the code? What code?"

"The account code. They used a font called Cyrillic. See here?" Lisa said as she pointed to the computer monitor which displayed the font and sample sentence.

Clay studied the screen and the paper. He was stunned. The bank had simply used a symbol-based font style. Clay was amazed. He looked and gave Lisa a hug before he really knew what he was doing. He let her go then returned his attention to the computer.

"Okay. Now let's see what this says," Clay said.

"That will take a while. Don't you have to print a copy of the alphabet in the font then figure it out?"

"We'll do it the easy way. We'll scan it, format it in WP, and change the font. Easy."

"Yeah, easy," Lisa agreed.

Clay placed the document with the Swiss bank information in the scanner and pressed Start. The document was scanned into the computer moments later. Clay pulled the new document up on his screen, formatted it to Word Perfect and highlighted the entire paragraph. He pressed Ctrl+C on his keyboard. Then he moved the cursor below the paragraph of symbols and pressed Ctrl+V. The paragraph of symbols was duplicated. He highlighted the second paragraph and this time chose Format on the tool bar. He selected Font, scrolled to Times New Roman, and pressed Enter. It worked. The screen now displayed one paragraph in Cyrillic font and one written in Times New Roman.

Πυρχηασε ορδερ νυμβερ 0273567 ιν τηε αμουντ οφ 100,000,000M Υ.Σ. δολλαρσ. Τψπε αχχουντ νυμβερ ΣΩΒ–8561–INT–7457. Χορρεσπονδινγ αχχουντ 212–285736825. Ιντερναλ αχχουντ ρεφερενχε 006743214. ΣΩΒ ΠΒΝ ϖαλυε 94,069,444.50 Υ.Σ. δολλαρσ.Τραδε γυαραντεε μινιμυμ τηρεε τιμεσ περ ωεεκ. Τερμ φιφτεεν μοντησ. Τερμινατιον δατε 9–25–95. Ρεσιδυαλ τρανσφερ ωιτηιν τωεντψ–φουρ ηουρσ αφτερ χομπλετιον οφ τραδε. Γυαραντεε μινιμυμ 3%.

Purchase order number 0273567 in the amount of 100,000,000M U.S. dollars. Type account number SWB-8561-INT-7457. Corresponding account 212-285736825. Internal account reference 006743214. SWB PBN value 100,000,000M U.S. dollars. SWB PBN PO0273567 discount 5.93%. SWB net PO0173567 value 94,069,444.50 U.S. dollars. Trade guarantee minimum three times per week. Term fifteen months.

Termination date 9-25-95. Residual transfer within twenty-four hours after completion of trade. Guarantee minimum 3%.

Clay studied the screen intently. He read through the detailed transaction summary, and to his surprise, he believed he understood its meaning. He knew that there was only one way he could prove to himself that he did understand it. To do it he would have to break his own rules. He would have to step over the invisible line he had always sworn he would never cross. He stared at the screen and made his decision. It was a decision that would change his life forever.

ARTICLE 13

July 27, 2005, 12:37 a.m.
Hoover Building, Washington, D.C.

The priority fax machine rang and the incoming facsimile slowly emerged from the receiving end of the machine. It read as follows:

EYES FACSIMILE

TO: SAC Whitfield   July 27, 2005
FROM: Special Agent Hendrix   Re: Case# 95-2213

No status change to report. Do not have enough information to predict suspect intentions at this time. Will keep you advised.

Hendrix

CHAPTER FOUR

ARTICLE 14

July 27, 2005, 8:00 a.m.
Hoover Building, Washington, D.C.

The fourth-floor conference room was once again full of SACs awaiting the arrival of Associate Director Stafford. There was a low murmur in the room as the agents spoke among themselves. Brian Whitfield sat in his chair quietly reviewing the report he had prepared for the director regarding his role in the pending operation. Director Stafford entered the room and walked to his chair at the head of the table.

"Gentlemen, I trust that everyone is prepared this morning. We have a lot to cover, so let's get started. Agent Bradley will be agent-in-charge of this operation, which we are calling Second Wave for obvious reasons. We want the Colombians and the Guatemalans to know that we are dead serious about this thing. They will understand that our forces in the United States are as one when it comes to fighting the war on drugs. I think they will think that U.S. operations will be weakened by deployment of personnel to Colombia. That is what they will think because we intend to publicize the fact that we have concerns about our ability to maintain our U.S. operations at the level they have seen in the past. We want them to believe that port inspections and air surveillance will be lax. Our hope is that they will ship greater quantities of drugs as a result. When they do, we will be there to greet them. Agent Bradley, why don't you brief us on what is expected and each area of responsibility?" Stafford asked.

Agent Leonard Bradley was sitting directly to Stafford's right. He was the special agent in charge of the FBI Narcotics Division.

"The DEA will deploy a 250-man task force to Colombia on July 29. They will deploy a one-hundred-agent task force to Guatemala on July 30. We know that the Colombians ship and fly cocaine to Guatemala. The drugs are then smuggled into the United States through Mexico on land. The base of operation for this is believed to be in the Guatemalan city of Huehuetenango. They also smuggle into the United States by sea along the west coast as far north as Oregon. The Guatemalan port cities, Champerico and San Jose, are the Guatemalan origination points for this operation. The Colombians ship the drugs to Guatemala through the Gulf of Honduras and into the port city of Puerto Barrios. The DEA will be working with the Guatemalan government troops in destroying the activity found present in all of these key locations.

"In Colombia, the DEA will be working with the Colombian army and several special forces units of our own in search-and-destroy missions concentrated in Medillin, Bogota, and the port cities of Tumaco, Buenaventura, Cartagena, Barranquilla, and Santa Marta. The special forces will concentrate their activities in the jungles surrounding Medellin, Bogota, Palmira, and Villavincencio.

"The intelligence operation has taken over a year. The DEA knows where it's going when it gets into both countries. This is full-scale war, gentlemen, and they expect heavy casualties to be sustained on the part of the drug cartel over the next 120 days. Their mission is seek and destroy, and shoot to kill. The operation is called Clean Sweep and that is what they intend to do.

"As for our responsibilities here at home, we step into positions which will be vacated by the DEA deployment. We will require three hundred agents in the field. We'll pull nonessentials from every department to meet this requirement.

I want a detailed summary of available agents from all field offices by 5:00. We'll meet at 6:00 to discuss Second Wave assignments. Agent Whitfield, I'll need to see you after this meeting. We need to discuss the telecommunications aspects of this operation."

Brian nodded in response to Bradley's request.

"Are there any questions right now?" Bradley asked.

The SACs looked around the table at one another then returned their attention to Bradley and the associate director.

"Good. Then you guys will meet back here at 6:00. I won't be here because I have to attend a briefing with the director at the White House. The president's COS is concerned that we may be committing some kind of act of war. The only war that son-of-a-bitch ever fought was trying to pull his pants over his fat ass. So I'll expect a briefing tonight from you Bradley when I get back here around 7:30."

"Yes, sir," Bradley responded.

"Let's go to work, gentlemen. This one's going to be fun," Stafford said as he stood and left the room.

When Stafford was gone, the SACs began to file out of the conference room. Brian Whitfield stayed in his chair as did Agent Bradley. When the room had cleared, Bradley spoke.

"I need your help in a bad way on this one, Brian. The telecommunications network the DEA has in place is archaic by our standards. I told them we would establish our own communication base in the field. Any ideas in terms of timing?"

Brian thought for a moment then looked intently at Bradley as he spoke.

"If I understand your strategy, Leonard, you plan to cover targeted port cities on the east and west coast, and borders in the Midwest and the southwest, and you intend to maintain air surveillance. You therefore need communications support on a local, regional, and national level. The communications system will need to be wireless, scrambled, and satellite based. How am I doing?"

"Excellent, when can you have it ready?"

"It's done."

"I don't understand, how could it be done?"

"We'll use our existing regional communications centers. I will assign personnel at each center to Second Wave. We will select an open frequency on the satellite system specifically for the operation. All calls made by field personnel to the field communications centers will be monitored from our communications headquarters in Potomac, Maryland. The system is already scrambled and we will have updates by the minute if you need them regarding field activity. I can have the entire system in place by 5:00 this afternoon. We will distribute the Second Wave phone numbers tonight at the 6:00 meeting."

"You're a damn genius, Brian. I hope that the rest of this operation goes this smoothly."

"What about the banking and financial information that the DEA targeted in their report? Is there anything that I can do on that end?"

"They're hoping to confiscate records during their seek-and-destroy raids in Colombia. I don't think they have been able to establish where the money trail starts and stops with the cartel. If you can do anything to assist them in those efforts, I don't see what it would hurt."

"I don't know if we can or not, but we'll give it a shot. In the meantime, I'll get the communications system ready to go. We'll be ready by 5:00."

Both men stood from their chairs. Bradley walked around the table to Brian and extended his hand. "Thanks, Brian, I really appreciate this. It's a load off my mind."

"No problem, Leonard. Just remember me when you make assistant director when this is over."

The two agents laughed at Brian's comment and walked out of the conference room together. Brian felt a sense of satisfaction about the fact that he was readily capable of assisting Leonard and the operation. He hoped his role in Second Wave would be this easy to fulfill while the operation was ongoing. Leonard was hoping that all aspects of the operation would proceed as this aspect had. They were both in for a surprise.

ARTICLE 15

July 27, 2005, 9:37 a.m.
Clay Peterson's House, Dallas, Texas

Clay sat at his computer looking intently at the screen. Lisa had not left until 11:20 p.m., and he had been up all night. He had called in sick that morning because he was intent on figuring out the structure of the trading account of D. Conrad Douglas. He had a basic understanding at that point as to how the trading account worked. Clay determined that on June 15, 1994, Douglas opened an account with the Royal Bank of Canada. Based on the transaction history, he knew now that the purpose of that account was collateral. The collateral was then used to purchase or control one hundred million dollars worth of Swiss World Bank prime bank notes. The Swiss World Bank sold the PNBs to Douglas at a discounted rate of 5.93 percent. Douglas or the corresponding bank, which in this case was RCB, then purchased the bank notes at face value or one hundred million dollars. This left Douglas with a spread profit of $5,930,555.50 each time he traded. The Swiss bank would issue the PBNs against the purchase order a guaranteed minimum of three times a week. Clay had a spread sheet displayed on the screen illustrating his hypothesis.

$ 100,000,000.00 x 10%	=	$ 10,000,000.00
$ 100,000,000.00 x 5.93%	=	$ 5,930,555.50
$ 5,930,555.50 x 3	=	$ 17,792,666.50
$ 17,791,666.50 x 4	=	$ 71,166,666.00

Purchase order number 0273567 in the amount of 100,000,000M U.S. dollars. Type account number SWB-8561-INT-7457. Corresponding account 212-285736825. Internal account reference 006743214. SWB PBN value 100,000,000M U.S. dollars. SWB PBN PO0273567 discount 5.93%. SWB net PO0173567 value 94,069,444.50 U.S. dollars. Trade guarantee minimum three times per week. Term fifteen months. Termination date 9-25-95. Residual transfer within twenty-four hours after completion of trade. Guarantee minimum 3%.

Clay had all of the numbers. He had been able to restructure the account activity. Now he wanted to see if his hypothesis was in fact correct. He focused on the Type Account Number option in the transaction history. He reaccessed the operating system, and when the computer requested the account number, he entered SWB-8561-INT-7457. He waited for the computer to respond. When it did, a new window was displayed. It showed two lists of purchase orders. One list had the heading of TRADING, the other PENDING SALE.

Douglas's purchase order was listed with eight others under TRADING. There were four purchase orders listed under PENDING SALE.

Clay highlighted the first purchase order listed under PENDING SALE. He waited for the computer to respond. A prompt screen appeared on the monitor.

SWB PBN TRADING ACCOUNT

PURCHASE ORDER #0273574		FCEV: 100,000,000U.S.
DISCOUNT RATE: 4.842%	TERM: 15 Months Fixed	TDEV:95,158,000U.S.
CORRESPONDING BANK:		COL.ACT:
COMMENCEMENT DATE:		TERM DATE:
MINIMUM TRADE GUARANTEE: 2 WEEKLY		INSURANCE: COLLATERAL

Clay surveyed the screen for a few moments. The cursor was positioned and blinking at the end of the Corresponding Bank information line, prompting him to enter the number of the corresponding bank. He reviewed the transaction history from the Douglas account and used the corresponding bank code for the Royal Bank of Canada, 2212. He entered the bank code and pressed Enter. The cursor moved and began blinking at the end of the Col. Act. information line. He needed a collateral account. He assumed that he needed a minimum of ten million dollars in it as well.

Clay instructed his computer to access the RCB operating system again. When the computer finished, he went to new accounts. The new accounts prompt screen appeared on the monitor and he began filling in the data requested. The screen asked for his name, which he gave as Sallad Rekcah, the anagram for Dallas Hacker. He made up and entered a social security number, address, date of birth, personal information, and employment history as he went along. When he reached the end of the prompt screen, the computer paused for a moment. Clay watched and waited intently. He had never gone this far; he did not know what would happen next.

The screen changed again, this time displaying a new account spread sheet. The cursor was blinking again requesting information, this time Opening Account Balance. Clay thought for a moment. He needed ten million dollars in this account. He decided he would withdraw ten million dollars from the Douglas account so he could finish his experiment. He exited New Accounts and entered Savings Accounts. He pulled up Douglas's account information again and requested a withdrawal. He again anxiously waited for the computer to respond.

The computer sounded a single tone and flashed a message: TRANSACTION DENIED—LOCKED ACCOUNT.

Clay sat back in his chair and looked disheartened at the flashing message. Then he had an idea and sat back up in his chair. He began typing commands into the computer, and when he finished, he waited.

When the computer finished the tasks Clay had requested, it displayed the Savings Account access screen of the Swiss World Bank. He looked at the print out of Douglas's SWB account and wrote the account number down on a pad he had next to the computer on the desk. Then he began his search for an account he could use. Douglas's account number was 006743214. Clay keyed in a set of numbers, 006743215, pressed Enter and waited. The screen responded with a tone and a flashing message: ACCOUNT NOT LISTED-CHECK ENTRY.

"Dammit. Why wouldn't there be. They have to be listed in some kind of chronological order."

Clay cleared the screen and tried again. This time the number he entered was 006743216. He pressed Enter and sat back in his chair. While Clay waited for the computer to respond, he spoke to himself.

"If this doesn't work, I'll try going the other way. If that doesn't work, I'll have to start with the inside numbers and that'll take a while."

He watched the screen for a few more moments and it still did not change. He leaned back, looked at the ceiling and rolled his head from side to side to loosen the tight muscles in his neck. His eyes were closed while he rotated his head. The computer sounded another tone and Clay did not look at the screen immediately as he expected to see another flashing message. When he did finally look at his monitor, he found that a new account was displayed. An account with quite a large balance and no activity indicated except several large deposits over the prior six months. Clay studied the account for a moment. The balance was close to eighty million dollars. Clay spoke to himself again.

"This one is perfect. No withdrawals, only deposits. And I won't be using the money for more than thirty minutes, so no one will ever know I was here. It's perfect."

Clay wrote the account number down on his notepad. He exited the account screen and went back to the main menu. He moved the cursor to the WIRES category and the prompt screen was displayed. Clay entered the account number from the Swiss Bank as the originating account. Then he entered the number of the new savings account he had opened with the Royal Bank of Canada. The cursor moved to the Wire Amount information and began blinking. It was prompting Clay to enter the amount he wanted to wire. He was nervous; his palms were sweating, yet he had this feeling of excitement and anticipation in his stomach. He wanted to see where this thing was going. He wanted to finish what he had started. He knew that he wasn't hurting anyone by doing this. He was playing a game; a game that few in the world could play. It was only a game.

After Clay had paused to reassure himself about what he was about to do, he keyed in the amount he wanted to wire. He did it slowly with one finger on the keys. 10000000 When he finished, he looked at all of those zeros. They were just numbers on a computer screen. Eight digits. Eight characters. In life, however, he knew that the numbers meant a lot more than just digits and characters. Men had killed for a lot less. Wars had started for a lot less.

Clay finished his philosophical thoughts about the money he was preparing to transfer and looked at his keyboard. He focused on the Enter key. He stared at it then lifted his index finger over the key and pressed. The screen flashed a message: PROCESSING. Clay watched the flashing message intently, waiting for the inevitable Access Denied or Invalid Entry message to take its place. He stared at the screen as though he were mesmerized by it. He waited, and he waited. After several minutes, he began rubbing his tired eyes with his fingers. Then he heard a tone. He kept his fingers over his eyes and thought for a moment.

"It's going to say Invalid Entry or Request Denied or any one of a hundred negative responses."

He peeked out between his fingers. Then he took his hands away from his face and sat up in his chair, looking at the screen in wide-eyed amazement. The screen displayed a message, only it was not the message Clay had expected. It was not flashing. It read simply TRANSACTION COMPLETED.

"I don't fucking believe it. I don't fucking believe it!" Clay shouted.

He looked at the screen then glanced at the phone. He wanted to tell someone what he had accomplished; he needed to tell someone what he had been able to do. Then he frowned as he realized that there wasn't anyone he could tell. This would always be his secret. He would be the only one who would ever know about this. Then he realized that he wasn't through. He still had to finish the game. He quickly exited the Swiss operating system and reentered the RCB system. He accessed the savings account he had earlier established and found that the account balance was indeed ten million dollars. Satisfied with that, he exited the RCB system and went back to the Swiss Trading Account Purchase Order window. He highlighted P.O. # 0273574, and pressed Enter. The prompt screen once again appeared on the monitor. Clay keyed in the RCB bank code on the Corresponding Bank information line. He keyed in the RCB savings account number on the Col. Act. information line. He entered 07-27-95 as the Commencement Date, and 10-27-96 as the Term. Date. Clay sat back in his chair and reviewed the information he had entered. It was all correct. He moved his index finger into position once again above the Enter key and pressed. The computer sounded a single tone, and another message flashed on the monitor: PROCESSING.

Clay again waited anxiously for several minutes. This time he did not take his eyes off the screen. He wanted to see the message as it was displayed. Moments later it was. TRANSACTION COMPLETED was the message and Clay's shout was his response.

"Yes! Son-of-a-bitch, I did it! I actually did it!" he shouted. Again he looked at the phone, then around the room and again he knew that there was no one he could tell. He ran to his back door, opened it and went out onto his concrete patio. He looked at the bright blue cloudless sky and screamed.

"I did it, world! You will never know it, but by god I did it!"

Clay stood there for a moment, his heart beating uncontrollably and sweat beginning to appear on his face due to a combination of his excitement and the midday summer heat. He was through talking to the world and was feeling the effects of the heat, so he opted to go back into the air-conditioned house. He walked through the living room and back into his office. He sat back at his desk and admired the monitor in front of him which still displayed the message that he had successfully completed his final transaction. Clay was filled with a sense of satisfaction. He looked at the screen and recalled the work it took to get to that point. To him it was as though he had finished a long journey of exploration or just completed climbing the highest peak.

Then he knew what he had to do. He had to fix it. Put everything back to the way it was before anyone would know he had been there. He had to erase all memory of his presence. He really did not want to do it this time. But he knew that he needed to, and he knew that he would. Still with a feeling of triumph and satisfaction inside, he sat up in his chair and positioned his fingers on the keyboard.

"Well . . . it was a trip. And it was fun while it lasted," Clay said to the monitor.

Clay exited the Trading Account screen and the Swiss system. He accessed the RCB system and pulled up his savings account which still reflected a balance of ten million dollars. He took a deep breath and proceeded to access the RCB WIRE prompt screen. He entered the savings account number from RCB then the destination account number which was the account he wired the money from in the Swiss bank.

He looked at the screen for a moment, reflected, then pressed the Enter key. He did not wait and watch the screen this time. Clay stood from his chair and started to leave his office. His departure was interrupted by a computer tone. Clay turned to look at the monitor. Another message was being displayed. Clay stood in shock and horror as he read the message out loud.

"Transaction denied . . . account locked."

ARTICLE 16

July 27, 2005, 4:45 p.m.
Alberto Rojas's estate, Medillin, Colombia

Tables were filled with a variety of gourmet food and all types of drinks. The ballroom was decorated with brightly colored piñatas and crepe paper streamers. Mariachi played as they walked through the small crowd of men, women, and children who had gathered for the celebration. Rojas waited with the other four members of the cartel in front of the house for the guest of honor to arrive. The five of them were smoking cigars Rojas had imported from Cuba.

"This is a great day, my friends. Truly a great day for all of us. It marks a new beginning in our history," Rojas said.

"I would offer my opinion, Alberto, but I know how much you dislike to hear the opinions of others," Joseffe Pinilla said in a sarcastic tone.

"Joseffe, my good friend, are you still angry with me?"

"Yes, Alberto, I am angry with you."

"Joseffe, please, my friend, I ask you in front of all of the other members who stand here with us, to accept my apologies for my comments and actions of the other day. I would never do anything to purposely anger you, my friend. And I welcome your opinions on any subject," Rojas said.

Pinilla looked at the other members who were awaiting his response to Rojas's speech. Joseffe was a stubborn man and he did not like to be insulted. But this was Alberto Rojas. And he had to accept the apology. To decline could mean an early grave.

"I accept your apology, Alberto," Pinilla said humbly.

Upon hearing this, Rojas moved to Pinilla and threw his arms around him in an embrace. "My good friend, Joseffe Pinilla. This makes my heart very happy. I will now, and only now, be able to enjoy the festivities of the evening," Rojas said as he continued to embrace Pinilla. Rojas drew back from Pinilla and grabbed both of his arms. "Come. Come, my brothers. We will drink to our friendship, to our brotherhood, and to our continued success together," Rojas said with a wide smile.

As the group started into the house, they heard a car enter the driveway. The group turned to see who it was. Rojas left the group and walked quickly to greet the new arrival. It was the guest of honor after all.

"Hulio! Hulio, my boy, it is so good to see you," Rojas exclaimed as Hulio exited the black Range Rover.

Rojas walked to him as he stood beside the vehicle. When the two were close, they embraced each other in a customary hug. When they finished their embrace, Rojas turned and faced the other cartel members who were still standing in the doorway.

"Look, my brothers, our future has arrived! Now let us celebrate together!" Rojas shouted. He walked with Hulio to the door where the others stood waiting. Hulio received a hug from each of them before they entered the house.

The group walked through the house toward the ballroom. It was a beautiful home; the largest home in all of Colombia according to Rojas. It had twenty thousand square feet of living area, an indoor tennis court, swimming pool, and riding arena. It had sixteen bedrooms, four master suites, twenty bathrooms, a huge formal dinning room, parlor, game room, three formal living areas, and of course Rojas's elegantly decorated office. There was a magnificent collection of art scattered throughout the home. Rojas did not have any taste when it came to art, nor did he appreciate anything about it except its price. If it was expensive, he purchased it. The collection was eclectic. It was reported to be worth in excess of one hundred million dollars. Rojas knew privately that he had spent well over a quarter of a billion dollars on his art collection. Each time he purchased a piece, he would have it masterfully copied. He had all of his original pieces in a fire-proof vault in Switzerland.

As the group entered the ballroom, everyone stopped what they were doing and gave the guest of honor a round of applause. As the applause died down, the crowd moved toward Hulio to greet him with a hug. Rojas and the other members went to their table in the corner to sit together. As they took their seats, a manservant served them each a drink from the silver tray he held in one hand.

Once all of the members had their drinks, Rojas stood at the table and raised his glass. "A toast, my brothers. A toast to family, friends, and a future together free from sickness and filled with success," Rojas raised his glass to his mouth and drank. The other members followed suit. Rojas sat down and surveyed the men at the table and then the room. He was delighted. He had made peace with Joseffe, who he considered a pain in the ass, but a cartel member nonetheless. Hulio had arrived safely from the United States after killing those who would betray the cartel. The organization was having a record year in terms of both sales and profits. His family was healthy; he was healthy. Times were good for Alberto Rojas. He thought that nothing could spoil this day. As Rojas sat contemplating what an extraordinary life he had, a manservant approached him. He stood in front of Rojas and Rojas was irritated at the man for blocking his view of the room.

"Get out of my way, you fool," Rojas demanded. The man obliged, and moved to one side. Rojas continued to ignore the man as he stood silent beside him.

Roberto Diego was amused at the situation. He had been watching Rojas and the servant. He knew that all of Rojas's servants were forbidden to speak to him unless spoken to first. Diego found this amusing. Diego spoke to Rojas.

"Alberto, I believe that this man has something to say to you."

Rojas glanced over his shoulder to find the servant standing behind him. Rojas turned in his chair and faced the servant. "What! What do you want?" Rojas barked.

"It is the phone, sir. You have a call."

"Goddammit, man, why did you not say something to me!"

"I am forbidden—"

"Shut up, you idiot. I will take the call in my office. Now go! Get away from me!"

Diego laughed to himself as Rojas left the ballroom to take the phone call. Rojas walked through the house to his office and sat at his desk. One light on the phone was lit and blinking, indicating that it was a call on hold. Rojas picked up the phone and pressed the flashing button.

"Hello!"

"Mr. Sanchez? This is Felix Messner. I'm calling long distance from Switzerland to speak with Mr. Sanchez."

"Oh . . . Yes, Mr. Messner, this is Ricardo Sanchez," Rojas said quickly remembering who he was supposed to be.

"Yes . . . well, Mr. Sanchez, I was calling to tell you that the wire did take place. The funds should be posted at opening of BVI business tomorrow."

"That is excellent news, Mr. Messner. I want to thank you for you attention on this matter. I will not forget it."

"You're welcome, Mr. Sanchez. The altered balance was somewhat of a problem because I had entered the wire into the computer after we spoke yesterday. I was here to catch it when the computer rejected the transaction. I corrected the balance and completed the transaction. It was fortunate that I was here."

Rojas listened to Messner, but was not sure if he had heard what he said correctly.

"What was wrong with the balance?"

"It was ten million dollars less than when we spoke yesterday. A withdrawal was made this morning in that amount. But as I said I simply adjusted the balance and closed out the remaining funds."

Rojas attempted to control the anger that was building inside of him.

"I made no withdrawal, Mr. Messner," Rojas said with clenched teeth.

"I am afraid you did, Mr. Sanchez. Funds were withdrawn this morning by wire transfer. The records are quite clear on that fact. I would be happy to let you speak to one of my supervisors, but they are all gone for the day."

"Mr. Messner, you listen to me. You listen to me very carefully. I am the only one who knew about the existence of that account. I am the only one who can deposit and withdraw money from that account. I am telling you that I did not withdraw one dollar or ten million dollars from that account today. Do you understand me? I did not do it!"

"Well someone did, because it's not there anymore."

"Well it wasn't me, you idiot! Now how do we find out who it was?" Rojas screamed.

"Now just a minute, Mr. Sanchez. I don't have to take this kind—"

"Oh yes! Oh yes, you do! And if you think this is abuse, you wait until I speak with your superiors in the morning! I will make sure they know about this! I will make sure that the press knows about this! Your precious bank will be the focus of international attention in the press, Mr. Messner. You will be the focus of a very messy investigation! Unless . . ."

"Unless what, Mr. Sanchez? Unless what?" Messner asked anxiously.

"Unless you find out where my money went, Mr. Messner. You have until 10:00 tomorrow morning! If I haven't heard from you by then, I will call the authorities. And your ass will be mine! Do we understand each other?"

"Yes, Mr. Sanchez," Messner said timidly.

"Now what are you going to do?" Rojas demanded.

"Well . . . because it was a wire transfer, our security log will have the modem information on file. I'll request it and we can trace the destination of funds that way. We should also be able to determine the bank and account information through the transaction history. I'll do both."

"When will you know where my money is?"

"Within the next couple of hours, sir."

"Call me then!" Rojas shouted. He then slammed the phone down on the receiver.

Rojas sat in his chair fuming with anger. His mind was reeling with questions regarding the missing ten million dollars.

"Who could have taken it? Who else knew about the money besides Ricardo, me and . . . Hulio? Hulio," he said with clinched teeth.

Rojas stood from his chair and walked quickly through the house and back into the ballroom. When he entered the festive room, he quickly looked around until he saw Hulio speaking to a group of people. Rojas walked to the table where the other members were still seated.

"My friends, we have a problem. Will you go to my office for a moment? I will meet you there in a few minutes. Please?" Rojas requested.

The group looked at one another, stood from their seats and filed out of the ballroom together. Rojas's eyes again turned to Hulio. He walked to the group of people who were standing around Hulio, and spoke.

"Would you excuse us for a moment, ladies and gentlemen? I need to steal him away from you," Rojas said calmly.

The crowd disbursed at Rojas's request. Rojas looked at Hulio with questioning eyes. "We have a problem, my young friend. We need to speak in my office with the others."

"What kind of problem, Alberto? What is wrong?"

"Let's go to my office and talk. This is not a good place."

The pair walked together and smiled at the passing crowd of people as they left the ballroom. They walked through the house without speaking and entered Rojas's office. The other members were seated around the six-seat conference table. Rojas closed the door to the office as Hulio took a chair at the table with the others.

Rojas remained standing as he spoke. "We have a problem . . . my friends. I arranged yesterday with the Swiss bank to have the money Sanchez was hiding from us to be transferred to our BVI account. I instructed the bank to wire the money this afternoon so that I could give you all the news of its return to us."

"That is good news, Alberto. Why then do you seem angry over this?" Pedro Bevearo asked.

"Because not all of the money was transferred. Ten million dollars was missing."

"Missing? How could it be missing?" Hulio asked in surprise.

"A good question, my young friend. The bank tells me that a withdrawal was made only this morning in the amount of ten million dollars. Who other than your father, me, and you knew about the money, Hulio?"

"No one, Alberto. My father is dead. He knew. You and I are the only two alive that knew about the money," Hulio said.

"Yes . . . you and I," Rojas said cryptically.

The room was silent. Rojas glared at Hulio who was looking at the floor and thinking about the situation. The other members shifted their glances between Hulio and Rojas. Hulio realized that the room was silent and he looked up to find all of the others including Rojas staring at him. Then he had a full understanding of the situation.

"What? You think I took the money? You think I stole from you?" Hulio said in complete surprise. The more he thought about it the more his anger began to show. "How could you possibly think I would take money from you? My father is dead because he stole from you! Do you forget who told you about what he was doing? Do you not remember that I betrayed my own father because he was disloyal to this organization? You insult me! All of you insult me and my name with your accusing looks! Think! Just for a moment, think! Why would I take only ten million? I could have taken it all! I didn't have to tell you of its existence! But I did, and my father paid for it with his life! Now you tell me what I had to gain from taking only ten million dollars of the money. Tell me if you can! Make sense of it to me!"

The room was silent as Hulio glared at the members around the table. He turned his eyes to Rojas who stood leaning against his desk. The others focused their attention on Rojas as well.

Jose Santiago broke the silence and spoke as he looked at Rojas. "Hulio makes sense, Alberto. He could have taken all of the money and we never would have known about it. He could have destroyed the banking records. It makes no sense."

Rojas studied the men at the table. He looked thoughtfully at them as they now all looked at him with suspicion in their eyes.

"I did not take the money either, my brothers. Do not look at me with that thought in your minds. Ten million dollars is nothing to me. Ten times that amount is still nothing to me. All of you know that," Rojas said calmly. The men knew that he was right. Rojas looked again at only Hulio. "I believe you did not take the money, Hulio. It doesn't make any sense for you to do such a thing. You have proven your loyalty to the cartel. Your honor is not in question here. Was there anyone else in the United States, Guatemala, or here in Colombia who was working with your father? Someone you may have missed? Someone who may have needed money to get away and hide from us?"

Hulio sat in his chair thinking about who it may have been. Of course there were others who knew about the money. But he could not tell Rojas about them. Besides none of them knew how to access the funds. They were not that sophisticated or intelligent. If there was someone else, he did not know who they were. And that worried him.

"I do not know of anyone else, Alberto. I swear it. All of those who I knew were involved with my father are now dead, except for three. Those three will be here tomorrow for you to interrogate. I do not have any idea who it could be," Hulio said sincerely.

"No matter, my young friend. The bank is tracing the money as we speak. They will be calling me this evening with the information. Where we find the money is where we find those who still work against us. When we find the money we will find them. And as god is my witness, they will die by my hand!"

CHAPTER FIVE

ARTICLE 17

July 27, 2005, 6:15 p.m.
Clay Peterson's House, Dallas, Texas

Clay Peterson sat at his computer looking weary and unkempt. He was slumped over the computer keyboard with his hands covering his face as he thought about what he would do next. He had been trying all afternoon to close the account he had opened with the Royal Bank of Canada. Nothing he tried worked. He had all of the codes; the account number would appear on the screen; he could obtain the account history; he could do everything except transfer the money back to the Swiss bank. The account was locked. Clay could not locate the lock-out formula in the RCB system. He was exhausted, frustrated, and frightened. He was startled by a knock at the door. Clay sat up in his chair with a panicked look on his face.

"Christ, they couldn't have found out it was me already. But what if they did? What if they are here to arrest me?" he said to himself quietly.

Clay got up from his chair and crept into the foyer. He tiptoed to the door, being very careful not to make any noise. He slowly moved his face toward the security viewing hole in the door. Just as he was about to look through the hole, the visitor knocked again, this time quite hard. Clay jumped away from the door, his pulse racing, feeling lightheaded. Then he heard a voice.

"Clay? Clay, are you in there? Are you all right?" the female voice called out.

Clay breathed a sigh of relief. It was Lisa. He walked back to the door and opened it. When she saw him her face grew concerned.

"Clay, you look like hell!" Lisa exclaimed.

"Come in quickly. Come in please," Clay said as he pulled Lisa into the house and quickly closed the door.

"Clay, what's wrong? Has something happened? Are you sick?" Lisa asked.

Clay stood with his back against the door. He looked as if he were attempting to keep someone from breaking it down. He looked at Lisa and he could see that she was truly concerned about him. He didn't know what to say to her. Clay moved away from the door and walked to her. He looked down into her eyes then embraced her. He held her tightly with both arms.

Lisa returned the embrace, stood with him for a moment then pulled away and spoke, her hands on his hips. "What is it, Clay? Please tell me," Lisa pleaded.

"I'm in trouble, Lisa. I'm in a great deal of trouble," Clay said as he moved away from her and started walking back into his office.

"What kind of trouble?" Lisa asked as she followed him.

Clay said nothing as he went back to his office and sat in his chair. He sat looking at the monitor which now displayed his flying toilet screen saver.

Lisa walked into the office and sat beside him at the computer. She looked at his unshaven face and eyes that were filled with a combination of sadness and fear. She put her arm around his shoulder and spoke. "What is it, Clay? Please tell me what's wrong with you," Lisa pleaded quietly.

Clay looked at her then returned his attention to the monitor. He pressed the space bar on the keyboard and the screen saver disappeared.

"That is my problem," Clay said as he continued to look at the screen.

Lisa also gazed at the monitor. She read the information that was displayed on the screen out loud.

"Royal Bank of Canada . . . savings account . . . account holder . . . Sallad Rekcah? Beginning balance . . . ten million dollars . . . current balance . . . ten million dollars."

Lisa thought for a moment. She initially could not see what this had to do with Clay. She did not understand why he would be upset about accessing another RCB savings account. It had been a game and fun for both of them the other night. She continued to look at the screen and think. Then she knew.

"Oh my god. You are this guy? You are Sallad Rekcah?"

"Yep," Clay responded.

"You opened a savings account with the Royal Bank of Canada for ten million dollars using this guy's name?"

"I opened the account. But it's not a guy, it's an anagram. I'm the Dallas Hacker."

"Jesus, Clay. That's really incredible. I mean it's really incredible."

They both sat there for a few moments staring at the computer screen. Lisa was amazed that Clay had actually been able to pull something like this off. She could not believe that a guy in Dallas could open a ten-million-dollar savings account from his home by computer. But there it was in front of her on the screen.

"So what did you do, just like enter ten million dollars when it asked you how much you wanted the balance to be?"

"No, I . . . well, I borrowed the money from another account."

"What account? Who isn't going to miss ten million dollars?"

"It's a Swiss account. I don't know who it belongs to but there hasn't been any activity other than deposits for the past six months. They will never miss the money if I can get it out of the Canadian bank."

"Well, just put it back."

"I can't. I've been trying and I can't. The account is locked and I can't find the origination formula to unlock it. It's like the account is locked from outside the bank system."

"Okay, listen. Let's just settle down for a minute and think about this. Start over. Go to the beginning and I'll bet you'll find what you're looking for."

"I've thought about it, Lisa, and there is a missing link-up here. There's an outside lock on the RCB account and I can't find it."

"Just try. Will you try for me?" Lisa asked with a pitiful look on her face.

Clay looked at her and sighed. No matter how upset he was over this whole situation, he couldn't turn her down. Besides, at that point he didn't have anything to lose.

"Okay, we'll start over."

"Great, where do we start?" Lisa said excitedly.

"I need to get back into the Swiss account and review the transaction history. Maybe there is a clue to the lock-out formula in there."

Clay keyed in the instructions which directed the computer to access the Swiss system once again. When he was in, he paused.

"You know . . . maybe the lock-out formula is tied to the Swiss account that I took the money from. Maybe that account has some kind of security lock that I missed."

"Go for it," Lisa said.

Clay requested access to the savings account from which he had transferred the ten million dollars earlier that day. He sat back in his chair and waited for the account to be displayed on the screen. When the account came up, he could not believe what he saw.

"Shit!" Clay exclaimed.

"What?" Lisa asked.

"The account . . . look at the balance in the account!"

Lisa scanned the screen. She looked at the account history which showed deposits of $854,000, $8 million, $10 million, $7 million, $14 million, $16 million, $12 million, and $10 million. Then there were two withdrawals. The first was for $10 million. The second withdrawal was in the amount of $66,854,000. Both withdrawals had been made that day.

"I'm fucked," Clay said.

"Why are you fucked?"

"The account was cleaned out today. Whoever has that account will most certainly miss ten million dollars. They'll come after me and they'll put me in jail. God, I can't believe that I got myself into this. I never would have done it if I thought I couldn't put the money back. They'll put me in jail."

"No, they won't, you can put the money back. We'll figure out a way to put it back. You have to, Clay. You can't give up now."

"It's too late, Lisa. They know the money is gone."

"Well, how do they know you took it?"

"They can trace the transaction. They'll find out that the transaction request originated from here, not Canada. They'll have a record of it."

"Didn't you know that would happen anyway?"

"If I could have put the money back in the account, they never would have questioned it. I was only going to use it for fifteen or twenty minutes. I didn't know I would be locked out. I didn't anticipate that, and I should have. I don't know what the fuck I was thinking."

Lisa looked at Clay as he placed his head in his hands. She knew that his intentions were good and that he had never meant to hurt anyone. Now she knew how he must be feeling. She knew that he must be frightened. She brushed the hair away from the side of his face. Then she spoke to him softly.

"Clay. Clay, look at me . . . please."

Clay uncovered his face and looked into Lisa's caring blue eyes. He studied her face, her hair, then moved his eyes down to her breasts and her legs. He slowly returned his eyes to hers. She placed her palm on the side of his face and leaned toward him. He drew back from her initially, not knowing if he should proceed and act upon the feelings he was experiencing. Then he did not care. He placed his hands on her cheeks and pulled her toward him. Their lips met and they kissed passionately. He wanted her, he needed her, and to his delight, she desperately wanted him.

The kiss lasted for several minutes, growing in intensity with each passing second. Clay moved his hands from Lisa's face down to her back. She moved her hands down to his thighs and began massaging them. Their tongues were dancing wildly inside each other's mouths. Clay brought his hands under Lisa's arms and around to her firm large breasts. He moved his hands over them outside her T-shirt for a few moments then he reached underneath and felt her soft warm breasts against his hands. Lisa's nipples were hard and erect. He caressed them as Lisa moved her hands up Clay's thighs and began massaging his groin area. Clay was aroused and he throbbed with intense desire. Lisa continued to massage Clay as she drew her lips away from his. Clay continued to fondle her breasts in his hands as she looked passionately at him. Then she spoke softly, unable to hide the excitement and arousal her body was experiencing.

"Let's go to your room," Lisa said.

Clay looked at her. He was about to explode. He wanted her and he wanted her now.

"Let's go to the living room. It's clean, and it's closer," Clay said as he breathed heavily.

"Great."

The two of them left the office quickly, removing articles of clothing as they walked out of the room. The computer screen was still displaying the Swiss account information. Clay

Peterson did not care about the account or the situation he had created for himself at that moment. He had other things on his mind.

Half a world away in Medillin, Colombia, however, the account was a concern for another man. That man would soon have one thing on his mind: finding Clay Peterson and killing him.

ARTICLE 18

July 27, 2005, 7:05 p.m.
Rojas estate, Medillin, Colombia

The six men sat around the table in Rojas's office waiting impatiently for the telephone to ring. It had been a little over two hours since Rojas had spoken to Messner in Switzerland. The group had gone back to the celebration in the ballroom for a while then one by one they returned to the office to wait for the call. Hulio and Rojas had discussed the matter thoroughly between them. Rojas was truly convinced that Hulio had nothing to do with the money being stolen. He was sorry he had even suspected him. Hulio on the other hand was baffled at the money's disappearance. It concerned him, not because ten million dollars was missing, but because he did not have a clue who could have taken it. If he did not know who else had access to the Swiss account, perhaps there was something his father had kept from him regarding the business. Maybe there was someone else in the United States who had been involved with his father, who knew about him, and Hulio did not know anything about it. The group's thoughts were interrupted by the ringing of the telephone. Rojas looked at the phone and allowed it to ring once again before he picked it up.

"Hello?"

"Mr. Sanchez?"

"Yes."

"Felix Messner here, Mr. Sanchez. I have some information for you."

"Very good, Mr. Messner. Tell me where my money is."

"Well, sir, it's kind of strange."

"What do you mean . . . strange?"

"We traced the wire transfer to an account in the Royal Bank of Canada. The account is registered to a Sallad Rekcah."

"Hold on a moment, Mr. Messner. Hulio, get a pad and write this down. Mr. Messner, did you say Sallad Rekcah?"

"Yes."

"Please continue."

"Well, here is where it gets strange. Our modem trace shows the wire path made from our bank to the Canadian bank. But there is no evidence of the bank requesting the wire. It was requested by a modem in Dallas, Texas."

"Dallas, Texas?"

"Yes. We do not have an address, but we do have a name and a number for you."

"Give me the name," Rojas demanded.

"Peterson, Mr. Sanchez. Clay Peterson is the name; the number is 2-1-4-5-5-5-2-7-4-3."

"Clay Peterson, 2-1-4-5-5-5-2-7-4-3. Thank you, Mr. Messner. You have redeemed yourself in my eyes. This matter will go no farther as far as I am concerned."

"Thank you, Mr. Sanchez. Thank you very much."

Rojas hung up the telephone, stood from his chair and began pacing around his office. The men sitting at the table watched him as he walked back and forth between walls.

Finally Jose Santiago broke the silence. "Who are these people?" he asked anyone who would answer. No one did. Jose spoke again, this time to Alberto. "Alberto, do you know this Peterson or this Arab-sounding name, Raka or Reeka something?"

"No, Jose. I do not know who they are. The name does sound like it is Arabic, doesn't it? Hulio, could your father have been involved with Arabs or the Iranians for some reason?"

"I would have known about it if he were, Alberto. These names mean nothing to me. I do not understand any of this. Let me go to Dallas. Let me find this Peterson and this Rekcah. I will find out where the money is and I will give them each a slow death!" Hulio said excitedly.

"No, Hulio. I need you here. We all need you here until we find out who these people are. If they find out about your father's death—and they may know already—you could be in danger. They may come after you."

"Then let me get them first. I will be the hunter; I will not wait for them to come for me!" Hulio shouted.

"I do not suggest that, Hulio. We will find them and we will get to them before they have a chance to get to you. But I will not risk your life. Roberto, you still have family that controls the trucking company in the Houston area of Texas?"

"Yes, Alberto, we use it often to distribute throughout the central United States."

"Are they loyal to us?"

"That is not a question you have to ask me, Alberto. They are loyal to me."

"I meant no disrespect, my friend," Rojas said humbly.

Rojas walked to the table where the others were seated and sat with them. He thought for a moment then turned his attention to Roberto. "I want you to call them. I want you to call them tonight."

"I can do that. What do you want me to tell them?"

"I want them in Dallas tomorrow. Tell them they are to go to Dallas and find this Clay Peterson and Rekcah."

"Alberto, how will they know where or how to find Peterson and Rekcah?"

"I will call Miami tonight. I will have our police contacts there find out who this Peterson and Rekcah are. I will have an address for you tonight before you call them."

"And what do they do with them when they are found?"

"They abduct them and we bring them here."

"How do we get them out of the United States, Alberto?" Pedro asked.

Rojas thought for a moment. They needed to avoid customs. They needed to deal with people who were friendly to the cartel.

"I will have my plane flown to the Dallas airport tomorrow night at the executive terminal. Roberto, you will be on the plane to meet your family."

"Alberto, I do not like the United States. They may detain me or even arrest me."

"Roberto is right, Alberto. We must assume that the Americans would arrest him if they knew he was in their country. I would advise against even using your plane," Jose said.

"You are right. But we need a plane to get them out of the country," Rojas said.

"I will arrange for that with my family," Roberto said.

"Good, my friend. We need to get them out of the United States and into Mexico. We need to get them to Oaxaca."

"In Oaxaca we have friends in customs," Jose said.

"Yes, and once they are in Oaxaca, I will have them put aboard my plane and brought here to Medillin."

"That will work. Now we only need to find these people. Dallas is not a small city, Alberto," Joseffe said.

"We will find them, Joseffe. Roberto, please tell your family that they will be rewarded handsomely. Tell them that I will be in their debt. Tell them that we will all be in their debt."

"They will be pleased to do this thing for us, Alberto. They are good people," Roberto responded.

"We are in agreement then?" Rojas asked.

"I would still like to go to Dallas, Alberto. I want to go," Hulio said.

"I know you do, Hulio. But you hold a position now. Pedro was right about the Americans. If they suspect that one of us is in the country, they will detain us. If they can, they will arrest us, perhaps even kill us. We can not risk that. We can not afford to risk that. Do you understand?"

"I understand, but I don't like it."

Rojas laughed. "Neither do I, my young friend. Neither do I. But know this and you will feel better. You will have the opportunity to take your revenge against these people. They will be brought here for that purpose. I will make sure that their deaths are lingering and they know who is to blame. I swore to you earlier, now I swear to you again. These two infidels will pay with their lives. They will die by my hand!"

ARTICLE 19

July 27, 2005, 12:30 a.m.
Clay Peterson's House, Dallas, Texas

A single light in the corner of the living room was on. It cast a soft dim glow over the room and on the glistening perspiration-covered naked bodies embraced in the middle of the floor. They were lying there holding one another. It was a beautiful and serene sight. They had been making love for the past five hours, showing how much they desired the other's body. Now they lay together manifesting how much they cared. Lisa lay back on the floor and looked up at the ceiling. Clay remained on his side surveying Lisa's body as she lay there.

"That was wonderful. I mean it was really wonderful, Clay."

Clay looked at her smiling face. He was pleased that he had satisfied her, he wanted that. And he had satisfied her many times while they made love that evening.

"You are so special. God, you have so much to give. You are beautiful, intelligent, you have a great personality, and christ, can you make love," Clay said as he laughed quietly.

Lisa looked at Clay. She admired his chiseled face and the way his hair draped over one eye as he looked at her. "You are the one who is special, Clay. You're a very special person."

"Can I tell you something?"

"Yes, anything."

"I'm not sure that I should."

"Please tell me. Really, you can tell me anything."

"I've always had this dream. A dream of meeting this really special girl. A beautiful girl. We would live on an island where the weather was always perfect and the sunrise and sunsets were always beautiful and even intense. In my dream, we would hold each other as we watched the sun rise and set each day. We would make love on the beach or wherever and whenever the mood struck us. We would swim naked in the moonlit sea and dance together slowly in the gentle rain. I would write her poems; she would greet me with a beautiful smile each morning. I would send her flowers; she would give me her heart. And I would love her with a passion she had never known before. Making sure each day we were together that she knew, she understood what a special woman she was, and how lucky I felt that she had chosen me to spend the rest of her life with."

Clay paused and looked deeply into Lisa's eyes. He was in love with her. He had to tell her, no matter what the consequences would be. He wanted her to know.

"I really care for you . . . I mean I . . . I think that I'm . . ."

Lisa looked at him and put her fingers gently on his lips. "No, please don't say that to me," Lisa said quietly. "You can't."

Lisa sat up, wrapped her hands around her knees and put her head down. She began rocking back and forth as she sat there. Clay was puzzled at her reaction.

"I shouldn't have said anything. It isn't that way with you. I'm sorry," Clay said.

Lisa looked at him with tears in her eyes. They sat for a moment staring at each other, and Clay brushed a falling tear away from Lisa's cheek.

"It's not that, Clay!" Lisa said in an aggravated voice. She then stood and began pacing the room. She ran her fingers through her hair as she paced back and forth. She looked confused and worried. Clay did not say anything, he just watched her pace. He was waiting on her to speak. Finally, she did. "Look, there's something that you don't know about me. In fact, there's a lot that you don't know about me."

Clay sat up and spoke to her. "I don't care about your past; I don't want to know about it if—"

"It's not my past, Clay. It's who I am now."

"I know who you are n—"

"No, Clay! No, you don't. No . . . you don't," Lisa said as she went to the couch to sit down. She brought her knees up to her chest and looked at Clay again.

Tears ran down her face and her lip quivered. She had a frown on her face as if to say she did not know how to tell him what she was talking about. The fact was that she didn't. Clay spoke to her in an attempt to ease her concerns.

"Look . . . Lisa, I don't need to know anything you don't want to tell me. Really. It doesn't matter. I have never felt this way about a woman before. It's the first time for me and I don't know the right things to say. All I know is how I feel, and if you don't have those same feelings—"

"That's the problem, Clay! I do have those same feelings, and I shouldn't . . . ya know, I just shouldn't!"

"You mean . . . I mean you think that you might feel—"

"Yes! Goddammit, yes! I love you . . . and . . . and I shouldn't . . . and you shouldn't . . . and I don't know what to do. I don't know whether to make love to you again or arrest you!" Lisa's eyes widened as she made her last statement. She hadn't mean to say it.

"Arrest me?" Clay questioned while laughing.

He watched Lisa for any sign that she might have been kidding him. There was none. She sat naked on his couch with a concerned look on her face. She wasn't kidding. She was serious.

"Lisa, if it's about the Swiss money, I'll figure out a way to put it back. You wouldn't call the police about that, would you? I swear to you I didn't mean to get stuck in the middle of that—"

"No, it's not the Swiss money. Although that makes everything worse. God!" Lisa said exasperated.

"Then what, what do you mean?"

"Clay, my name isn't really Lisa Tinsley. My real name is Christine Hendrix. I'm a field agent for the FBI."

Clay's mouth dropped open. His face reflected the shock that he felt inside regarding Lisa's comment. He couldn't believe it. He did not believe her.

"Come on. You're not. Tell me you're not," Clay pleaded.

"I am, Clay. Really."

Clay looked at her for a moment, then got up and began pacing the room and shaking his head. He couldn't believe it. He was shocked, angry, frightened, confused, all at the same time. He would pace for a while then stop and look at this woman who he now knew as Christine. He would feel anger while he walked, then he would look at her and the anger would be replaced with a feeling of love and passion. He composed himself then spoke to her.

"Why? I mean why me?"

"In February you breached the Pentagon's computer system. All you did was access the system; you didn't try to get in once you broke the code. They traced the breach to you through your modem. That's when we started investigating you. Then in March you breached the U.S. Treasury's computer security system and accessed their operating system. Oh, you didn't do anything once you got inside the system, but you did get in. The bureau decided to send me undercover to find out what your intentions were. They didn't know if you were a hacker with antigovernment or terrorist intentions, or just a guy playing computer games. I was supposed to find out."

"And what did you find out?"

Christine looked at him, tilted her head and sighed. "You're just a guy. You're just a really nice, shy, cute, innocent guy who likes to play on his computer, and who stole my heart," Christine said softly.

"I stole your heart? Really?" Clay said smiling.

Christine looked at him with her head still tilted to one side and smiled while nodding. Then she remembered who she was again, snapped her head up, and spoke to Clay.

"Yes, and you also stole ten million dollars!" Christine snapped.

"I didn't steal it. I was only going to use if for a few minutes."

Christine stood up and began pacing the room again.

"I don't think that excuse is going to hold any water, 'Sallad.' You have to figure out a way to get that money back into the Swiss account, or both of us are going to be in really deep shit."

Clay stood up and blocked her way as she was pacing. She looked up at him with questioning eyes. He looked down at her with love and compassion.

"Does that mean you're not going to arrest me, Detective Hendrix?"

Christine gazed into his eyes and felt her heart begin to pound with excitement again. "Agent," Christine corrected.

"What?"

"It's not detective, it's Agent . . . Christine . . . Hendrix, and . . . no, I'm not going to arrest you. But we really have to figure out a way to put that money back or I won't be able to help you."

"Then let's go to work. I'll figure something out. I'll make it work," Clay said as he leaned close to her and they kissed passionately. Clay drew away from her slowly.

"We better go to work now," Christine said. "Before I lose focus again."

"Okay."

They walked toward the office still naked, their arms around each other. As they got to the hallway, Clay spoke.

"You really think I'm cute?"

"I think you're adorable. And so will all the guys in prison if we don't get this thing worked out," Christine responded.

ARTICLE 20

July 27, 2005, 8:45 p.m.
Rojas estate, Medillin, Colombia

The celebration had ended several hours before. All of the guests were gone except the six members of the Medillin cartel. Five of them sat at the conference table in Rojas's office. Rojas sat at his desk talking on the phone.

"I have the information you asked for. At least I have part of it," the detective said.

"What do you mean part of it? I do not want just part of it," Rojas barked.

"Well, that's all I was able to get. If you don't want it I'll hang up the fucking phone."

"Wait. Do not hang up the phone. You Americans, you are a very touchy people, did you know that, Detective?"

"We just don't like to be chastised, Rojas. We like to be appreciated."

"I appreciate you, Detective. Really, I do appreciate you."

"How much?"

"Ten thousand."

"Make it twenty."

"You tread a dangerous line, Detective!"

"Hey! Who the fuck called who? Now, do we have a deal?"

Rojas composed himself. He hated this man, he hated all Americans. But he also knew that he needed him and he needed the information he would give.

"Yes, Detective, we have a deal. Now give me the information."

"Okay, this guy Sallad Rekcah, I can't find anything on him. No wants or warrants. No address or phone number in Dallas. I think he's foreign."

"Very astute assumption, Detective. With a name like Rekcah, one wouldn't expect him to come from the United States," Rojas said sarcastically.

"Anyway, we did get an address on the Paterson guy. You got a pen?"

"Yes."

"Twenty-three seventeen West Sage in Dallas."

"Twenty . . . three . . . seventeen . . . West . . . Sage . . . Dallas. Very good, Detective. I appreciate your assistance."

"When will you appreciate it in the form of two hundred one-hundred-dollar bills, Rojas?"

"When we have what we are looking for, Detective."

"Hey, I can't control your people. I gave you the information and you owe me whether you get what you're looking for or not."

"Sue me, Detective," Rojas said as he hung up the phone.

Rojas stood from his desk and carried the notepad to the conference table. He sat with the others.

"We have the address, Roberto. When will your people be in Dallas?"

"They will be there tonight. They are familiar with the Dallas area and will be staying at the Marriott Hotel in North Dallas tonight."

"I don't want them spending the night, Roberto. I want Rekcah and Peterson tonight. Please?" Rojas asked sternly.

"Very well, Alberto. They are to call when they get to Dallas. I will tell them to get Rekcah and Peterson then leave Dallas. I don't know if the plane will be ready tonight."

"No matter. Just tell them to get these men and get them out of Dallas tonight."

ARTICLE 21

July 28, 2005, 12:27 a.m.
Hoover Building, Washington, D.C.

Brian Whitfield was on his way out of the office after a very long day. He had been successful in formulating the telecommunications network for Second Wave. Agent Bradley had made it a point to congratulate Brian very publicly on several occasions. Bradley's motives were a bit self-serving, however, and Brian knew it. Bradley wanted everyone to know that the job Brian had done was the kind of work he expected from everyone during the operation. Brian's timeliness also boded well for Bradley and his administrative ability. That did not hurt him in the eyes of the associate director, whom Brian did not like or get along with.

On his way down the hallway to the elevator, Brian stuck his head into the priority communications department. He saw Agent Criswell sitting with his back to him, working on a computer.

"Criz!" Brian shouted.

Criswell nearly fell out of his chair. He composed himself and turned to look at who had nearly scared him to death.

"Goddammit, Brian. You nearly gave me a heart attack, man."

Brian could not control himself. He was laughing at Criswell's reaction.

"Better cut down on the caffeine intake, Criz, you're way too jumpy."

"You go to hell. What do you want, you pain in the ass."

"Get anything from Hendrix tonight?"

"Haven't seen anything. Hey, what's Hendrix working on anyway?" Criswell asked.

"I would tell ya, Criz, but then I'd have to kill ya," Brian said with a smile.

"Get outta here, man. Leave!"

"See ya."

CHAPTER SIX

ARTICLE 22

July 28, 2005, 1:15 a.m.
Clay Peterson's home, Dallas, Texas

Clay sat at the computer keying instructions in what so far had been a futile effort to access the RCB lock-out code. He had tried everything. He ran a CASE analysis on the Douglas account and it did not indicate anything regarding a lock-out code. He tried the same thing with the Swiss account without any luck. He traced the wire from the Swiss account to a British Virgin Islands bank, but could not break the access code with COBAL or PASCAL. Clay did not utilize the Fibonacci Sequence for this exercise because he first had to find out where the lock-out originated before he could break it. Christine walked into the room with a freshly poured cup of coffee for Clay.

"Any luck?"

"No, no luck at all. I can't figure out where the lock-out code originates. The only answer I have is that there must be a third party involved in the trading account. There must be someone or some institution in the middle who controls the flow of funds and also the accounts at both ends. You must not be able to access the money until the end of the trading term, which in this case is fifteen months."

"Fifteen months?"

"Yes, that's the length of the trading program. I don't think the funds can be accessed until then."

"Fifteen months. Clay, you've got to figure something out. You just have to."

"Why can't I just go to the FBI and tell them the whole thing is just a mix-up? That I was just playing around?"

"Clay, think about it for a minute. You accessed the Pentagon computer system. You deciphered one of the most sophisticated security systems in the world to do it. Then you broke into the U.S. Treasury system, again a very sophisticated system. You didn't do anything, but you got in. Now you have an account in Canada with ten million dollars of someone else's money in it. They won't believe that all you were doing was playing some kind of game."

"So what do I do? Tell me and I'll do it. I don't want the money, I never did. But now I can't put it back."

"We need to show them that you did not want to keep the money. We need to show them that you found out you couldn't put it back, but you tried. They need a trail to follow, something to show that you tried."

They sat for a moment and thought about what Clay might do to show the FBI a trail. Christine didn't have a clue. Clay had an idea.

"I got it. I got it!" Clay exclaimed.

"Tell me."

"Okay, what if I set up an account at the Swiss bank, and all of the funds from the trading account would be wired into that account. I can't put the ten million back because it's locked into the RCB account. But I can direct the proceeds from the trading account back into the Swiss bank account. That would at least show good faith on my part, wouldn't it?"

"I don't know. It may just show that you were trying to dilute the paper trail. Are you sure you can do that, I mean with the trading account profits?"

"I think so."

"Well go ahead. While you're doing that, I'll keep thinking."

Clay began typing commands into his computer. He was going to attempt to have all of the proceeds from the trading account intercepted prior to deposit into the RCB account. He would have the funds directed into the Swiss account from which he took the ten million dollars. The account holder would be reimbursed of the original ten million, plus tens of millions more in trading profits; and Clay would hopefully avoid going to prison.

Christine left the room while Clay worked on the computer. She went into the living room wearing only her T-shirt, carrying her cup of coffee, and sat down on the couch to think. She had a lot to think about. She was an FBI agent with responsibilities to the bureau and to the government. She wondered how she could feel the way she did about Clay, a man she met just three months prior and had only really known for the past three days. That didn't happen to people in real life, it only happened in the movies. But it had happened to her, and she was in love with him. She did not know why, she could not explain it; she only knew what she felt in her heart. She had never had this feeling, and wondered what she was willing to give up to hold on to it. It could mean her job; it could even put her behind bars. She did not want that to happen and the only way it wouldn't was for Clay to show the FBI that he in fact didn't have any intention of keeping the money. He was facing only minor charges regarding his activities as they related to the U.S. Treasury and the Pentagon. Although they were major breaches of security and the punishment could be quite severe, she felt that because Clay had only looked and not touched, that would have an impact on his punishment. The FBI had been quite clear about not wanting the matter made public. They would want to handle it quietly. Any kind of trial would certainly bring unwanted publicity to Clay and the fact that he had breached the government's systems. Christine believed that if Clay could take care of the money situation, he would more than likely get a slap on the wrist. The government would do nothing more than take away his modem. This was her hope, and she would do everything in her power to make sure that it was handled that way. Christine's thoughts were interrupted by a shout from the other room.

"Shit!" Clay shouted.

Christine leapt off the couch and ran into Clay's office. He was looking at the monitor shaking his head.

"What? What's wrong?"

"The Swiss account. It's got a security lock on it. It's a secondary system interface and it will take me all night to break it if I can."

"Are you locked out of the Swiss system altogether?"

"No, just this account."

"What about the RCB system?"

"It's all set. I'm ready to set it up but I don't have an account to put it in."

"Can you open up another account at the Swiss bank?"

"Yes."

"Then do it, open an account. Can you use numbers instead of a name on the account?"

"Yes."

"Then open a new Swiss account and use the numbers from the locked account as the account holder reference. That will show that you at least tried to get in, couldn't, and opened the new account with the old reference number as the account holder."

"Will that work?"

"I don't know, but at least it's something. It will show them that you tried. It gives them and the old account holder something to consider."

"Okay, Agent Hendrix, here goes," Clay said as he began typing.

Christine watched him as he worked in his boxers. She hoped that she was right about the punishment he would receive for the Pentagon and Treasury breaches. But she also knew that the FBI was unpredictable. Then she had another thought. Perhaps the bureau could actually use Clay and his talents. Perhaps they could put his abilities to work for them in certain situations. She convinced herself that it was a real possibility and felt better about the whole situation for a moment.

"How's it going?" She asked Clay.

"Almost got it. I just have to enter the new account number into the RCB system then it should do the rest."

Christine watched him as he entered the number then pressed the Enter key. He sat back in his chair and both of them watched the screen together. Christine's attention was taken away from the computer monitor. She thought she heard a noise in the kitchen.

"Do you have a cat or something?"

Clay continued to watch the monitor while he answered her. "I have enough trouble taking care of myself and I don't really like cats. Why?"

"I thought I heard a noise in the kitchen."

"I didn't hear anything," Clay said still concentrating on the screen.

"Well, I need to use the restroom. Can I get you anything?"

"Is there any more coffee?"

"Yeah, you want a cup?"

"That would be great."

Christine got up and left the room as Clay continued to concentrate on the monitor. Then a tone sounded and a message began flashing. Clay was pleased with the message this time. TRANSACTION ACCEPTED was displayed. Clay stretched his arms above his head and looked at his watch. It was 2:20 a.m. and he was beat. He stood from his chair and started to walk out of the room. He froze suddenly as he heard a piercing scream of terror. It was a woman's scream, it came from the kitchen and Clay knew it was Christine's.

Clay frantically looked around the room for something he could use as a weapon. He didn't see anything he could use to defend Christine or himself. Out of desperation, he grabbed the calculator off his desk and crept out of the office. As he entered the hallway, his pulse was racing and he could feel his knees shaking in terror, anticipating the confrontation about to take place. He did not hear Christine anymore and he grew concerned that something terrible had happened to her. Clay was at the end of the hallway now. He had his back against the wall. He was perspiring profusely and his heart felt as though it was going to leap out of his chest. He nodded his head quickly as if to tell himself that he knew what he had to do. Then with a leap and a yell, Clay burst around the corner.

"Yaaaaaaaa!" Clay screamed as he stood like a linebacker waiting for a tackle.

"Ahhhhhhh!" Christine screamed in response to his yell and sudden appearance.

Clay crouched and looked at Christine who was on her hands and knees cleaning something off the floor.

"What are you doing?" she asked him in an irritated tone. "You nearly scared me to death!"

"You screamed. Why did you scream?"

"I spilled the coffee and burned my leg. Why are you holding a calculator?" Christine asked as she chuckled.

Clay looked down and saw the calculator in his hand. He suddenly felt quite silly crouched there in his boxers, holding a calculator, ready to attack.

"It's all I could find. I thought you were in trouble or something."

"So what, you were going to use fractions on my attacker?" Christine laughed.

"No, I was—"

Clay's sentence was interrupted by the ringing of the telephone. Clay and Christine looked at one another. The phone rang again.

"It's 2:20 in the morning, should I answer it?" Clay whispered.

"They can't hear you, Clay. Yes, answer it," Christine said.

Clay walked to the phone hanging on the wall in the kitchen. It rang a third time and Clay picked up the headset. He slowly brought the phone to his ear and spoke.

"Hello?"

"Clay Peterson?" the detective asked.

"Yes," Clay answered nervously.

"This is a friend, Mr. Peterson."

"A friend?"

"Yes. Apparently you have made some very important people very angry. They want you, or they want something you have."

"Who? Who did I make angry?"

"It doesn't matter. But if you don't get the hell out of Dallas immediately, they'll be finding pieces of you scattered all over the state of Texas."

"Why do they want me?"

"That's all, Mr. Peterson. Oh and you might give this same message to Mr. Rekcah. It applies to him as well."

"But who are—" Clay didn't finish his sentence. The man at the other end hung up.

Clay stood with the phone still pressed against his ear. He was pale and noticeably shaking in fear. He looked at Christine who was staring at him in concern.

"Who was it, Clay? What did they say?"

"I don't know who it was. He said I have made some important people mad. He told me that if I didn't get out of Dallas immediately, there would be pieces of me all over the state of Texas," Clay said as though he were in a transcendental state.

"What people? Did he say who was mad at you?"

"No. No, he didn't. But he did say to tell Mr. Rekcah that the same message applied to him."

Lisa stood in a panic. "We need to get out of here, and get out of here now. That account must have belonged to a criminal, or a criminal organization. That's the only reason you would get a call like that. A legit corporation or individual would let the authorities handle a problem like this. No, this isn't good. Get some things together, you can come stay with me until I can contact my office and we can get you some protection and get you some place safe."

Both of them began moving quickly around the house. They found their clothes, got dressed, and met back in Clay's office. Clay shuffled around his desk. He put his backup disks, file disks, and several files in a duffle bag with clothes he had brought from his room.

"What are you doing?" Christine asked.

"I'm getting my stuff."

"I don't have a computer, Clay. I don't think you'll be needing your disks."

"Well, I'm taking them anyway. I'll need them when I try to explain what I've been doing. Your bosses will want some evidence and this is all I have."

"Hurry up, we need to go," Christine said as she left the room.

Clay placed all of his disk holders in the duffle bag. Then he surveyed the office one last time before turning the light out and leaving the room. He walked to the kitchen and found Christine on the phone.

"Who are you calling?"

"Washington. There's usually someone in the communications office twenty-four hours a day."

Christine listened as the phone rang for the eighth time. She grew impatient and hung up the telephone.

"Let's go," she ordered.

The pair walked to the front door. Christine held Clay back and walked in front of him. She reached into her purse and took out a gun. Clay's eyes widened at the sight of the weapon. Christine noticed Clay's expression.

"Works better than a calculator," she said sarcastically.

Clay gave here a look that let her know he thought that she was being a smart ass. Christine opened the door slowly.

"Turn out the hall light," she ordered.

Clay obliged and Christine could see that there was no sign of anyone between the house and her car parked in the street. Christine signaled for Clay to follow her out the door. They moved slowly down the walk toward the street. Just as they reached the end of the wall of the garage which paralleled the walk, Clay spoke and startled Christine.

"Christine," Clay whispered.

Christine turned and looked at him sternly. "What!"

"I didn't lock the door."

"Well, go lock it then, but hurry!" Christine whispered.

Clay turned to walk back up the walk to the front door. As he approached the door, he heard a scuffle behind him. As he turned, something struck him squarely in the back of the head. Clay fell to the concrete walk unconscious.

ARTICLE 23

July 28, 2005, 12:15 p.m.
A jungle encampment near the Magdalena River, Colombia

The small camp was located in a clearing near the river. It had eight small shanties with palm-leaf roofs which served as living quarters. There was a tower at the end of the makeshift road leading into the camp. A lone lookout stood watching the road, holding a semiautomatic weapon and dressed in army fatigues. In the center of the camp there was a rectangular structure approximately fifty feet in length and thirty feet in width. This is where the cocaine was processed.

Alberto and Hulio had arrived in the camp earlier. They were concluding a tour of the production facility. It had once belonged to Hulio's father and now belonged to Hulio. The men were inside the production shack when a commotion began outside. They walked out of the shack to investigate.

An old pickup truck with a cattle cage on the back was entering the camp. As the truck drove past Hulio and Alberto, they saw three bound and gagged men in the cattle cage. The truck proceeded to the back of the camp and parked near the river. Alberto and Hulio walked to the truck as the men were being unloaded from the cattle cage. They were terrified as evidenced by the look on their faces. As they were taken from the cage, they fell to their knees at Rojas's feet. They were sobbing and attempting to beg for their lives through the gags that covered their mouths. Rojas stood over them showing no compassion for the men whom he considered to be a disgrace.

"You are a pitiful lot," Rojas said in disgust. He turned to the men who had been driving the truck and spoke to them. "Take them to the trees near the river. Chain them. I will be there momentarily," Rojas ordered.

The men obeyed immediately. They jerked the prisoners off the ground and forced them into the jungle. Rojas walked back toward the production shack with Hulio in tow. When Rojas reached the shack, he unzipped a black leather bag he had carried with him on the trip from his home. He took out a pair of camouflage pants and a pair of black combat boots. Rojas disrobed to his underwear and dressed in the camouflage pants and boots. After he had finished tying his shoes, he stood and took a machete out of the black bag. He pulled the sharp stainless-steel weapon out of its sheath and held it in front of him.

"Do you know what this is, Hulio?"

"It's a machete, Alberto."

"No, my young friend. It is the law. It is my law," Rojas said with an angry tone.

Rojas placed the sheath back into the bag and walked toward the jungle holding the machete. Hulio followed him down a narrow path leading through the dense green plant life. As they moved deeper into the jungle, the light grew dimmer. The path ended at a small circular clearing. It had obviously been purposefully cleared by man. In the center of the clearing stood a single large tree. It's branches spread well above and beyond the clearing and hid the small area from the sky above. One of the prisoners was chained to the tree. He had been striped naked and stood quivering at the sight of Rojas. The other two prisoners were chained together and sitting close to the tree. A fire was burning in a pit near the tree. The flames burned high above the rim of the pit and tips of iron rods protruded from the fire. Rojas surveyed the scene as he entered the clearing. He glared at the man chained to the tree as he walked toward him. When he stood in front of him, the chained man began crying uncontrollably while begging for his life.

"Please . . . Please . . . I didn't do anything. I have a wife and three daughters. I am an honest man . . . . Please! Do not—"

Rojas had heard enough. He slapped the man's face, spit at him then glared with hate-filled eyes.

"You are a liar and a thief! You are a pig! You will tell me what I want to know!" Rojas screamed.

Rojas walked to the two men chained together and sitting on the ground. They too were both sobbing. Rojas looked at them with disgust. He spit on them then turned back to the man chained to the tree.

"You say you have a wife and three daughters?"

"Yes . . . Yes, I do," the man said, hoping that it would soften Rojas's heart.

"Do they live with you?"

"Yes," the man answered quickly.

"Hulio, do you know where this pig lives?"

"Yes, Alberto. I know."

Alberto took two steps away from the men on the ground and focused his eyes on the man chained to the tree.

"Then we will find your wife and daughters. First they will be raped. Each of them many times. They will be raped by many men. I would guess that three or four would satisfy themselves at the same time."

"No! Please, mother of god, no!" the man screamed.

Rojas slapped him again. "And after they have been raped, do you know what will happen to them? Do you know what I will have done to them?"

The man could not speak. He was too frightened to speak. He stood with his mouth open; saliva mixed with blood flowed down his chin and onto his chest. He was crying but there was no sound. He could not make a sound.

"I will do this!" Rojas said as he suddenly wheeled around with the sharp gleaming blade he held in his right hand. The blade hit one of the men sitting on the ground at the base of the neck just above the shoulder blade. The blade sliced quickly and cleanly through the skin, muscle, and bone. Rojas spun completely around and now faced the man again. The severed head of the prisoner fell to the ground with a muffled *thud*. The headless body spewed blood and quivered. Rojas held the blade in front of him. It was dripping with the blood of his victim. The man chained to the tree looked at Rojas in horror. Again his mouth was open; he was hyperventilating and was unable to generate any sound. The man stood there shaking his head from side to side, signaling to Rojas that he did not want to die. Rojas walked toward the man. He held the machete at the man's throat.

"Now you will tell me what I want to know. Who else was working with Ricardo Sanchez? Who else knew about his operation?"

The man could not speak; he was too terrified to speak. All he could do was shake his head from side to side. He wasn't telling Rojas that he wouldn't tell him anything, he was trying to tell him that he did not know anything. Rojas looked deep into the man frightened eyes. Rojas was filled with rage and anger.

"You will tell me what I want to know, and you will tell me now!" Rojas screamed.

The machete moved swiftly and Rojas's aim was precise as the blade cut through the man's shoulder severing his arm from his body. The man screamed in wild fright and pain as his arm fell to the ground. Blood spewed uncontrollably from the gaping wound on the side of his body. As the man continued to scream in utter agony, Rojas walked to the fire pit. He picked up a padded towel which lay next to the pit and retrieved one of the hot irons from the fire. He walked back to the man and studied him for a moment.

"Do you want to die?"

The man was weeping and gasping for breath, but he did not want to die. He shook his head from side to side in answer to Rojas's question. Rojas brought the end of the glowing red-hot iron rod up to the man's body. He looked at Hulio who was standing behind him and smiled. Then he jammed the hot iron into the man's wound. The smell was repulsive as the hot iron burned the blood and skin, cauterizing the wound. The man again let out a brief piercing scream then his body went limp. The man was unconscious. The pain had been more than he could bear.

Rojas turned and walked toward Hulio. He tossed the iron rod to the ground. Hulio looked pale and he had a sick feeling in his stomach. He knew that these things happened; however, he had never been witness to such an incident. He couldn't let Alberto know that the sight had sickened him. He had to be strong in front of him. As Rojas approached, Hulio took a deep breath and attempted to swallow in an effort to clear his throat. His mouth was dry, however, and he felt as though he were going to throw up.

"You look peaked, Hulio. Are you all right?"

Hulio cleared his throat and spoke. "Yes, Alberto, I'm fine. I don't think you will get any information from these men. If there was someone else working with my father, they wouldn't know about it. I didn't even know about it."

"I know."

"You know? But why kill them if they know nothing."

Rojas looked at Hulio. Again his eyes changed expression, and Hulio could actually see the hate and rage inside of them.

"Did they not work for your father? Did they not betray me, you, and the cartel with their actions? I do this to make an example of them. I do this to show those who would think about placing their needs above those of the cartel what will happen to them!"

Rojas turned his head and pointed to the man still alive chained to the headless body.

"Do you see him? He will be the one to tell. I will let him live to tell what happened here today. He will go back to the United States and tell people what he saw, and how these men died. He will tell people why they were killed and who held the blade that brought their deaths!"

Rojas looked at the three who brought the prisoners to the clearing.

"Turn him around! I want him to face the tree!" Rojas ordered.

The three men ran quickly to the prisoner and positioned him so that he now faced the tree. Rojas walked to him.

"Do you see this man?"

The prisoner was shaking and was afraid to answer.

"Answer me! Do you see him?" Rojas screamed.

"Y . . . Yes, I . . . I . . . see him."

"He is here because he betrayed the cartel! I am going to kill him as I killed the pig you are chained to, only his death will not be so swift. He will die in agony. He will know what hell on earth really means! He will beg me to kill him before I am finished. No one! No one betrays the cartel and lives! You go back to the United States and you tell this to people. Do you understand?"

The prisoner nodded his head.

"Good! Now you watch as your friend suffers in his death," Rojas said as he walked toward the tree again.

The chained man was still unconscious. His body hung limply, held up only by the shackle around his remaining arm.

"Bring me water and a rope!" Rojas ordered.

The men scattered. Two ran to the river to fetch the water and one brought a long chain to Rojas. Rojas studied the chain the man nervously held in front of him.

"That will do. Secure his head."

The man wrapped the chain around the tree trunk and around the man's neck. He tightened the chain and drew his neck back securely against the tree. The two men returned from the river with the water Rojas had requested and gave him one jug. Rojas threw the murky brown water in the man's face. He did not respond. Rojas then dumped the entire jug of water over the man's head and he slowly regained consciousness. When he opened his eyes, he saw Rojas standing in front of him holding the machete. He glanced to his left and saw the wound where once there was an arm. His eyes widened as he returned his attention to Rojas.

"You are awake. That is good. Do you still want to live?"

The man struggled to nod his head which was tightly held against the tree by the chain. Rojas looked into the man's eyes. Rojas showed no emotion as he spoke.

"I can not let you live. And I can not let you die swiftly," Rojas said calmly. He spun around again twice. Each time he turned, he landed a blow with the sharp blade in the middle of the man's thighs. The man gaped and his eyes looked as if they would explode out of his head. The veins in his neck were pressed tightly against the skin. He tried to scream, but the excruciating pain overpowered his ability to make sound. The man's legs were attached by the thigh bone and skin in the back of the thigh. This angered Rojas and he began chopping wildly at first one leg and then the other until both legs fell to the ground. Rojas stood back from the quivering body and watched as the life spurted from the wounds he had inflicted. Rojas walked to the prisoner sitting on the ground. He was in shock. He did not move, he just sat and stared at the horrific sight before him. A severed head lay at his feet, the arm and legs of a man he did not know lay on the ground at the base of the tree. His limbless body quivered and he looked as if he were attempting to speak. He was still alive, barely, but he was still alive. Rojas looked at the prisoner.

"Tell them what you saw here today. Tell them that Alberto Rojas does not tolerate traitors. This is the destiny of a traitor," Rojas said.

He walked away from the prisoner and toward Hulio. Rojas was covered in blood. The closer he got to him, the more Hulio felt as though he would become ill. When Rojas reached him, Hulio could smell the sickening sweet scent of the blood that covered Rojas. Hulio could no longer stand it. He ran toward the woods and began violently throwing up. Rojas watched him from a distance and began laughing.

The two-hour drive back to the Rojas estate was a quiet one. Hulio had to ask Rojas to stop several times along the way. When they arrived at the house, Rojas went to his master suite to shower and change clothes. Hulio went into the parlor and sat down. A servant entered the room and stood quietly before him, waiting for his instructions. Hulio looked at the servant and sighed.

"Bring me a soda. Any kind of soda, please."

The servant left the room and Hulio sat thinking about what he had experienced in the jungle that day. The sight of the man chained to the tree still sickened him. The image was burned into his mind. Hulio didn't have a problem with killing people; he himself had killed seven men during his young life. But they had been swift killings, always with a gun and always with one bullet. He did not stand around and watch as his victims died. He would simply pull the trigger and walk away. Today he had watched the dismemberment and slow death of a man. Hulio had not liked it.

The servant entered the parlor with a soda on a tray for Hulio. He walked to him and presented the tray. Hulio took the glass without saying anything and the servant exited the room again. Roberto Diego then entered the parlor.

"Hulio! How are you? Oh . . . you don't look so good," Diego said.

"I'm fine, Roberto. I had a rough day."

"I heard. Alberto is in a good mood. He enjoys days like today. He knows that his reputation will be strengthened and that people will continue to fear his name when it is spoken."

"Is that such a good thing, Roberto? Do his people have to fear him? Why doesn't he want their respect?"

"Fear is respect in our business, Hulio. In this business it is the most powerful and influential kind of respect a man can have."

"He enjoyed it, Roberto. I mean he truly enjoyed watching those men die. I have killed before and I will kill again, but I will not kill that way. Not that way."

Roberto walked to a jar of candy sitting on one of the parlor tables. He flipped through the mints, picked out one he liked and popped it into his mouth.

"Killing is killing, Hulio," Roberto said matter-of-factly.

"I thought that as well, until today. Today I saw a man butchered."

"Did Alberto not get his point across to the one left alive?"

Hulio thought for a moment before answering. "I suppose he did. The man was scared to death."

"Then do not question the methods, look at the result. You are still young; you have a lot to learn about running your own business. As you grow older and your own business grows in strength, your people will have ideas of their own. They will become jealous and envious of your wealth and your power. If you have demonstrated your leadership ability correctly, they will think twice before crossing you. They will also do whatever they can to impress you; they will try to gain your favor. That is the world you want to live in, my young friend. That is the way you will want your people to respect you one day."

Ricardo was a wise man with many years of experience. Hulio respected him and listened to his advice. Hulio sat thinking about what Ricardo had said to him when Rojas entered the parlor.

"How are you feeling, Hulio?" Rojas asked with a wide smile.

"I'm feeling better, Alberto. I'm sorry I became ill," Hulio said timidly.

"Do not be sorry, Hulio. You grew today. And I trust that you learned something?"

"Yes, I did. I learned that I still have a lot to learn."

Rojas and Diego laughed at Hulio's comment. Rojas walked to the couch and took a seat. He sighed deeply and looked as though he was feeling good about himself. He was.

"Did you tell him the good news, Roberto?"

"No, Alberto, I was waiting for you to come down."

"Well, I am here. So tell him."

"What news, Alberto? Roberto, is it good news?"

"It is good news, Hulio. We have captured Peterson and Rekcah in Dallas. They are on their way here as we speak."

"You got them both?"

"Yes. A man and a woman. We captured them early this morning at Peterson's house. It was easy really."

"Have they talked?"

"No, they will not be asked to talk until they arrive here. Then we will ask them to talk won't we, Alberto?" Diego said with a smile.

"Oh yes, Roberto. Hulio, you may enjoy it. It is one thing to make a man confess what is hidden in his mind. It is another to make a woman talk," Rojas said.

Rojas and Diego laughed at the thought of making the woman talk. The two of them had done it many times. Both of them enjoyed it. Hulio did not find humor in the comment. He could only imagine what Rojas had in store for her and he knew it would not be pleasant.

ARTICLE 24

July 28, 2005, 5:25 p.m.
Hoover Building, Washington, D.C.

Special Agent Whitfield was on his way out of his office. He had worked two very long days in a row and wanted to spend some quiet time at home with his family that evening. He walked down the hallway toward the elevators then stopped abruptly and snapped his fingers.

Brian walked backward for a few steps then turned around and walked toward the communications office. He walked into the office and surveyed the room. There were four agents working at different stations positioned in different corners of the room. The walls were lined with computers, receivers, and all kinds of sophisticated communications equipment. In the center of the room sat the COMSAT telecommunications computer. It coordinated satellite communications for the bureau throughout the United States.

Brian walked to Agent Marshall who was seated at a workstation with a communications headset on. Brian tapped him on the shoulder to get his attention. Agent Marshall turned to see that it was Brian and held his finger in the air to let Brian know he would be with him in a moment. Brian stood behind Agent Marshall and waited patiently for him to finish his call. When Agent Marshall was finished, he turned and greeted Brian with a smile and a handshake.

"Special-Agent-in-Charge Whitfield, what brings you to the cave?" Marshall asked.

"Slumming it today, Marshall. Listen, do you have any correspondence from Agent Hendrix? Maybe something from real early this morning or during the day?"

"Let me pull Hendrix up on the computer," Marshall said as he swiveled around to his computer.

Agent Marshall keyed Agent Hendrix's name into the computer. Her name came up and next to her name the computer displayed her communications security code. Marshall highlighted the security code and pressed the Enter key. Her communications record then appeared on the monitor. Agent Marshall studied the screen.

"Looks like the last transmission we received from her was at 12:37 a.m. on July 27."

"Nothing after that?"

"No, sir. Don't show a thing."

"Do me a favor and get in touch with the Dallas field office. Tell them I want them to do a drive-by of the Peterson house. Also tell them to check out Hendrix's apartment."

"You think something's wrong?"

"No, I'm sure everything's fine. It's her first field assignment and I'm sure she just hasn't checked in. I'll chew her ass out when we get hold of her."

"Man, I'd like to be in on that!" Marshall said with a laugh.

"Just call Dallas. I'm goin' home."

"See you tomorrow," Marshall said as he began completing the task the Brian had just requested.

Brian walked out of the communications office and back toward the elevators. He couldn't help but worry about Christine Hendrix. It was her first field assignment. She was fresh out of the academy. He knew that she was probably okay, but it irritated him that she hadn't called in with a report. He walked to the elevator and decided he would worry about her in the morning. Tomorrow he would give her the ass chewing she deserved.

CHAPTER SEVEN

ARTICLE 25

July 29 2005, 5:30 a.m.
Central Cordillera Region, Colombia

There was no moon in the early morning sky over the jungle. The C-130 transport plane could be heard but not seen as it flew ten thousand feet above the hills and trees. The rear hatch slowly began to open and the special forces personnel stood and prepared for their exit. They were difficult to see in the darkened plane. They all had black and green painted faces and wore dark camouflaged pants, jackets, helmets, and backpacks.

The rear hatch of the plane was open and the platoon commander who was standing at the hatch raised his fist in the air. The troops moved into two lines and stood waiting for the commander's signal. The commander intently watched a red light on a box adjacent to his head. Suddenly the red light went out and a green light illuminated the side of the commander's painted face. Without a word, the commander dropped his arm and the troops began jumping in pairs out of the back of the C-130. As the massive transport plane continued along its path, the sky was filled with a cluster of dark sinister-looking parachutes slowly descending toward the trees. It was an ominous sight; however, no one on the ground saw it. They were unaware of the fate that was about to befall them. There were two platoons. The men had a single purpose. They were there to wipe out what the United States government had labeled "a plague." And they were ordered to kill anyone who got in their way.

ARTICLE 26

July 29, 2005, 7:50 a.m.
Hoover Building, Washington D.C.

SAC Brian Whitfield walked into his office to find Agent Criswell waiting. Brian stopped in the doorway when he saw Criswell sitting with his back to the door.

"Criz!" Brian shouted.

Agent Criswell jumped out of the chair and turned quickly toward Brian.

"Dammit, Brian! God, I swear you're gonna give me a heart attack one of these days," Criswell said holding his chest.

Brian laughed at Criswell's reaction as he walked to his chair, laid his briefcase on the desk and sat down. Criswell's pulse rate returned to normal as he took his seat as well.

"To what do I owe such an early morning visit from my director of communications?"

"I have news on Hendrix," Criswell said with a serious look on his face.

"Bad?"

"Well, it's not good. The field went to her apartment last night. There wasn't anyone home and the car was gone. They went by Peterson's house early this morning. They were initially going to drive by and report. But Hendrix's car was parked in front of the house. They took a look around the house. And . . ." Criswell paused.

"What? What did they find?"

"The house appeared vacant and they found blood, Brian. Blood on the sidewalk in front of the door."

"How much blood?"

"Drops, just traces. But Hendrix and Peterson are nowhere to be found."

"Goddammit! I knew I shouldn't have given her the assignment. Peterson probably found out who she was or she blew her cover and he took her. The son-of-a-bitch took her!"

Brian sat with anger and concern showing on his face as he thought about the situation and what he would do about it.

"What's the status in Dallas?"

"We have an APB out on Hendrix and Peterson. We don't know what he is driving because his car was in the garage and Christine's was still parked in front of the house."

"We didn't have any information that he was working with anyone else. All of our data on this guy says he was working alone and was probably just a hack. He had a squeaky clean background. Not even a traffic ticket. Lived alone. Didn't date. And he was an excellent employee. Christ, Criz, I didn't think this guy was anything to worry about. And goddammit, I swear I didn't think he could be violent. The history wasn't there. I never would have sent her into a situation like that!"

"I know that, Brian, and you have to quit beating yourself up about it. Shit like this happens, and it happens to veterans, man. We'll find her. This guy Peterson isn't a convict; he's not a seasoned criminal. He doesn't have that mentality, so he'll screw up. And when he does, we'll get the bastard. You know we will."

"Who's in charge in Dallas?"

"Murphy, he's a good man. He'll find her, Brian."

"Well, I can't sit on my ass around here. I'm goin' to Dallas."

"You might want to reconsider."

"Why? I've got an agent missing. She's my responsibility, and on top of that, I put her in this situation. I'm going down there and I'm going to find out why a mild-mannered computer nerd with no history of criminal activity suddenly turns into a kidnapper. I'll go nuts if I stay here, Criz."

"You want me to arrange your flight?"

"Yeah. I'll leave this afternoon."

"Don't worry, Brian, we'll get her back. Hell, we don't even know that she's in any danger. It's all speculation at this point."

"I can feel it, Criz. I felt it last night when I checked with communications. Something is wrong. Very wrong."

"What do you need for the trip?"

"Get me all of the information on Peterson. The whole file. Send Dallas a copy of what we have."

"I did that this morning."

"Good. Then I'll take a copy with me. Call Dallas. Let Murphy know I'm on my way. I want a briefing late this afternoon when I get in. You tell him that this is priority one on his agenda. We have to assume that Peterson has abducted Hendrix. He is to be considered armed and dangerous. I want him on the list as well. He may have gotten out of Dallas by now."

"Anything else?"

"I'm sure there will be. I have to go brief Stafford. I'll talk to you after I've seen him. Go ahead and get started on what I've given you," Brian said as he stood from his chair and walked to the door and exited his office.

Associate Director Stafford's office was on the same floor at the end of the long hallway outside Brian's office. He walked down the hall thinking about Christine and the conversation he was about to have with Stafford. He didn't get along with the associate director. Brian respected the man professionally due to his position; however, he did not like him personally. He avoided contact with him whenever possible. Stafford had a way of belittling his people even when they performed well in their duties. He would always focus on what had gone wrong with an investigation rather than the positives. And when there was a problem with a division, the SAC of that division felt the full impact of Stafford's outrage and sarcastic criticism. Brian was not looking forward to telling Stafford about Hendrix.

Brian entered Stafford's office reception area. Margaret Campbell sat at her desk working on her computer.

Brian approached her desk and spoke. "Is he in?" he asked with a serious tone.

"Yes, would you like to see him?" Margaret said with a smile.

"Is he in a meeting?"

"No, sir."

"Not really, but I have to."

Margaret pressed her intercom which prompted the speaker in Stafford's office to buzz.

"Yes?" Stafford answered.

"Special Agent Whitfield would like to see you, sir," Margaret said.

"Whitfield? Tell him to wait," Stafford said sternly.

Margaret looked at Brian as if to tell him she couldn't do anything about her boss's indignant manner. Brian was angry. Stafford had done this to him for twelve years. When the other SACs asked to see him, they were asked right in unless Stafford was in a meeting. The longer Brian stood in the reception area, the more upset he became. He knew that he didn't deserve this kind of treatment from Stafford.

"Hell," he thought. "I'm the senior SAC in the bureau. I don't have to take this shit." Brian looked at Margaret with determination on his face. He had waited long enough. He had waited twelve long years.

"Margaret, I don't have to take this shit. And I'm not going to anymore."

With that, Brian walked past Margaret's desk and walked through Stafford's door. He closed it behind him noticeably hard. Margaret sat at her desk smiling broadly in approval of Brian's actions.

When Brian entered the office, Stafford was holding a putter and practicing his putting stroke in one corner of the massive room. He looked at Brian with indignation.

"Just what in the hell do you think you're doing? You don't barge into my office. I didn't tell you that I was ready to see you."

"You gonna hit the nigger with that stick, Director Stafford?" Brian said sarcastically.

Stafford realized that he was wielding the putter in the air as he spoke to Brian. He brought the club down to his side and responded to Brian's remark.

"I didn't use that language with you, Whitfield."

"You didn't have to. For the past twelve years, each time I came down here to see you, expected or not, you made me wait in your reception area. Why am I the only one who has the pleasure of waiting? You don't ask any of the other SACs to wait."

Stafford put the putter back in the golf bag leaning against the wall in the corner of the room. He then walked to his enormous desk and sat down.

"Perhaps it is because I am busy when you come to see me, Agent Whitfield," Stafford said sarcastically.

"Like you were busy today working on your fucking golf game?" Brian snapped.

"You're out of line, Agent Whitfield!"

Brian walked quickly toward Stafford's desk. He placed his tightened fists on the desk and glared at Stafford.

"Out of line? No, no, I'm not out of line. I've put up with your bullshit for twelve years and I don't have time for your petty little power games today. I've got a missing agent!"

"A missing agent? Who have you lost, Agent Whitfield?" Stafford asked again sarcastically.

"I didn't lose anyone. It's Hendrix, Agent Christine Hendrix. She was in Dallas undercover for me. She was investigating a computer fraud case and disappeared last night."

"Hendrix? The new agent? You sent her undercover? A woman who'd been out of the academy less than six months and you send her undercover? What a brilliant executive decision, Agent Whitfield."

"She wanted the assignment and I felt that the circumstances were such that she wouldn't be exposed to any danger. The guy didn't have a history—"

"You thought? Well, Agent Whitfield, you better pray to your god that nothing happens to that agent as a result of your ineptitude. Your insolent behavior in this office today is enough to have you suspended. I'll have your job and your ass if something happens to Hendrix."

Brian turned and started to walk to the door. "I'm going to Dallas," he said as he walked away.

"The hell you are! You're not going anywhere! You get your ass back here, goddammit. I'm not finished with you!" Stafford shouted.

Brian kept walking toward the door.

"I'll have your job anyway, you stupid black asshole," Stafford said under his breath. The room acoustics were excellent, however, and Brian heard the comment. He stopped and very slowly turned to face Stafford.

Stafford realized that Brian had heard the racial slur. He watched anxiously as Brian walked with a confident and determined stride back to the desk. Brian leaned over the desk and glared at Stafford who dared not move at that point. Brian had a look of deep lingering hate on his face as he spoke in a soft calm voice to Stafford.

"I heard that, Director Stafford. It confirms a suspicion I've had about you for twelve years. You're as ignorant as you look. Now you listen to me. I am going to Dallas to find Agent Hendrix. I'm not coming back here until I've found her and I know she is safe. When I'm finished, I will come back here. I will come to see you. And when I do, I'm going to shove my ID so far up your racist ass that people will be able to read my name when you smile. Now, do you have anything else to say to me, Director Stafford? Any more brilliant anecdotes on your mind that you want to share with me?"

Stafford responded by shaking his head from side to side quickly. He looked at Brian with fright in his eyes.

"Good. Now if you will excuse me I'm going to leave. The stench in this office is turning my stomach."

Brain turned to leave the office and Stafford spoke. Brian stopped with his back still turned to Stafford.

"Whitfield, about that comment you supposedly heard? No one else heard it. Just you. It's your word against mine, Whitfield, and who do you suppose people would believe? Enjoy your trip to Dallas, Whitfield. It'll be your last for the bureau."

Brian stormed out of Stafford's office, slamming the door behind him. As he walked past Margaret's desk she spoke.

"Agent Whitfield?" she said softly.

"What!" Brian shouted in anger as he stopped and looked at her.

Margaret was startled by Brian's tone, and sat back timidly in her chair. Brian realized that he was directing his anger at the wrong person.

"I'm sorry, Margaret, really. What did you want?"

Margaret sat up in her chair and tapped the intercom speaker with her fingers. She smiled at Brian as she spoke.

"I heard it too, Agent Whitfield."

Brian looked at her with a look of pleasant surprise on his face. He smiled and winked at her.

"Thanks, Margaret."

"No problem."

Brian walked out of the reception area and started down the hallway to his office. He put the incident with Stafford out of his mind. He had to. His focus needed to be on a young rookie agent named Christine Hendrix. He did not know where she was and chances were that she was in a great deal of danger. He thought about Peterson and how he could have been so terribly wrong about this man. His actions didn't fit his personality profile at all. He knew desperate people were capable of desperate things but this was over the edge. He grew angry as he thought of the possibility of Christine being hurt or worse at the hands of Peterson. He stopped at his door. He stood there for a moment thinking about Peterson.

"I'm gonna find you, Peterson. And if you've harmed that girl, I'm gonna make sure you wish you'd never been born," he said to himself as he entered his office.

ARTICLE 27

Roberto and Jose had gone on an inspection trip somewhere in the central Cordillera Valley area. Four of the six cartel leaders sat around an umbrella-shaded table. The table was adjacent to the enormous pool behind the Rojas main house. The black-bottomed pool had three beautifully sculptured rock waterfalls, a twisting water slide, and an oversized Jacuzzi on one end. On the other end of the pool sat the main guest house of the estate. It was a large Greek-styled structure built of white marble and trimmed in gold. The guest house had white marble columns surrounding it and black marble steps leading from the pool to its front door.

Rojas liked to sit by the pool and conduct his business. He liked the fresh air and the clean chlorine scent that emanated from the pool. The four men all had drinks in hand and cigars lit. Rojas was speaking as was the norm in this situation.

"We will deal with our Guatemalan friends in an appropriate manner," Rojas said.

"They want more money, and I have heard from our people in Puerto Barrios that they may even ask for a percentage of the product shipped in and out of the port. We don't control the port, Alberto, they do," Pedro said.

"What do you think about the matter, Joseffe?" Rojas asked.

"I think we should take the port. If not, then we stop doing business with them until they begin listening to reason.

I can reroute our shipments to Honduras tomorrow. They are begging me to."

"Why don't we then?" Rojas asked.

"Our air support is in Huehuetenango, Guatemala. If we upset the port, they will make sure we have problems at the airfield. If the Guatemalan demands are unreasonable, however, we can spend the money needed to set our air distribution up in Honduras or even El Salvador."

"How much would this cost?" Rojas asked.

"A couple of million in payoffs, and maybe five million to get the operation set up."

"Then let's do it, regardless of what the Guatemalan demands are. It will give us options that we need in place anyway. If we are in agreement here, we will ask the others what they think when they arrive. I know that they will—"

Rojas was interrupted by the appearance of one of his many armed guards running from the main house toward the table where they were sitting. As the man drew closer Rojas shouted at him.

"What do you want?"

The guard stopped. He was still roughly fifteen yards away from the table.

"Come here, you fool, tell me what you want," Rojas demanded.

The guard walked quickly to the table looking at the ground the entire time. He spoke when he reached Rojas. "A crate has arrived," the servant said.

"A crate? What crate? From who?" Rojas asked impatiently.

"It came here, but it is for Senior Diego. I think there is something living inside of the crate."

Rojas looked around the table at Joseffe, Pedro, and Hulio. He had a look of satisfaction on his face.

"Peterson and Rekcah have arrived gentlemen," Rojas said with a broad smile.

The four men stood quickly from the table and followed the guard back to the main house. They walked through the house and out the oversized front doors. They stood at the entry to the house and studied the large wooden box sitting in the middle of the driveway. Rojas walked to the box and yelled at one of the armed guards who was standing nearby.

"Get me something to open it with. Now!"

The guards all scattered in different directions. Moments later one appeared holding a crowbar. He ran to Rojas and presented it to him. Rojas grabbed the crowbar from the servant and pushed him away. He inserted the bar between the lid and the side of the box and strained as the top began to pull away from the side. He worked his way around the box until the top was loose enough to lift off by hand.

"Come here and help me get this thing off," Rojas ordered his guards.

Two of them ran to the box and assisted Rojas in lifting the top off. When the top had been removed, Rojas looked into the container. Another broad smile appeared on his face. He looked up from the crate and back to the three men still standing in the doorway.

"Gentlemen, may I present our guests, Peterson and Rekcah."

The three men walked quickly from the doorway of the main house to the box in the driveway. They looked inside the container and saw Clay Peterson and Christine Hendrix lying back to back. They were bound from head to foot and had gags around their mouths. Their eyes were covered as well with duct tape. Clay's duffle bag and Christine's purse lay at their feet.

"Do not untie them. But take them to the back and hose them off. We will join you there after the stench has been washed off them. Bring their belongings to me. Come in and get us when you are done," Rojas ordered the guards.

As the four men walked back to the house, four of the guards struggled to get Clay and Christine out of the crate.

They could not lift them out, so they all stood on one side of the box and tipped it over. Clay and Christine rolled out of the box and hit the gravel driveway face first. The servants then grabbed the pair by the rope around their feet and dragged them to the back of the house laughing as they walked.

When they reached a grassy area in the rear of the main house, one of the servants used a hose to wash Clay and Christine down. The trip had taken almost fifteen hours. They had been in the box from the time they left Dallas. The guard sprayed them with the hose for at least fifteen minutes before he was satisfied that most of the stench had been removed. Clay and Christine didn't mind the bath; in fact, it felt quite good to them. They both remained terrified, however. They did not know where they were; they didn't know who had abducted them. They only knew that they must be a long way from Dallas. As they lay soaking wet in the grass, one of the guards went into the house to get Rojas. Clay and Christine struggled, as they had many times during their trip, to free themselves. It was a futile effort. The ropes were tied well. There was no escape.

Rojas, Pedro, Joseffe, and Hulio walked out of the house and onto the grass where Clay and Christine were lying. Rojas looked at them and smiled.

"Untie them," he ordered one of the guards.

The guard took a knife from his pocket and began cutting through the rope that bound the pair together. He cut the rope around their ankles first, then around their waist, and finally around their shoulders. When their shoulders were cut loose, both of them rolled onto their stomachs and lay there. Rojas walked closer to them. He kicked Clay in the side and Clay responded with a moan. Rojas was making sure that he was alive. He walked to Christine and did the same. Christine too moaned when the toe of his shoe connected with her ribs.

"Roll them over and cut their hands free. Remove the gags and tape as well," Rojas ordered.

Two of the guards worked to free the rope from around their wrists. When the rope was taken off, the guards rolled them over, pulled the gags out of their mouths and jerked the tape from their eyes.

Clay and Christine lay on their backs, trying to focus their eyes. The late afternoon sun made it difficult for them to see the men standing around them. Both shielded their eyes from the sun after a moment and sat up as their eyes slowly focused. They looked around at the armed guards and the four casually but well-dressed men who surrounded them. Clay attempted to stand, but a guard moved forward and struck him in the back with the butt of his machine gun. Clay cried out in pain and slumped back to the ground. Christine did not attempt to move.

"Welcome. Now I would like to know which of you is Peterson and which of you is Rekcah?" Rojas asked.

Clay sat looking at the ground, still in pain from the blow to his back. Christine was frightened and still said nothing. When Rojas did not get a response to his question, he signaled his guards with a swipe of his hand. The guards moved toward the pair and cocked their guns in preparation to fire.

"Wait!" Clay screamed holding his hand in the air. He slowly raised his head until he was looking at Rojas. Clay studied him for a moment. Then he spoke.

"I am Peterson. I am Clay Peterson."

"Ah . . . then this must be Rekcah. Ms. Sallad Rekcah."

"No she's no—"

Before Clay could finish his sentence he was struck again in the back by one of the guards. Clay again cried out in agony. This time the force of the blow was so strong that Clay fell all the way to the ground.

"You will soon learn, Clay Peterson. You do not speak unless you are first spoken to. You do not move unless you are told to move. Are you starting to understand the rules, Clay Peterson?" Rojas asked.

Clay did not answer. Rojas nodded to one of the guards. The guard moved toward Clay and kicked him viciously in the side. Clay let out a cry as the breath was knocked out of his body and he rolled to one side on the ground.

"Stop!" Christine screamed. Two of the guards put their guns to her head and she was still.

"I will ask you again if you understand the rules, Clay Peterson?"

"Yes, I understand the rules," Clay answered in obvious pain.

"That is good. Slow learners do not live long in Colombia as you might now well imagine."

Rojas turned his attention to Christine. She was weathered from the long trip in the wooden box and wet from the bath she had received, but Rojas still admired her beauty.

"Get her up," he ordered.

Two guards grabbed Christine under her arms and jerked her small frame off the ground. She was wearing Clay's white Trojan T-shirt and a pair of cutoff jeans. The wet shirt clung tightly to her breasts and her large brown nipples were plainly visible to Rojas and the men standing around her.

Rojas admired her from the front for a few moments then walked slowly around to look at her from behind. He admired her firm athletic body. He walked back in front of her and smiled. Rojas looked into her eyes as he spoke.

"I told you that interrogating a woman could be much more interesting than interrogating a man. Didn't I, Hulio?" Rojas said with a wicked smile.

"Yes, you did, Alberto. Now I see what you mean, my friend. She is lovely."

Rojas continued to look at Christine, then without warning slapped her hard with the back of his hand. The blow sent Christine to the ground.

"She is a thief and a traitor to the cartel. And that is all that she is. Take them behind the pool house. Tie them each to a tree. I am going to change my clothes," Rojas commanded.

The guards grabbed Clay and Christine and started walking away with them. Rojas turned his back and started walking back to the house. Suddenly Clay broke free from the grasp of the guards and turned to speak to Rojas.

"Wait! You don't understand! We didn't—"

Clay did not finish his sentence. A guard hit him again, this time in the back of the neck. The blow rendered him unconscious. The two guards each picked up one of Clay's feet and dragged him face down toward the pool house. Rojas turned back toward the three cartel leaders who were standing on the steps leading up to the house.

"This Peterson, he is a very slow learner, is he not?" Rojas quipped.

The men laughed together as they walked into the house. Once inside the house, Rojas stopped to talk to them before proceeding to his room to change.

"Would you gentlemen like to change clothes and assist in the interrogation?"

The three men exchanged glances.

"I have seen enough killing this week, my friend. I will wait in the house while you are busy with them," Pedro said.

"I will wait with Pedro also, Alberto. I too do not have the stomach for a killing today."

"And you, Hulio? Would you like to interrogate the girl?"

"I will interrogate her if there is anything left of her after you are through. My stomach is just now beginning to feel better, Alberto. I had better stay with the others."

"Very well, my friends, I will have to do this myself. I don't mind; you will just be missing some fun with the girl, that's all. Go into the parlor and make yourselves at home; I do not anticipate that this will take very long," Rojas said as he exited the room.

The three men walked to the parlor to get themselves drinks.

The guards dragged Clay and walked Christine past the pool and the pool house to a shaded area behind the house. They shoved Christine against one of the trees. One guard stood in front of her with his gun pointed between her eyes. The other pulled her arms back and tied her hands together. He then tied her ankles and wrapped the rope around the trunk of the tree. When they were finished, she could not move. The guards who were binding Clay to the other tree were having some difficulty with him because he was still unconscious. The two guards who tied Christine to her tree went to assist with Clay. Once they had secured him, the four men walked back to Christine and began admiring her. They flipped her hair with the barrels of their guns. One guard put the end of his gun under her chin then slowly moved it down to between her breasts. Christine closed her eyes and began to cry as he circled both breasts then moved the gun down her stomach and finally stopped between her legs. He moved the barrel of the gun forward then backward between her legs, pressing the gun against her crotch. He whispered something in Spanish to the other men and they laughed. Christine held her eyes tightly shut as the man continued to besmirch her body.

Suddenly the man stopped and she didn't hear them laughing anymore. She waited a moment then slowly opened her eyes. The guards were gone. Christine looked toward Clay who was tied to the tree next to her. His head was leaning forward on his chest as he was still unconscious. Christine called out to him while she attempted to free herself from the ropes.

"Clay! Clay, wake up! Dammit, Clay, wake up. We have to get away from here!"

Christine continued to struggle with her ropes. Clay began moving his head. He was beginning to regain consciousness.

"Clay! That's it, Clay, wake up!"

Clay slowly lifted his aching head and opened his eyes. As the surroundings began to come into focus, he saw that Christine was tied to the tree. His first instinct was to move toward her to help. When he couldn't, he looked down his front and saw that he too was tied to a tree at the shoulders, waist, and ankles. He looked sadly at Christine. He watched her as she desperately struggled to get away.

"I can't move, Christine. I can't help you."

"I know. I can't get out of these ropes either. They're too tight. Is your head okay?"

"I think so. I have a hell of a headache though."

Christine continued to struggle, while Clay surveyed the surroundings. He could see the pool and a portion of the main house in front of him. To his left was Christine and a garden area beyond her. To his right he could look over a small wall and into the valley below them.

"I don't think we're in Dallas," Clay said.

"Hell, no we're not in Dallas. Didn't you hear that guy? We're in Colombia."

"Colombia? You mean like Colombia, South America, Colombia?"

"They don't walk around with machine guns in Columbia, South Carolina, Clay. Yeah, we're in Colombia, the country. Where a lot of very wealthy drug people live. My guess is that this is the guy who had the Swiss account you took the money out of. He thinks I'm Sallad Rekcah. He thinks I have his money."

"So we'll just tell him the truth. We'll tell him it was all a mistake. He has to let us go."

"No, Clay, he can do anything he wants. And I doubt that he has plans to let us go."

"Then what are we going to do? Let him kill us? Christ, Christine, he has to understand it was a simple mistake. We have to make him understand. I'm going to try when I see him again."

"No . . . you won't! You'll keep your mouth shut. Now let me think for a minute, please."

Christine leaned back against the tree and thought about the predicament they were in. She knew that this man planned to kill them. She knew that given the surroundings and the trouble he had taken to have them brought there that he had to be very powerful and very wealthy. She had to think of a way to buy time. They had to show this man they were more valuable to him alive than dead. Then she had an idea. She was about to tell Clay what to do when she heard someone approaching.

"You keep quiet and follow my lead, Clay," she whispered.

Both watched as Rojas and two of his armed guards approached them. The guards stopped at the back of the pool house and Rojas continued toward them. He carried a gleaming stainless-steel machete in his right hand. He wore camouflage pants, black combat boots, and no shirt. He walked into the grassy area and stood for a moment studying his soon-to-be victims. Rojas snapped his fingers. One of the guards quickly walked to where Rojas stood and placed a chair down beside him. Rojas sat down and continued to look back and forth at his prisoners. He smiled and then spoke.

"My name is Alberto Rojas. Do you know why you are here?" He asked.

Clay and Christine both shook their heads no in response to the question.

"You are here because you were working with Ricardo Sanchez. Ricardo Sanchez used to be a member and a leader in the Cartel. Tell me what you know about Ricardo Sanchez."

"We weren't working for Ricardo Sanchez. We don't know who Ricardo Sanchez is," Christine said.

"Why do you lie to me, Sallad Rekcah? I know that you had Ricardo's money wired to your bank in Canada. That money is money that Sanchez stole from me, from the cartel!" Rojas screamed as he stood abruptly from his chair.

Rojas walked toward Christine. He moved very close to her and gazed into her eyes. Clay watched helplessly as Rojas placed the palm of his hand on Christine's face firmly. He left it there for a moment and studied her eyes as he squeezed her cheeks. They were filled with fear and he could see it. Rojas liked it. He moved his hand slowly from her cheek down her neck and grasped the collar of her T-shirt. He paused and smiled at her. Then he squinted his eyes a bit, clinched his teeth and pulled with all of his might. The front of the T-shirt ripped away from Christine's body. Her breasts and stomach were now exposed. Clay was fighting to hold back his desire to scream at this man. He struggled to break free from the ropes that held him firmly against the tree. The two guards watched Clay and smiled at one another. They knew that he had no chance of getting free.

Rojas paid no attention to Clay. He was concentrating on Christine. He looked at her without any sign of emotion on his face now. He studied her, admired her stunning upper body. He reached out with the machete and moved the remainder of the T-shirt which hid portions of both breasts. He flipped the shirt away from her breasts and moved closer to her. Christine didn't scream, she just looked at Rojas now with hate in her eyes. Rojas could see this and he liked it as well. He placed a hand gently on one of her breasts and began massaging it. Then he grasped it firmly in his hand and slowly began pulling his fingers toward him until her nipple was between his fingers. He watched her eyes intently as he pinched the nipple hard. Christine clinched her teeth, but again said nothing. Rojas let go of her nipple.

"You are a very strong-willed woman, Sallad Rekcah. I like strong-willed women. Would you like more? You will tell me what I want to know before I am through with you. Your will is not as strong as you think."

Christine did not answer. She just continued to glare at Rojas. Rojas moved close to her. She could feel his breath on her face. He placed his hand on her breast again then moved it slowly down her stomach. Christine closed her eyes and continued to clinch her teeth. Clay had to turn away, he could not watch. Rojas's open hand continued down Christine's tight flat stomach, onto her-cut off jeans and down to her crotch. He grabbed her firmly when he reached her crotch causing Christine to moan in pain. He moved his open hand up and down for a moment before continuing farther. Rojas placed his hand between her legs. He started to work his fingers inside her cut-offs between her thighs when she finally cried out.

"Wait! Please!" she screamed.

Rojas drew back away from her. He looked at her terrified face and smiled.

"Are you ready to talk to me?"

"I don't know what you want me to say, we didn't work for anyone named Sanchez. I just want to know why you have to take something from me that I will give. Untie me and I will give you what you want. Please," Christine pleaded.

She reasoned that she had a better chance of getting out of this situation if she were free from the ropes that bound her to the tree. She had no idea what she would do, but if he let her loose, she would try something, anything to get away.

"It is more fun for me to take it from you," Rojas responded.

With that, he moved toward her quickly and placed his mouth on one of her nipples. He sucked on it for a moment then bit down on it causing Christine to cry out in pain.

"Stop! Stop, you son-of-a-bitch!" Clay cried out.

Rojas's eyes got wide while he still held Christine's nipple between his teeth. He jerked away from her and spun around to face Clay. Rojas looked at him with hate in his eyes. He walked toward Clay, drew back the machete and lunged forward.

"Nooooo!" Christine screamed.

The machete hit the tree just inches above Clay's head. Rojas was in Clay's face as he spoke.

"Do you have something to say to me, Clay Peterson? If you do, you had better say it because you will be dead in a few more minutes."

"We're here because of the money. Because of the ten million dollars."

"You are not telling me anything I don't already know! You will die now!"

Rojas pulled the machete out of the tree and drew it back again.

"Wait! We took the money, but we didn't work for this Sanchez guy! If you listen to me I will tell you how to turn that ten million into almost a billion dollars in just over one year. We can do it, we've done it."

"You are lying. You are just trying to save your life with lies!" Rojas screamed.

"He's not lying. We can do it, and that's why we took the money. If you kill us you won't ever know the truth. What do you have to lose if you just hear us out?" Christine said.

Rojas stepped away from Clay and looked at Christine. He walked back to his chair and sat down. After thinking for a moment, he spoke to them.

"All right. All right, I will give you three minutes to tell me what you have to say. If I am not convinced, you will both die. You will die first, Sallad Rekcah, only after I have had you, and taken your body as only I can. You will die, Clay Peterson, after you have watched me rape this woman. You have three minutes from now . . . . Begin!"

Christine and Clay looked at one another. Clay spoke before Christine could stop him. "We accessed an account in the Royal Bank of Canada on my computer in Dallas. It was a savings account belonging to D. Douglas Conrad. He is a bill—"

"I know who he is. Continue," Rojas interrupted.

"Okay, well the opening balance in the account was ten million dollars. Then over the course of twelve months the balance grew to almost nine hundred million dollars. We wanted to know how the account grew so quickly, so we traced it.

"We traced it to an account in the Swiss World Bank. It was a Trading Account belonging to Douglas also. He leveraged the ten million to buy prime bank notes, one hundred million dollars worth of prime bank notes from the Swiss Bank. The prime bank notes he bought were discounted, and when he resold them he got almost a 6 percent spread on every trade. After the trades were concluded, the profits were wired into the Canadian bank account and more PBNs were issued against the purchase order and the process started all over again.

"Douglas was making almost six million dollars every time the purchase order was traded. The Swiss guaranteed that they would make a minimum of three trades per week, which they did. That meant Douglas was putting close to eighteen million dollars a week in trading profits, or seventy-two million a month, in the bank," Clay concluded.

"We tried to use money from the Canadian account to open our own account, but it was locked. So we searched the Swiss bank system until we found an account with a large balance and little or no withdrawal activity. We found one. It must have been your account. We transferred ten million dollars out of it into an account we opened in the Canadian Bank. Then we structured our own trading account through the Swiss bank. That's all we were going to do. We just wanted to see if we could open the trading account. When we tried to put the money back, the balance of the money had been withdrawn and the account had a lock on it that we couldn't break. That is the truth. We didn't work for anyone named Sanchez; we don't even know anyone named Sanchez. Clay is a computer programmer at Comp-Link in Dallas; I work at the same company in distribution," Christine said.

"And her name isn't Sallad Rekcah. It's—"

"Clay?" Christine questioned him in surprise.

"Her name is Lisa Tinsley. Sallad Rekcah is an anagram," Clay said.

"An anagram?" Rojas asked.

"Yeah, turn the letters around and it spells Dallas Hacker. That's the name we used to open the account. Look, if you don't believe us just call our company. They'll tell you that neither of us is in, that will prove to you that we work there."

"And what of this account business? How would you propose to prove such a thing exists to me?"

"Do you have a computer?"

"Of course. I have three computers. All of them IBM."

"They'll have to do, but I can show you the accounts on your computer. All I need is a phone line and a modem and I can show you."

Rojas sat and studied them both for a moment. Then he stood from his chair and picked up the machete. He looked at Clay.

"Very well, Clay Peterson. I will give you a chance to show me that what you say is the truth, that I can turn ten million dollars into one billion dollars in a year. You will not die today," Rojas said as he looked away from Clay and turned his attention to Christine.

"And you, Lisa Tinsley. I will have your body and then I will kill you while Clay Peterson watches us," Rojas said as he grabbed Christine's breasts again.

"No! You can't! She has the codes!" Clay screamed.

"What? What codes?" Rojas asked while he still held Christine's breasts.

"The security codes, she has them memorized. I can't get into the bank systems without the codes. That's why we worked together on the whole thing. If you kill her you will be losing almost one billion dollars in very easy money," Clay said.

Rojas looked at Christine and clinched his teeth. He held on to her breasts and then pinched her nipples again as he backed away from her. He smiled as she grimaced in pain. Rojas stood between the two trees and spoke softly to them.

"Know this, if what you tell me is true, you are to say nothing to anyone in my organization about it. If what you say is a lie or if you tell anyone about this conversation, this is what I will do to both of you."

Rojas turned and walked to the guards. Clay and Christine watched as he spoke to one of them and he walked back to the main house. The other guard stayed by Rojas's side and walked to the grass area with him.

"Do not take your eyes off them!" he ordered.

The guard obeyed and stood at attention watching both Clay and Christine. Rojas backed away from the guard. He then quickly spun in a circle and hit the guard in the middle of the neck with the machete. Blood spurted everywhere, covering both Christine and Clay. The head fell to the ground and the body wilted after it. Christine was shocked at the horrific sight. She tried to close her eyes, but the blood burned her eyeballs when she closed them. Clay simply turned away when he saw what was going to happen. The guard never knew what happened.

Rojas walked to the guard's severed head which lay at Christine's feet. He bent down and picked the head up with one hand. He held it up so that he could look at the face. He laughed when he saw it.

"You don't think that I have my people trained well? You do not think that they obey me even in death? What were the last orders I gave this man?"

Neither Clay nor Christine answered as they watched Rojas in horror. He turned the head around so that they could see the man's face. Blood was dripping out of the nose and mouth and it flowed from what was left of the neck. But it was the man's eyes. His eyes were open as wide as they would go, as if he were staring at something that frightened him.

"I told him to keep his eyes on both of you!" Rojas began laughing uncontrollably.

Clay and Christine knew then that this was a mad man and it would take a miracle to get them out of Colombia alive.

CHAPTER EIGHT

ARTICLE 28

July 29, 2005, 5:20 p.m.
Executive Terminal, Love Field, Dallas, Texas

The FBI Citation taxied toward the executive terminal building. Three unmarked blue Chryslers were parked on the tarmac. Six executive-looking clean-cut men in suits stood next to the vehicles. All of them wore sunglasses and all of them watched as the jet came to a stop in front of them. As the jet engines died down, the cabin door was opened. A small hatch opened below the cabin door and steps began descending to the tarmac. SAC Brian Whitfield appeared at the cabin door and waited as the steps were locked into position. He then walked down the steps and toward the waiting entourage. As he approached the vehicles, one of the men walked to greet Brian. He extended his right hand to Brian. He was a young man, Brian thought, maybe in his early to mid-thirties. He was tall, standing over six feet three inches. Brian knew because he himself was six feet one inch tall.

As the young man extended his hand to Brian, he smiled. "Agent Whitfield?"

"Yes."

"Agent Bob Murphy, sir. Pleasure to meet you."

"Thanks for meeting me, Agent Murphy," Brian responded as the two walked toward the vehicles. "Update, Agent Murphy?" Brian asked.

"Well, sir, we don't really know much at this point. We've interviewed all of the neighbors and no one saw anything.

The lab has the blood samples and is running their analysis as we speak. It should be ready within the hour."

"I would like to go to the Peterson house, then to Agent Hendrix's apartment. Have you spoken to Comp-Link?"

The men had arrived at the vehicles and Murphy opened the passenger door of the first car for Brian.

"Yes, sir. They haven't heard from Agent Hendrix or Peterson. Peterson did call in sick yesterday. Hendrix was at work though. She mentioned something to a co-worker, a Brenda Thomas, that she might go by and check on Peterson after work. We are assuming she went to see him some time after 5:45," Murphy said.

Brian got into the backseat of the Chrysler. When he was seated, he looked up at Murphy who stood outside the car.

"Let's go see the house," Brian ordered.

"Yes, sir," Murphy replied.

Murphy closed the door and sat in the front seat next to the driver. Brian opened his briefcase as the car pulled away from the terminal. He pulled out his file on Clay Peterson and began reviewing it for a third time that day. He still didn't believe that Peterson was capable of such a crime.

The FBI three-car motorcade turned off Commerce onto Sage Street twenty minutes later. Brian surveyed the neighborhood as the vehicle sped toward Peterson's house. Brian was impressed with the upper-middle class neighborhood. It was clean; the homes were all new, he thought, perhaps two or three years old. There were no trees, just grass and landscaping in front of the houses. Brian noticed a man crouched at the end of one of the driveways. The man was picking up what remained of a small pile of news papers. The papers were not lying on the ground loose, they were individually tied. As the vehicles came to a stop in front of Peterson's house, Brian looked at the scene. The home was brick with a two-car garage on the north end of the house. The garage doors faced the street and the main part of the house was recessed roughly twenty feet from the end of the garage. The garage wall bordered a walkway leading to the front door. There were two arched windows in front, to the right of the door. The yard was well-manicured and summer flowers were planted along the walk and below the windows in front of the house. It was exactly what Brian had imagined it would look like.

Brian got out of the car and looked up and down Sage Street, surveying the neighborhood once again. He looked three houses down to the south of the Peterson house and saw the man picking up newspapers struggling to walk back up to his house with his arms full. Brian studied him for a moment then spoke to Agent Murphy, who was surveying the neighborhood also.

"Murphy."

"Yes, sir?"

"Send a man down to that fellow with the newspapers in his arms. See if he will let us have a newspaper."

"A newspaper, sir? I'll have one of the men go to the store for you if—"

Brian turned and looked at Murphy. He raised his eyebrows and let Murphy know by his look that he wanted his order to be followed exactly as he had said.

"Yes, sir."

Murphy turned to the agent standing next to him. "Randy, go down and ask that man for one of those newspapers."

The agent obeyed and started walking down the street immediately. Brian walked toward the Peterson house. He walked slowly, surveying the ground as he walked. He found nothing that looked out of the ordinary while searching the sidewalk bordering the street. He started up the driveway. Halfway up the concrete pad, he noticed something. He crouched down and looked at what appeared to be dried blood droplets.

"It's blood, sir."

"How much did you find and where?"

"Traces. Traces on the driveway and on the front walk. We believe Peterson somehow disabled Hendrix in the house then brought her outside. He took her down the walk and across the driveway at an angle off to this side. Then he drove away with her."

"In what?"

"Sir?"

"What did they drive away in, Murphy? I was told that Peterson's vehicle is still in the garage and I believe that's Hendrix's car at the curb. So what did they drive away in?"

"We don't know, sir," Murphy replied.

Brian continued up the driveway to the walk leading to the front door. He stopped again where he assumed the blood droplets started. There was a large cluster on the walk roughly halfway between the front door and the end of the garage wall bordering the walk. Brian surveyed the area.

"This is where the blood starts outside?"

"Yes, sir," Murphy replied.

"What about inside?"

"We haven't been able to find any traces inside the house, sir."

"None?"

"No, sir, the lab was here all day. The only thing they found was . . ." Murphy paused.

Brian looked at Murphy and waited for him to continue. When he did not, Brian snapped at him. "Come on, Murphy, this isn't a guessing game. What did they find?"

"Semen . . . sir. They found fresh semen on the living room carpet and on the living room sofa."

"Semen," Brian said shaking his head and turning away from Murphy.

Brian continued to survey the sidewalk and the area surrounding it. The flowers which neatly bordered the walk were trampled down near the site of the blood.

"What do you make of these damaged flowers?"

"Probably knocked over when Peterson was dragging her or she was stumbling down the walk."

"No, they are flattened out. No one was dragged over them; someone fell on top of them."

"Maybe Peterson dropped her. Maybe he was carrying her at first and she became too much for him to carry. He may have dropped her here which would explain the cluster of blood and the flowers."

"Maybe," Brian responded.

Just then the agent returned to Murphy and Brian. He held the paper in his hand as he spoke to them.

"Here is your paper, sir," he said as he handed it to Brian.

"Thank you. What did the man say to you when you asked him for it?" Brian asked.

"Well, sir, he thought it was funny. He said he'd had trouble this past year getting a paper and this morning when he left for work, there was a stack of them in front of the house. I offered to pay him but he wouldn't accept."

Brian thought for a moment as he studied the paper he held in his hand.

"Murphy, what time do we estimate Peterson left the house with Hendrix?"

"Between one and five this morning. Best guess based upon the condition of the blood samples."

"Okay, I want you to call this newspaper. Find out who delivers the paper in this neighborhood. I think we may have a paper carrier out there that saw what happened here last night."

"Sir?"

"The date on the paper is today's date. It's the morning addition. Did you ever have a paper route, Agent Murphy?"

"Well . . . no, sir."

"It's a bitch of a job. You have to get up at three or four every morning in all kinds of weather. You have to tie the papers with a rubber band and pack them around the neighborhood on your back or on your bike. It's hard work, man. And the thing of it is you never have any extra papers left at the end of the route. If anything, you were short a couple. My guess is that the carrier was sitting down at that house watching what was happening here. When he saw whatever it was he saw, he got the hell out of Dodge. When he took off, he dropped a load of papers in that man's driveway."

Brian looked at Murphy who was obviously impressed by the hypothesis. Murphy looked at Brian and said nothing, he just smiled.

"Well? Go make the call Murphy," Brian ordered.

"Oh . . . Yes, sir," Murphy said. He walked into the house to make the call, leaving Brian alone on the walk.

Brian looked around the quiet Dallas suburban neighborhood with one thought on his mind. He was going to find Agent Christine Hendrix and when he did he would personally deal with Clay Peterson.

ARTICLE 29

July 29, 2005, 6:00 p.m.
Rojas estate, Medillin, Colombia

Hulio, Pedro, and Joseffe sat in the parlor talking quietly among themselves. They each had a drink and waited for Rojas's return from his interrogation of Peterson and Rekcah. Their quiet conversation was interrupted by the sudden appearance of Rojas. He entered the room with a broad smile on his face. His blood-covered arms, chest, and pants indicated to the others that Rojas had been brutal in his interrogation of the prisoners.

"Well, my brothers, you missed out on all of the fun. The woman was quite interesting. Unfortunately, Hulio, there isn't enough of her left to share with you," Rojas said with a chuckle.

"Did they talk?" Hulio stood and asked.

Rojas looked at Hulio while using a damp towel to wipe blood from his body.

"No, they said they knew nothing. They denied any connection with your father. They said they stole the money for their own benefit after they broke into the Swiss Bank computer system. They claimed to be computer programmers. That is all."

"And what about the money?" Hulio asked.

"We will have it back in our hands by late tomorrow afternoon. Now, if you gentlemen will excuse me, I must go clean myself up."

Rojas started out of the room then stopped suddenly and turned to speak again to the others. "Gentlemen, could I trouble you to reschedule our meeting for tomorrow afternoon? I have some business I must attend to this evening and I'm afraid it can not wait."

"What about Roberto and Jose?" Pedro asked.

"When they arrive, I will brief them on our discussion regarding expansion into El Salvador and Honduras. We will finalize everything tomorrow. Are we in agreement?"

The three other members looked at one another and nodded in agreement.

"Good then. I will see you all here tomorrow, say around four thirty."

Rojas then exited the room leaving the three men standing in the Parlor. Pedro looked at Hulio and Joseffe.

"Well, I guess we're done here for today," he said.

"I guess so," Hulio replied.

"Well, I don't know about you two, but I'm going home to take a siesta," Joseffe said as he walked toward the hallway leading to the front door. The other two walked with him.

"A siesta sounds good to me as well, Joseffe. Ah . . . but our young friend does not need to rest. What will you do for the rest of the day, Hulio?"

"Think, my friend. I am going to go home and think," Hulio responded.

The armed guards had taken Clay and Christine into the pool house and bound them both securely. They sat in the middle of the white marble floor in the living room. Both were struggling to free themselves from the ropes that constricted their wrists and feet.

"Do you have a plan?" Clay asked.

"We have to get out of these ropes. If we can get free, then we have a chance. If we can't, he'll kill both of us," Christine replied.

"Well, that sounds like a hell of a plan, Agent Hendrix," Clay said sarcastically.

"Can you do better?" Christine snapped.

"I'm not the FBI agent here . . . remember? What the hell did they teach you guys in that academy anyway? Don't you have something text book for a situation like this?"

"Shut up, Clay. We're in this mess because you played your little computer game and took it a bit too far. I should have arrested you when I had the chance. If I had, neither of us would be here right now."

"Yeah . . . well, why didn't you?"

"Because . . . Because dammit, I fell in love with you!" Christine snapped with an angry tone.

Clay looked at her as tears began to fall from her eyes. She continued to struggle; she would not give up on her attempt to free herself.

"Christine," Clay said calmly. "Christine."

"Oh . . . what!" she said desperately.

"I love you, Christine. And I will do something to get us both out of here alive. I promise you that I will."

"Don't make promises . . . to me . . . that you can't keep, Clay Peterson," Christine said as she continued to fight with the ropes.

"I will keep that promise to you. I know that we're going to be okay."

"Well, if we do get out of this thing by some miracle, you can open your own psychic line. But I don't feel anything but fear, Clay. This is real and that Rojas is nuts. He'll kill us if we don't get away. God! Where did these guys learn to tie these knots?" Christine said in frustration.

"They have had a great deal of practice, my dear," Rojas said from the back of the room.

Clay and Christine were startled by Rojas's sudden appearance and the sound of his voice. They watched anxiously as he walked across the room toward them. He wore white from head to toe; his thick black hair was slicked back and his deep brown skin seemed darkened even more by the loose white silk shirt he wore.

Rojas walked to the black leather couch which was the centerpiece in the living room, and sat down. He crossed one leg over the other and studied the pair sitting on the floor in front of him. "You are both right. You, Clay Peterson, are right in the belief that you will be all right if what you tell me about this trading account is true. You, Lisa Tinsley, you are right as well. I will kill you if what you tell me is false. And even if it is true, I will not need both of you around. So, one of you will most certainly die either way.

"I thought about making the decision myself, however that would not be fair to either of you. And believe whatever you wish, but I am a fair man. Therefore, I leave the decision to you. If what you tell me is the truth, one of you must still be killed. You decide between you who it will be.

"My guards will bring my computer to this house for you to work on. You will have until 10:00 tomorrow morning to show me that you speak the truth about the money. If you can not, both of you will die. Do you understand?" Rojas asked.

"What if the computer isn't equipped with the hardware needed to complete the transaction?" Clay asked.

"What do you need?" Rojas asked.

"A modem, hard drive . . . I need a lot of things. And I need my software out of my duffle bag."

"The computer has a modem. I do not know about anything else. I will have your duffle bag brought to you as well. Is there anything else?"

"I could use a bath," Christine said.

"Yes, that you could. You will be taken to the main house. You will bathe in my master suite. If you would like to clean up before you start I will tell the guard to allow you to shower, Clay Peterson. Some fresh clothes will be brought to you as well. I will burn those which you now have on. Now if there is nothing else, I would suggest that you get started. The computer will be here by the time you finish cleaning up."

Rojas stood from the couch and walked to the front door. He signaled the guards who were outside to come to him.

"Take the girl to my room in the main house. Allow the man to clean himself up. I will have some clothes sent down. Help set the computer up when they bring it down from the house if you need to. If either of them tries to escape . . . do not hesitate to kill them," Rojas ordered.

Rojas walked out the door and back toward the main house. The guards walked into the room and jerked Clay and Christine to their feet. They cut the rope around their ankles and left their hands tied. As the one of the guards started out of the house with Christine, she looked at Clay who was watching her.

"I love you, Christine!" Clay shouted only to receive the butt end of a gun jammed violently into his midsection.

Christine watched him as he slumped over in pain. She mouthed the words she knew better than to speak. He did not see her lips mouth the words "I love you" back to him.

Thirty minutes later, Clay emerged from one of the guest house bedrooms refreshed from a shower, and in clean clothes. He was escorted to the living room by an armed guard. As promised, Rojas had the computer set up in the middle of the room on a table with a desk chair in position for him to begin working. His green duffle bag lay on the floor next to the table.

Clay walked to the table and sat in the chair. He looked at the computer which was several years outdated and took a deep breath. He looked around the CPU to find the power switch, located it behind the unit and switched the machine on. He watched the monitor as the machine system booted itself up. Clay was relieved as he watched the monitor display the booting functions. The system was MS DOS based and had Microsoft software installed. The computer may have been old, but the software had been maintained. This meant that all of his file disks would be compatible.

While the computer continued with its start-up procedures, Clay reached down and picked up his duffle bag. The sudden movement prompted the guards to cock their weapons and point them at Clay. Clay stopped moving forward and raised his hands. He sat slowly back up in his chair and turned to look at the guards.

"Disks . . . I need to get my disks out of my bag. That bag. You guys get 'em if you want, but I need the disks," Clay said in an irritated tone.

The guards looked at each other then one of them motioned with the barrel of his gun for Clay to go ahead. Clay reached slowly for his bag and dragged it to the base of his chair. He reached inside the bag and rummaged through the clothes and files until he found the two disk holders he was looking for. He slowly brought them out of the bag and held them in the air for a moment so the guards would know he wasn't up to anything.

The computer had completed its start-up procedures and now waited for Clay to enter his first instructions. Clay keyed in a command for the computer to run a modem diagnostics. The computer obliged. While the computer was analyzing its own modem, Clay flipped through the file disks and selected those he needed to prove that what he was telling Rojas was true. He located three disks he would use in the effort. He looked back to the monitor to check the status of the modem diagnostic and there was a problem. The diagnostic had been completed and the modem was in good operating condition. However, the information screen indicated that the phone line check proved the phone line to be inactive. Clay started to get up from the chair. Again the guards moved forward with their weapons pointed at Clay's back. Clay raised his hands in the air and looked at the guards again.

"The phone line. I need to check the phone line," Clay said.

Again the guard signaled him to go ahead. Clay stood from his chair and walked around behind the computer. He saw that the phone cord was attached correctly to the CPU but as he followed the cord, he found that it was not connected to a phone jack. He picked up the end of the cord and surveyed the room in an effort to locate a jack. There was a phone jack on the wall next to the large fireplace. He knew that the cord wouldn't reach. Clay looked at the guards and attempted to communicate with them.

"The cord won't reach. We have to move the table closer to the wall."

The guards showed no sign that they understood Clay. They just stood and looked at him. Clay did not speak Spanish and he didn't think that the Colombian guards understood English so he improvised.

"Telephono el cordo donto el reacho," he said.

Again the guards just stood looking at him this time seeming to show signs of confusion at the words that he had spoken.

"Come on, guys, we have to move the fucking table!" Clay shouted.

The guards looked angry now as they moved toward Clay. Clay raised his arms again and backed away from them. One guard placed his weapon over his shoulder and began pulling the table and computer toward the wall. Clay raised his eyebrows in surprise.

"Okay . . . that's . . . that's good . . . we're communicating now," he said in approval of the guards actions.

When the guard had moved the computer and table to the wall, he took his weapon from around his shoulder and pointed it again at Clay. He motioned with the gun. Clay knew that he wanted him to continue with his work. Clay obeyed. He took the end of the phone cord and plugged it into the phone jack. He then walked over to the chair and brought it back to the table. He glanced back at the guards who were both glaring at him then sat and took another deep breath as he looked at the monitor.

He keyed in a repeat command prompting the computer to run another modem diagnostic. This time the procedure proved to be a success. The phone line was functional and Clay was in business.

Rojas's master suite was enormous. A fireplace spanned one complete wall in the room and a huge solid-oak poster bed with an ornate canopy highlighted the furnishings. A sitting area was in the center and in front of the giant fireplace. The floor was covered in a plush beige carpeting and the ceiling was at least fifteen feet high. A beautiful crystal chandelier hung in the middle of the room and brightly lit the whole area. Rojas was seated in front of the fireplace. He was waiting for Christine to finish her shower. He looked at his watch noting that she had been in the bathroom for over forty-five minutes. He was growing impatient, and just as he made up his mind to go in and get her she appeared through the doorway leading to the bathroom. He was taken by her as she walked into the room. She stood, surprised by the sight of him, with a white towel covering her body. Christine looked at Rojas anxiously.

"You look refreshed, Lisa. How do you feel?"

"Better. I feel better," Christine said quickly.

"Good. I am pleased. I took the liberty of picking out some clothing for you to wear. I often have female visitors and like to keep things on hand. I believe that I even had some things that were close to your size. They are in the boxes on the credenza. Please . . . try them on," Rojas said politely.

"I will, as soon as you leave the room."

"Try them on . . . now!" Rojas demanded.

Christine jumped as she was startled by Rojas's command. She looked at him then quickly surveyed the room around her. She checked the windows and the door with her eyes. Then returned her gaze to Rojas. He was smiling at her.

"Do not be foolish. There is no escape. There are two guards outside the door. Guards at every window. You are like a bird in a cage. A very beautiful bird, I might add. Now try on the clothes!" Rojas shouted.

Christine knew he was right. There was no way out right now. She would appease him, and when the opportunity presented itself, she would escape. Christine took a deep breath and dropped the towel. Rojas sat up in his chair at the sight of her. He had seen many women; however, Christine had a magnificent body. He watched her as she moved to the credenza against the wall. Her naked tan body glistened under the light emanating from the crystal chandelier.

Christine opened the first box. Inside was a white lace bra with half cups. She studied the bra and knew that when she put it on most of her breasts including her nipples would remain exposed. She looked at Rojas who sat up in his chair watching her intently.

"I don't like wearing bras. They hurt my breasts and I find them uncomfortable," she said.

"Put it on!" Rojas commanded.

Christine glared at him this time with hate in her eyes. She turned her back to him and slowly put the undergarment on. When she had finished, she continued to stand with her back to Rojas.

"Turn and let me see it on you," he said.

Christine slowly turned around and Rojas was aroused by the sight of her. Christine stood there for a moment, feeling degraded as her anger toward this man grew.

"Continue . . . please continue," Rojas instructed.

Christine moved to the next box. She opened it and found a white garter belt, white T-back panties, and white thigh-high stockings. She looked at the garments for a moment, looked at Rojas who nodded at her to proceed, and started dressing. It took her a few minutes to put the ensemble on. Rojas was excited as he watched her dress. When she was finished dressing in the underwear, Rojas spoke again.

"The next box, open it," he ordered.

Christine opened the final box. Inside she found a white silk dress and a pair of white leather pumps with four-inch spike heels. She put the dress on over her head and let it fall down around her body. She attempted to pull the hem of the dress down a bit but it would go no further. It was very short. It barely covered the tops of her stockings. She took the shoes from the box and placed them on the floor. Christine tried to put them on but they were too small for her feet.

She looked at Rojas and spoke. "The shoes are too small," she said.

"You don't need the shoes. Tell me, how do you feel?" Rojas asked.

"Like a twenty-five-dollar hooker," Christine said in an angry voice.

Her comment prompted Rojas to laugh out loud. After a few moments, he stopped laughing and composed himself.

"You underestimate yourself, Lisa. In Bogota you would command at least five hundred dollars an hour," Rojas said as he smiled and stood from his chair.

He walked across the large room until he stood in front of Christine. He put his hand gently on her shoulder and moved it down her arm. Christine looked into his eyes. She was frightened, but this time, she would not allow him to see it. She trembled slightly as he continued to stroke her arm. His touch made her sick to her stomach.

"Here, however, in my house, I will have you for nothing," Rojas said as he leaned forward to kiss Christine.

As he drew closer, she put her hands on his chest in an attempt to stop him. He was too strong for her and continued forward.

She finally cried out. "Wait! Please . . . wait a minute."

Rojas drew back with anger on his face. He glared at her, waiting for her to speak. She had thought about what she was going to do while she was in the shower. She didn't expect him to try to take advantage of her quite so soon. She had to stall him; she had to buy some time.

"I want to prove that I am the most important one. I want to live. The only way I can do that is to work on the trading account and prove that we were telling the truth. I will get the information that I don't know from Peterson and then you can kill him. And . . . you can have me. I want you to have me," Christine said as she tried to look seductively at Rojas.

Rojas studied her for a moment. He could not figure this woman out. He did not trust her, he knew that. But he found her intriguing and a challenge. He wanted her and yet he wanted to play out her game. After thinking for a few moments, he spoke.

"All right. You can work on the computer with Peterson. You can prove that you are telling the truth about the bank account. But first you have something to prove to me now," Rojas said with a smile.

"What? What do you want me to prove?" Christine asked.

"That you do in fact want me to have you, and you want to be the one who lives," Rojas said.

He placed his hands on her shoulders and slowly forced her to her knees. He looked down at her and she looked up into his eyes. She knew what was coming. It sickened her inside. Rojas's smile grew broader as he unzipped his pants and exposed himself to her.

ARTICLE 30

July 29, 2005, 6:30 p.m.
Central Cordillera Region, Colombia

Roberto Diego and Jose Santiago were concluding their business at the production and distribution facility. It was the second largest drug operation in the Central Colombian Valley Region. It was a joint effort of the cartel and jointly administered by Diego and Santiago. The airfield could be used day or night; three planes were on the ground being loaded with cocaine for transportation into Guatemala at that very moment. The drugs were manufactured on site in two large shacks that sat back off the runway in the perceived safety of the heavily wooded jungle. Surrounding the production shacks were ten small shanties which served as living quarters for those who worked at the facility. Diego and Santiago were talking to Carlos Montega, their man who was in charge of the operation on site.

"I am not happy with the quantity we have been seeing out of here lately, Carlos. We doubled the size of the production building; we should see double the output of product. What is the problem? We are seeing half that amount out of the new building," Diego asked.

"We are producing as much cocaine as we are able, Roberto. If we don't get the coca in, we can't produce the cocaine. It is as simple as that. Each week, we run out of coca. This is not my problem."

"It is your problem! Why have you not said anything before now, Carlos? Do you not know how to use a phone? If you do not tell us there is a problem, how do you expect us to fix it?" Santiago shouted.

"My apologies, Jose, you are right. It is my fault."

"I do not want your apologies! I want results! You are responsible for this operation. That is your job and you are paid very well for it. If there is something that you need, you have only to ask for it. You know that if you ask, it will be given. That is my job! That is Roberto's job! We will get you the coca, you get us the results, or Alberto Rojas will have all of our heads!" Diego screamed.

"It will be done, Roberto. Please give me the chance to prove it to you, it will be done. On my mother I swear it," Carlos pleaded.

"We will see, Carlos. One of us will be back here in two weeks. I will arrange to have double the shipment of coca delivered to you. You will see that the production levels are where they should be, or you will explain the matter to Alberto. Do you understand?" Diego asked.

"Yes, Roberto. I understand."

"Good. Then we will not have this conversation again. Jose and I are late returning to Medellin. We have a meeting tonight with Alberto. This incident will not be mentioned for your sake, Carlos," Diego concluded.

"Thank you, Roberto. I am forever in your debt, and I will not fail you."

Diego and Santiago shook hands with Carlos and walked away from him toward their vehicle parked near one of the hangars near the airstrip.

As the men walked together, Diego spoke to Jose. "I think we will see a great improvement in the production level, what do you think, Jose?"

"I agree, Roberto. Carlos is not a fool. He wants to keep his head. Alberto's reputation is a good motivator, don't you think?"

"I do, my friend. I haven't had to kill anyone myself for over a year. I just threaten them with Alberto's name and the problems seem to disappear," Roberto said, prompting both men to laugh. Suddenly a huge explosion shook the ground beneath their feet, and the force of the blast sent them both to the ground. Shrapnel whizzed by just above their heads and gunfire erupted all around them. Diego looked back at the makeshift camp and production buildings. He watched as one by one the buildings exploded violently and burst into flames. Flames and smoke rose high above the jungle trees. Bodies were on fire as they were tossed high into the air by the explosions. Some men and women who weren't killed instantly by the blasts were running around frantically, attempting to extinguish the flames that engulfed their entire body. Others were being slaughtered by the rapid machinegun fire that seemed to be coming at them from every direction.

In panic, Diego looked to Santiago. "We have to get out of here, Jose. The government troops—"

He stopped talking to Jose Santiago. He would not be able to hear him any more. One side of his head had been blown away. Diego stared at the gaping hole in the back of Jose's head. What used to be the side of his face was now a tangled mass of bone, flesh, hair, and brain matter. Jose Santiago was indistinguishable. Diego panicked at the sight of Jose and started running toward the vehicle several hundred feet from where he had lain. Explosions and gunfire could still be heard behind him as he dashed to his car. The machinegun rounds hit the ground all around Diego as he ran. His car had already been hit many times, as evidenced by the bullet holes on the passenger side of the vehicle. Once he had reached the car, he paused for a brief moment to look at the destruction going on behind him. He could not believe what he saw, it was an inferno. Everything was being destroyed; burning bodies were scattered all about. He could see a long flame from a flamethrower working its way through the encampment. There would be no survivors, and he had to get out of there.

Diego got into his car and started driving quickly away from the direction of the gun fire. The machinegun rounds were still hitting the car as he drove wildly away. The rear window of the car shattered from a bullet. Then he saw them, three low-flying aircraft moving at high speed toward the camp. He depressed the accelerator in an effort to make it to the road and the safety out of the jungle before the aircraft could see him. It was a futile effort. One of the U.S. F-15s opened fire on Diego's vehicle. Diego watched the ground in front of him as the trail of bullets made their way toward the car. The rounds were precise and nearly cut the Range Rover in half. Diego's body sustained two direct hits. Diego's body was ripped apart and he was killed instantly.

The F-15s passed over the airstrip alerting the ground forces to their presence. The planes circled and flew back for a second pass. This time as they flew over, they fired their missiles and dropped their bombs on the airfield and surrounding camp. In an instant everything was destroyed. The F-15 artillery worked with the precession of a surgeon's scalpel. Within minutes after the attack had begun, it was over, the destruction devastating and complete. The distribution and production encampment now lay in ruin. The three airplanes that were being loaded with cocaine were now burning piles of fiery twisted metal. If there had been a question about survivors during the air attack, there was none now.

It had been a very good day for the special forces personnel. This was their second successful seek-and-destroy mission of the day. They would now hike three hours into the jungle and make camp for the night just outside of their next target. Their mission was only partially complete, and the carnage would begin again at first light.

CHAPTER NINE

ARTICLE 31

July 29, 2005, 8:37 p.m.
Ronald Perry's House, Dallas, Texas

Special-Agent-in-Charge Brian Whitfield and Agent Murphy sat in the Perry living room. They were speaking with Mr. and Mrs. Perry regarding the reason for their visit. Murphy's men had contacted the newspaper as Brian had requested. The paper informed the FBI agents that a fourteen-year-old boy named Ronald Perry was responsible for the paper route on Sage Street. The paper told the agents that Perry had not completed his route and they received numerous complaints from their customers that morning as a result. The paper had not heard from Ronald Perry all day.

"Mr. and Mrs. Perry, we would like to speak with your son," Brian said.

"Why? I mean has he done something wrong?" Mr. Perry asked.

"No, sir. We believe he may have seen something a bit unusual this morning while he was delivering his papers. We just need to ask him a few questions," Brian responded.

"I'll go get him. He's been in his room since he got home from school," Mr. Perry said.

Mr. Perry left the room to go get Ronald. Mrs. Perry sat in front of the two agents, obviously nervous and uncomfortable at their presence. Brian looked at the woman and attempted to calm her.

"Mrs. Perry, I can assure you that Ronald didn't do anything wrong. He may in fact be able to assist us in an investigation we are currently involved in. He could be a big help to us."

"That's what worries me. I know my son. I know he wouldn't do anything wrong. But if he saw something last night and you people are involved, he may be in danger. I don't want my son to be in any danger," Mrs. Perry said as a tear fell from her eyes.

"Mrs. Perry, Ronald is not in any danger. Please try to remain calm and know that we would not do anything to change that. We just want to ask him if he saw anything last night. He may have seen nothing. But we have to ask him," Brian said in an unsuccessful effort to put the woman at ease.

Mr. Perry then walked back into the room with his arm around Ronald. Ronald was big for his age. He was at least five feet nine inches tall, and Brian guessed that he weighed roughly 180 pounds. He was a good-looking kid with short hair, and his clothes were clean and free of holes; they fit him and matched. Not quite the style of most of the kids he knew through his daughters back in D.C. Ronald walked to an empty chair and sat down. He didn't look at the agents or his parents. He sat looking at the floor instead.

Brian studied him for a few moments before he spoke to the young man.

"Ronald, my name is Brian Whitfield and this is Bob Murphy. We're with the FBI. Do you know anything about the FBI?" Brian asked.

Ronald continued to look toward the floor, bouncing the heel of his shoe up and down on the hardwood. Mr. and Mrs. Perry looked at one another when Ronald did not answer Brian's question.

"Answer Mr. Whitfield, son," Mr. Perry instructed.

"Yes, I know about the FBI," Ronald said as he raised his head and looked at Brian.

"Do you know why we're here tonight?" Brian asked.

Ronald looked at Brian then turned to his parents. He had a look of concern on his face. Mr. and Mrs. Perry nodded at the boy in an attempt to give him confidence to speak to the agents.

Ronald turned back to Brian and spoke. "It's about . . . this morning I guess."

"What about this morning, Ronald? What happened this morning?"

"There was a truck, a truck with like a big box on the back of it."

"You mean a semi?"

"No, not that big. It was smaller. It had a front end like a pickup, but the back of it was like a big box with a garage door in the back."

"What else did you see, Ronald?" Brian asked.

"I saw a man and a woman. They walked out of this house."

"Had you ever seen the man or the woman before?" Brian asked.

"I'd seen the man. I'd seen him on Saturdays when I delivered the evening route. He didn't take the paper, but I always saw him working in his yard when I rode my bike by his house."

"What did you see the man do, Ronald?" Brian asked.

"Well, he and the woman came out of the house. They started walking and then the man turned around and started walking back to the house. That's when this other guy grabbed the woman."

"Other guy? How many people did you see, Ronald?" Brian asked.

"There was the man and the woman and three other guys hiding in front of the garage. The man and woman couldn't see them when they walked out of the house."

"What happened then, Ronald?" Brian continued.

"When the guy grabbed the woman, the man stopped and started to turn around. Another guy ran up behind him and hit him with something. He hit him really hard and the man fell. That's when I jumped off my bike and hid."

"Where did you hide?"

"I hid behind a big green trashcan sitting next to the driveway of the house I had just delivered. I didn't want those guys to see me. I didn't know what they would do if they saw me," Ronald said.

"You did the right thing, Ronald. Really, you did exactly the right thing. Did you see anything else?"

"The other guys put the man and woman in the back of the truck and closed the door. Then they got in the truck and drove away."

"Which way did they drive, Ronald? Did they drive by where you were hiding?"

"They drove the truck into the driveway of the house where the man and woman were and sat there for a minute. Then they backed out and drove off the other way."

"I don't suppose you could see any of license plate on the truck from where you were, couldn't you?" Brian asked.

"No, I didn't see it. But I could see the writing on the side of the truck."

"What did it say, Ronald?" Brian asked.

"It said 'Digo' or 'Dego' Moving and Storage."

"Digo or Dego. Can you spell the first word for me?" Brian asked.

"D-I-E-G-O," Ronald said.

"Diego. Diego Moving and Storage. Okay, good, Ronald, very good. Is there anything else you can remember? Anything at all?" Brian asked.

"No, sir, that's all I can remember. Am I in any kind of trouble or anything? I mean because I didn't tell you guys or anyone about this? I mean, gaw, I was really scared and I thought that if I told—I don't know," Ronald said as tears began to form in his eyes.

"Ronald, listen to me. Listen to me, son. I've been with the FBI for over twenty-four years. And I can tell you that you are one of the bravest young men it has ever been my pleasure to meet. You don't have to be afraid; you don't have anything to worry about. You did exactly the right thing. You should be very proud of your son, Mr. and Mrs. Perry. He's a special young man," Brian said as he stood from his chair. "Now, Agent Murphy and I need to be going. We have a lot of work to do. Mr. and Mrs. Perry, I thank you for allowing us into your home. And Ronald, thank you for all your help, son," Brian said, extending his hand to the boy.

Ronald stood from his chair and shook Brian's hand. Ronald smiled at the FBI agent, and for some reason did not feel afraid any longer. Instead, he felt satisfaction and pride.

"It was good to meet you, sir," Ronald said smiling.

"The pleasure was all mine, Ronald. We'll let ourselves out, Mr. and Mrs. Perry. Thank you again and have a good evening," Brian said as he and Murphy left the living room.

They walked out of the house, down the driveway and to their automobile without speaking. Brian was thinking about Ronald's account of what happened in front of the Peterson house. Both agents got into the car and Murphy drove the car away from the Perry residence.

Murphy was first to speak. "What do you think?"

"I don't know, I really don't know what to think. Peterson may have been involved in something we didn't know anything about. He was quite capable of doing about anything he wanted to on his computer. Maybe he was working for someone. Maybe he pissed them off or they wanted him silenced. Or maybe someone or some organization found out what he could do and they wanted his technology. The guy knows how to break computer security codes, and he does it in a way that no one else has been able to. Based on what we know about him, he could access any computer system in the world. That kind of access equates to power. Christ, I don't know what to think."

"Let's go back to your office. I want to start a track on this Diego Moving and Storage. Let's see if it's real; and if it is, where they're located. Also, did we get Peterson's phone records from the phone company? The current records?" Brian asked.

"Yes, sir. They should be waiting for us when we get to the office. The lab results on the blood and semen should be there as well."

"Good. I don't know what our Mr. Peterson was up to, Murphy, and I don't like to think about what Agent Hendrix might be going through right now. Things don't look too good for her right now. We don't have much time. We may already be too late."

ARTICLE 32

July 29, 2005, 11:20 p.m.
Rojas estate, Medillin, Colombia

Clay had been working feverishly on the computer for four hours. The guards had lost interest in Clay's activities several hours prior, and now sat talking to one another behind him. Clay made the decision to work on a plan of his own when he sat down at the computer. He had all of the back-up regarding the trading account on disk. He could prove to Rojas that the account existed by showing him the information contained on the back-up disks and accessing the Canadian account if he desired. That process wouldn't take any time at all.

During the past three hours, Clay had accessed Rojas's Swiss account once again. The account had a security block on it which prohibited any transactions such as withdrawals or deposits to the account. However, Clay was still able to access the account history and run a CASE analysis on prior transactions. He had done that. He traced the last wire transaction listed on the account history. Clay then accessed the receiving banks operating system and completed the first phase of his plan. He worked in the BVI bank system for quite sometime.

Clay then accessed the U.S. Treasury operating system using his Fibonacci Sequence interactive disk. He spent forty-five minutes working through the Treasury files and entering information. He knew that the Treasury would be tracing the breach into their system, but he didn't care. In fact his work was made easier because he did not have to concern himself about the trace.

After Clay had completed his work in the treasury system, he exited and instructed the modem to dial the Pentagon. He used the Fibonacci Sequence disk again to break the access code. Because the codes to the treasury and Pentagon systems had already been accessed by Clay using the Fibonacci Sequence, the disk already had the code structures on file for both systems. Clay gambled that neither entity would completely revamp their coding system due to one isolated security breach. This process would not only be time consuming, but also cost prohibitive by government standards. Clay believed that the government would spend eighty thousand dollars on developing a toilet seat for the space shuttle before they would spend the money it would take to revamp a computer security system as trivial as the Pentagon or the U.S. Treasury.

Clay surfed through the Pentagon system and accessed the files he needed. The Pentagon system was fascinating. He accessed the Pentagon Global Plotting System (GPS), a satellite-based locator or tracking system which will plot exact locations anywhere in the world. Clay was able to determine that his present location was twelve miles south of Medillin, Colombia. Once he had determined where he was, the remainder of his work in the Pentagon system was made a great deal less complicated. Clay had finished his work in the Pentagon and was attempting to access another system when the front door of the guest house abruptly opened.

Clay turned to see Christine walk through the door accompanied by a pair of Rojas's armed guards. The two guards who had been watching Clay were startled by the sudden appearance of the other guards and Christine. They stood quickly from their seats as did Clay. This prompted the guards to point their weapons at him again. Clay raised his arms and sat slowly back down in his chair while he kept his eyes on Christine. She looked shaken and pale. She had her arms wrapped around her as if she were frightened. She would not look at him as the guards forced her over to Clay where they placed a chair for her to sit in. Christine sat down next to him, and the guards backed away.

Christine sat silently in the chair looking down at the floor. Clay reached up and gently put his hand on her shoulder. Upon feeling his touch, Christine instinctively jerked away from him. This prompted the guards to laugh among themselves. Clay turned and gave the guards a look of disdain. They glared back at him as if to taunt him into doing something. He didn't. He looked back at Christine and spoke to her softly.

"Are you all right?"

Christine was trembling, and shook her head from side to side quickly to signal to Clay that she was not all right. The anger grew within Clay. He looked back at the guards with hate branded on his face. They stood waiting and hoping that this ignorant American would try something, anything that would allow them to kill him. Again he did nothing. It would have been a foolish effort, and he knew it. The only way he could help Christine was to remain alive and finish what he had started on the computer. He looked away from the guards and back to Christine again.

"I need some information from you. I don't know what you have been through. I know that whatever it was, there probably isn't anything that I can say that will make you feel any better right now. But you need to know something. You need to listen to me. I love you. I've never loved anyone the way that I love you—"

"You don't understand, you don't know . . . You don't know what—"

"No, I don't. I don't know. But you're wrong that I don't understand. We're in a situation here that only you and I could possibly understand. I'm going to do whatever I have to do to get us out of this thing alive. So will you. What happens while we're here happens. When we're out of here, we can put it behind us. But you need to know this, and you need to remember this always, no matter what happens. I love you, Christine Hendrix. I love you, and there is nothing on this earth that could happen to change the way I feel about you. Nothing. Now, I need your help. Can you help me?"

Christine raised her head and looked at Clay with her watery eyes and tears flowing down her cheeks. She could see the love and compassion he felt for her in his eyes. Clay could see the hurt and remorse she felt in hers. Christine nodded and spoke to him softly. "Yes . . . . I can help you."

"Good. We're going to get out of this thing all right. I have a plan, and I think it will work. You and I have to be out of here before nine tomorrow, though. That part I haven't figured out yet. But we have to be out of here."

"Why, what have you done?"

"Don't worry about it. But by the time I'm through, every law enforcement agency and military arm of the government will know where we are. Do you know how to access the FBI computer system? Do you have an access code?"

"No, I correspond through the communications center in Washington."

"How? How do you correspond?"

"By fax."

"Perfect."

Clay exited the screen he had been working on prior to Christine coming into the house. He keyed in some instructions, typed a brief message then turned to Christine again.

"What's the number?"

"Two-zero-two, five-five-five, six-zero-six-zero."

Clay keyed in the phone number as Christine spoke. When he was finished, he pressed the Enter key and sat back in his chair. Christine and Clay watched the monitor together. The modem was working to connect to the FBI's communications system. Nothing was happening on the screen, it remained unchanged. Clay grew impatient as he continued to watch the monitor. Then the monitor flashed a message: CARRIER FAILURE.

"Dammit," Clay said under his breath.

He quickly started the process over again. He keyed in the system instructions, retyped the brief message and turned to Christine again. As he was about to speak, he heard voices outside the guest house front door. It was Rojas speaking to one of the guards. Christine heard the voice also and began to tremble as she looked at the door in terror. She knew that he was coming for her. She knew what he would do to her again.

"Give me the number," Clay whispered.

Christine did not respond to Clay. She just sat and glared at the door, thinking Rojas would enter at any moment and take her away with him.

"Christine, give me the fucking number again!" Clay demanded again trying to keep his voice low.

Rojas's voice drew closer to the house and his steps could be heard as he walked onto the front porch. Clay was frantic. He had to send the message now, he didn't know if he would have another opportunity. Everything was ready, the system was set; he just needed the number. He remembered the area code, and keyed it in without Christine's assistance. Then he turned to her one last time as Rojas stood just outside the door speaking to one of the guards.

"Christine, please, honey. Give me the number. I have to have the number," he said as he nudged her in her ribs this time to get her attention.

"Two-zero-two . . . five-five-five . . . six-zero . . . six-zero," Christine said without turning away from the door.

Clay keyed in the number as she spoke. As he entered the final two digits, Rojas entered the house. Clay looked toward the door and saw him enter. Then he looked back at the keyboard and found the Enter key and pressed it with his trembling index finger. Clay watched the screen anxiously as he waited for the computer to respond to his instructions. Rojas looked at the two prisoners briefly then greeted his guards. Clay continued to watch the screen. It didn't change, and didn't give him any sign that the message was going through. He wasn't even sure the modem had connected to the FBI system. Rojas finished conversing with the guards and looked toward Christine and Clay again. He began to walk toward them. Clay knew he couldn't allow Rojas to see the screen. He would surely kill them both if he did. Clay looked anxiously at the monitor as he heard Rojas's steps grow near. As Rojas spoke, the computer flashed a message: TRANSMISSION COMPLETE.

"How are my computer programmers getting along?" Rojas said as he walked to Christine and put his hands on her shoulders.

Clay quickly keyed in the exit command and pressed the Enter key. Rojas's attention was on Christine and not the screen. Had he looked at the screen he would have been furious, and no doubt would have had both Christine and Clay killed. The computer responded to the exit command and the screen went blank. Clay sat back in his chair looking at the monitor. He knew how close he had come. He knew he was lucky to be alive at that moment.

Christine closed her eyes and grimaced as Rojas began to massage her shoulders as he spoke to both of them. "How are you coming along, Clay Peterson?" Rojas asked.

"I am ready to show you the account now. It will prove to you that we are telling the truth about the money," Clay responded.

"Then show me. Show me now," Rojas ordered.

"Okay," Clay replied.

Clay picked the trading account back-up disk up from the table and inserted it into the computer. He then keyed in the program commands which would allow the computer to read the information contained on the back-up disk. When he had finished keying in the commands, the computer started processing the information. Clay waited for the trading account file to appear on the screen. He glanced back at Rojas who was still focused on Christine. He was paying no attention to the computer screen or Clay. The trading account appeared on the monitor and Clay spoke to Rojas.

"Here it is."

Rojas moved away from Christine and stood next to Clay. He studied the screen and the numbers it displayed for a moment. He did not have a clue what he was looking at, but he wasn't about to let the Americans know it.

"So? What does this prove?" He asked sarcastically.

"It proves what we were telling you is true. Look at the beginning balance. It is a number. That is the account number of the Canadian account with the ten million dollars in it. It's the collateral account for the trading program. That ten million was hypothecated and allowed the purchase of the one hundred million in prime bank notes. The PBNs were traded three times a week and that generated the seventy-one million and change you see here each month. The deposits were made on the twenty-fourth of each month and wired out to the Canadian account on the twenty-fifth of each month. That's it. That's how the trading account works."

"And how did you do this without the help of my beautiful companion, Mr. Peterson? I thought you needed her to give you the codes for this transaction?" Rojas asked.

Christine looked at Clay anxiously. She did not know what his plan was that he spoke of earlier. And she did not think that he would be prepared to answer the question Rojas had just asked him. She knew that one of them was about to die. Clay looked at Christine with confusion on his face then he looked back at Rojas.

"I'm sorry. I must have misunderstood you."

"Misunderstood me? How could you possibly have misunderstood me?" Rojas demanded.

"I thought you wanted us to establish a trading account for you. For your personal use. In order to accomplish that, I need Lisa's input. I need the codes from her."

"I already have a trading account for my own use, you fool. You have already used ten million of my dollars to set up a trading account for me. You told me that it would produce almost one billion dollars over the next year. I am happy with that return on my investment."

"Why?" Clay asked.

"Why! Why do you think? It is free money, you idiot."

"It's nothing. I thought that you wanted to make a lot of money. Enough money to make you one of the most powerful and wealthy men in the world. If I was wrong, I apologize," Clay said.

Rojas drew his hand back and hit Clay firmly across the mouth. Clay's head was forced back by the blow. Christine screamed when Rojas hit Clay. Rojas looked at her and yelled, "Shut up!"

Rojas then turned his head slowly and looked at Clay who was holding his hand over his bleeding mouth. Rojas glared at him as he spoke.

"I am already one of the richest and most powerful men in the world, you insolent fool. And I am the most powerful man in this country. I control the government, the police; I rule this country. So what is it you can give me that I don't already have, or that I can not take on my own?"

"More money and greater power. I thought that you wanted us to structure a trading program that would generate a hundred times what the first account we set up would. Instead of one billion, I thought you wanted us to set you're account up so that it would generate ten billion. Ten billion would then turn into one hundred billion. And that's over a period of just over two years. One hundred billion dollars in just over two years. I thought that's what you wanted from us. That's the program I set up for you. I'm sorry I misunderstood," Clay said as he looked away from Rojas toward the floor.

"You set it up?" Rojas said in surprise.

"I've gone as far as I can go right now without the codes. After Chri—Lisa gives me the codes, we'll have about five or six hours worth of work left to do. But it's ready to go. I'm sorry, Mr. Rojas, I thought that is what you wanted."

Rojas thought about what Clay was telling him. He could be satisfied with one billion dollars, or give this American six more hours of life and have one hundred billion dollars at his disposal. He was rich, he thought, but he wasn't that rich. His power could span the globe if he had access to that kind of money. He looked at his watch then down at Clay and smiled.

"Do not be sorry. Finish your work. Complete the transaction as you have structured it. It is just a little after midnight. I will be back here to check on your progress at eight o'clock tomorrow morning. Have it finished by then. I will rest during the night and contemplate your fate if you are successful in your efforts."

Rojas looked at Christine.

"You will come with me. I do not wish to sleep alone tonight, and I want to finish what we started earlier."

Christine looked at Clay with fear and panic in her eyes. Clay turned to Rojas and spoke. "But there is no way that I can finish without her now. Each time I access an account it requires a very specific code. I never know when they will present themselves in the system. The security systems are very complicated and Lisa has the expertise to break the codes. I don't. I can't do it without her."

Rojas grabbed her arm and pulled her toward him. "You will have to try."

"Look! I don't care what you do with her after we get this account in place. But you said that you would kill me if I didn't get it done. I can't do it without her and she can't do it without me. So . . . well, you might as well just kill me now and get it over with. I'll die tomorrow anyway when you come in and find that I couldn't complete the transaction!"

"Give me your gun!" Rojas ordered one of the guards.

The guard obeyed and gave his machinegun to Rojas. Rojas took the weapon and pointed it between Clay's eyes. Clay closed his eyes when he heard Rojas cock the weapon. He thought he was going to die.

Rojas looked intently at Clay as he sat trembling with his eyes closed. Rojas loved this moment, he felt strong. He had the power to decide who would live and who would die. He had the power to extinguish any life he chose, and now he had a decision to make regarding the life of Clay Peterson. He jammed the end of the gun against Clay's forehead and his index finger began to pull the trigger back.

Christine cried out. "Don't . . . don't kill him. Not yet please!" she shouted as she stood from her chair.

Rojas stopped applying pressure to the trigger of the gun but continued to press the barrel hard against Clay's forehead. "Why should I not kill this man! Give me one reason!"

"I'll give you one hundred billion reasons. He's right, I can't structure the account without him. And I am the only one who can break the codes in the system. Think about what one hundred billion dollars could mean to you. What it could mean . . . to us," Christine said seductively and convincingly.

Christine was so convincing that her comment prompted Clay to open his eyes in surprise. He looked at Christine. She wouldn't look at him. Instead she was looking at Rojas and began stroking his cheek with her hand. Rojas's glare dissipated and he pulled the gun away from Clay's head. He turned to Christine and put his arm around her waist. He jerked her toward him and they kissed passionately. Clay watched and a sick emptiness grew inside of him. Rojas pulled away from Christine and looked at her while still tightly holding her with his arm. He smiled at her then turned to look at Clay.

"This is a wise woman, Clay Peterson. You choose your partners well. She will work with you tonight. You will be finished by eight tomorrow. If you are successful, and my mood is good, I may spare your life."

Rojas turned back to Christine. He pulled her toward him and they kissed passionately, longer and harder this time. Clay had to turn away. When they finished their embrace, Rojas freed Christine from his grasp and walked toward the door. He threw the machinegun to the guard who had given it to him earlier. When he reached the door, he turned and spoke to Christine. "It will be a lonely night with out you. I will be thinking about our time together tomorrow."

"And I will be thinking of you as well," Christine replied.

Rojas smiled at her, then opened the front door and left the guest house. Two guards left with him and two remained to watch Clay and Christine. Christine sat down in her chair beside Clay. She looked at him for a moment then looked back down at the floor as she spoke to him.

"I'm sorry," she said.

"You don't have to be sorry, unless you're sorry about saving my life."

Christine looked up at him and smiled. She had been afraid of what he thought of her after what he had witnessed, and the things he heard Rojas say about what had happened earlier.

"Where did you come from, Clay Peterson? Why haven't you always been in my life?"

"I don't know. But if we get out of this thing alive together, I'm going to make sure you're a part of the rest of my life."

"Do I have anything to say about that?" Christine asked with a smile.

"Not a goddamn thing. You're stuck with me whether you like it or not. Is that a problem?" Clay said in a determined voice.

"No . . . that's not a problem," Christine replied as another tear rolled down her cheek.

"Good. Then let's get to work on this thing. We have to have something ready for Rojas in the morning. And I would suggest that you start thinking of a way to get us out of here shortly after eight o'clock. There's a good possibility that this place will be one giant crater sometime after nine. If we can just get to Medillin, we have a chance to get out of Colombia . . . alive."

"And if we can't?"

"Well . . . if we can't, he'll probably kill us both. That isn't the eternity that I had planned to spend with you."

ARTICLE 33

July 29, 2005, 11:40 p.m.
FBI Regional Field Office, Dallas, Texas

The regional office of the FBI was located in an industrial park in North Dallas, just south of Plano. The outside of the warehouse was nondescript and from all appearances looked as though it was just another commercial warehouse distribution facility. Behind the generic reception area in front of the building, however, there was a maze of offices. Forty field agents worked out of this building and it looked as if the majority of them were present even given the late hour. They were there because one of their own was missing. Finding Agent Hendrix had become a nationwide FBI priority. The investigation was concentrated in the central region of the United States, however, every agent in the country knew about the disappearance of Agent Hendrix. All of them were looking for possible clues to her whereabouts. They wouldn't stop until she was found.

Brian Whitfield sat in the conference room that had been converted into the strategy and planning room in the search for Agent Hendrix. Calls were coming in from all over the central United States from field offices that had questions or clues regarding the investigation. Brian sat at the conference table looking at the laboratory results regarding the blood and semen specimens found at the Peterson house. Murphy entered the conference room carrying two fresh cups of black coffee. It was going to be a long night.

"Here you go, sir," Murphy said as he put the cup of coffee in front of Brian.

"Oh . . . thanks, Murphy. These lab results on the blood support the Perry kid's account of what happened outside of the house. One blood type and it doesn't match with Hendrix's blood type we have on file in Washington."

"What about the semen?" Murphy asked.

"What about it? It doesn't belong to Hendrix," Brian snapped back.

Brian had tried to put the semen specimens out of his mind. He did not want to think about what may have happened to Agent Hendrix while she was in the Peterson house.

"Sorry, sir, I . . . Well, I didn't mean to—"

"No, Murphy, I'm sorry. I didn't mean to bark at you. I don't know what happened to Hendrix inside that house. We have four male suspects now. We know from the Perry kid's account that Peterson was in the house with her before the abduction. We have to assume that the semen is Peterson's, and that Hendrix was involved in some kind of sexual activity or abuse with Peterson. I don't know what that was; I can only hope that she will be all right when we locate her."

"We'll find her, sir," Murphy said in a futile attempt to ease Brian's mind.

They were interrupted by the appearance of another agent entering the room. The agent walked to Murphy and handed him a document. The agent left the room as Murphy slowly read the information on the sheet of paper. When he was finished, he looked at Brian. He couldn't hide the concern he felt inside.

"It's a report on Diego Moving and Storage," Murphy said.

"Well . . . what the hell does it say?" Brian demanded.

"There are two companies by that name in the United States. One is located in the Bronx, New York. It is owned by two brothers and they are a small mom-and-pop operation with a clean history. The second company is located in Houston, Texas. It is owned by a family, the Diego family. The family has been under investigation and is a suspected drug smuggling front. We haven't been able to prove any of our suspicions, and the DEA has had them under surveillance for over a year."

"Who do they smuggle for? Who is the supplier?"

"The report suggests that they could have ties that lead to Colombia. Possibly even to the cartel itself."

"The cartel? Shit! Goddammit, Murphy, none of this fits. We start looking at this guy a couple of months ago because he breaches the security at the Pentagon and the U.S. Treasury. Now we do a background on him and he comes up squeaky clean. The kid is nothing less than a genius in school; everybody likes him; he's a good employee. The guy has no history of drug abuse or alcohol abuse; he was raised in a good home. The son-of-a-bitch didn't even have a fucking traffic ticket. So, we think, or I think, that what we have here is nothing more than a computer nerd who happens to be a genius at breaking cryptic security clearance codes. Instead, what we have now is a guy who has kidnapped and possibly sexually abused one of my federal agents, and who is in someway tied into the Colombian drug cartel. Does any of that make sense to you? Any of it at all?" Brian asked.

"No, sir, but if Peterson somehow found out who Hendrix was, who knows what he could have done? Desperate people do desperate things."

"Can the clichés, Murphy. This guy wasn't a bank robber. He didn't kill anyone, and all we probably would have given him was a stern slap on the wrist and probation for what he had done. Hendrix knew that and she would have told him that if he was out of control. We discussed it before she went under."

"So what do you think?" Murphy asked.

"I think that our Mr. Peterson may have accessed a computer system that he shouldn't have. That's what he did, that's what he was good at. If he accessed the wrong system and they traced it back to him, I think one of two things has happened to him and possibly to Agent Hendrix."

"What?"

"These people who abducted them, they either took him because of what he found out when he got into their system, or they abducted him because they want to know how he got in. They want the technology that is in his brain. If they took him because of what he found out, he's a dead man right now. If they took him for what he knows, there's a good chance he'll cooperate with them and he's still alive. If the cartel is involved and they get Peterson to tell them what he knows, they'll have the key to the kingdom, Murphy."

"And Agent Hendrix?"

"In the wrong place at the wrong time. She's dead too if they took Peterson because of what he found out. She's dead if they found out that she worked with us. She may still be alive if he is cooperating with them and they don't know she's with the bureau. I don't know. If they are still alive, we don't have a lot of time to find them.

"Call our Houston office and tell them what we have on Diego Moving and Storage. Tell them I'll be there in the morning by eight. Then get in touch with the DEA and let them know that we have an agent and a suspect that may both have been abducted by the moving company or someone affiliated with them. I want to know everything that they know about Diego Moving and Storage. For the time being, we'll keep our base of operation here in Dallas. I'll contact you every hour for updates, and you will contact me immediately if there is any change in status. Are we clear, Agent Murphy?" Brian asked.

"Crystal, sir," Murphy responded.

"Get someone to call the airport and have my plane ready to leave for Houston by seven in the morning. Which airport is closer to the field office, Hobby or International?"

"Hobby, sir."

"Okay, let the field-agent-in-charge know that I want him to meet me at the Hobby executive terminal when I arrive in the morning."

"Anything else, sir?"

"None that I could think of right now."

"I'll see to these items right away," Murphy said as he stood to exit the room. Before he got to the door, another agent entered the conference room and nearly ran into Murphy.

"What do you want?" Murphy snapped.

"A message, sir. It's a message from Washington for Special Agent Whitfield."

"Well . . . there he is, give it to him," Murphy said sarcastically.

Brian looked at Murphy with a frown on his face. He didn't like Murphy. He thought he was an ass kisser, and Brian didn't like ass kissers. And he did not like the way Murphy treated the people that worked with and for him.

The agent walked timidly to Brian and gave him the two-page document from Washington. Brian took the message from the agent who looked exhausted from the long day they all had experienced. As the agent turned to leave, Brian spoke.

"Excuse me, Agent . . . ," Brian said waiting for the agent to speak his name.

"Ryan, sir, Agent Ryan," Ryan said timidly.

"Yes, Agent Ryan. I would like to apologize for Agent Murphy's tone. We have been under a great deal of pressure today as I am sure you have as well. He meant nothing by it, and I'm sure he is sorry for addressing you in such a manner. Aren't you, Agent Murphy?" Brian said as he looked with anger toward Murphy.

Murphy fidgeted for a moment. He was obviously uncomfortable and taken by surprised at Brian's comment and question. Murphy cleared his throat and adjusted the collar of his shirt before responding.

"Yes . . . Yes, Agent Ryan, I am sorry if my tone was harsh. Good work, really . . . good work. I appreciate your efforts."

Ryan looked back at Brian who winked at him. Ryan then walked out of the office feeling much better about himself and the bureau in general. Murphy looked at Brian who still had his eyes fixed on him.

"Sir, I mean no disrespect, but do you really think that was called for?" Murphy asked.

"Agent Murphy, do you want these people around here to respect you, or do you want them to think that you are an asshole?"

"I want them to respect me of course, and I believe that they do. And, sir, for the record, I think that chastising me in front of one of my men was uncalled for and out of line. I feel it my duty to make a full report on the matter. I hope you understand."

"Oh by all means, Agent Murphy, make out your report. I'll even sign it if you like."

"Thank you," Murphy said as he turned to leave the room.

"Oh and, Murphy . . . ," Brian said.

Murphy stopped and turned to hear what Brian had to say.

"For the record? I think that you are an asshole. And I feel that it is my duty as your superior to report that to you. If you don't change the way you deal with these people, you'll find your candy ass in a junkyard at midnight playing security guard with a Doberman by your side to keep you company. Do I make myself clear, Agent Murphy?"

Murphy looked pale and timid, just like the agent who had delivered the message to Brian moments earlier.

"Yes, sir . . . I understand."

"Good! Now don't forget to put that in your fucking report. That will be all, Agent Murphy."

Murphy looked at the floor and left the room when Brian had finished with him. Brian smiled as the look on Murphy's face lingered in his mind. He knew what he had done wouldn't change Murphy or his attitude, but he enjoyed giving him some of his own medicine. He didn't immediately concern himself with the correspondence from Washington because he assumed it was from Associate Director Stafford. He'd had enough bad news for one day, and wasn't in any hurry to get anymore. He unfolded the two documents and saw right away that the correspondence wasn't from Stafford, it was from communications.

FBI COMMUNICATIONS DIVISION—WASHINGTON

TO: SAC WHITFIELD   JULY 30, 2005
FROM: COMMUNICATIONS LAB   RE: P.FIELD COM.

ATTACHED COMMUNICATION RECEIVED .... JULY 29, 2005

SOURCE: .... UNKNOWN/UNAUTHORIZED
ORIGINATION: .... MEDELLIN, Colombia
TIME 11:41:44

Brian read the cover page, and then quickly turned to the second page of the Washington correspondence.

Priority Message

To: Someone In Charge
Re: Agent Christine Hendrix and Clay Peterson

We are being held captive at a residence ten miles south of Medellin, Colombia. The man who is holding us here goes by the name of Alberto Rojas. The GPS coordinates of our location are 22s:23w:005-727-45-00745.

We need you to get us out of here or we need a diversion in the morning. Something that will allow us to escape. If you get here and don't find us we will be in Medellin sometime tomorrow afternoon. Check the hotels for the name Rekcah.

If you do not find us in Medellin, chances are we're dead. This is not a prank, Christine gave me this number. Hurry!

Clay Peterson

Brian read the message twice. If it was real, and at this point he believed it was, it meant that as of eleven forty-one, Agent Christine Hendrix was alive. That was the good news. The bad news was that there was no way he could possibly get to Medellin, Colombia, before midafternoon the next day. He would have to work from Dallas and hope that he would be able to get his agent out of this situation alive. At that moment, he did not hold much hope of that happening.

CHAPTER TEN

ARTICLE 34

The night scope gave the platoon leader an eerie light-green view of the encampment. He watched as his men moved quickly and stealthily to each building. This was a smaller production facility than the two that they destroyed the day prior, but it was a primary target nevertheless. The configuration of this camp was not unlike that of the others. The large building in the center was where the cocaine was manufactured. The seven smaller buildings housed the workers.

The platoon leader panned the camp and was able to locate each of the four men he sent in. Then he saw unexpected movement. A dark figure walked out of one of the smaller buildings and stood in front of it. The platoon leader watched as the figure lit a cigarette, exhaled a plume of smoke then stretched his arms, waking his body to the day. The platoon leader could see one of his four men crouched adjacent to the building where the figure stood smoking. As the figure began walking in his direction, the soldier slowly lay flat and still on the ground. The figure smoking the cigarette ambled to within inches of the soldier then stopped. For some reason he felt that he needed to stretch once again. The attack was swift and silent. The blade cut with precision. The figure did not have a chance. Compared to that which the others in the camp would suffer in a short while, this man's death was humane.

Under the watchful and protective eye of their platoon leader, the four men completed their mission within the camp. They joined the remainder of the platoon one hundred yards from the camp. Once they were together again, the platoon leader raised his hand and signaled in two directions. Two groups of men left to take their positions for the attack. The platoon leader waited patiently for his men to situate themselves. When he was sure they were positioned, he gave a silent thumbs-up signal to his demolitions specialist who sat directly behind him. The soldier pressed the transmitter button and the ground began to shake as the buildings exploded one by one in front of them. When the explosions stopped, the soldiers eyes were fixed on their platoon leader who had one arm raised in the air. When the platoon leader saw the first sign of human life, he dropped his arm. Gunfire erupted from three different directions. The machineguns worked together like a chain saw, cutting away anything left standing.

After only a few minutes, the platoon leader raised his arm once again, and the firing ceased. The jungle was quiet again. There was a secondary explosion in the camp as the flames found and ignited several barrels of chemicals. Then nothing but the crackling and popping sound of burning wood. Again the destruction had been complete. All human life extinguished. The mission was a success.

The platoon watched the village for any sign of movement. When the platoon leader was satisfied that the area was clean, he gave the silent order to move out. Their next two targets were seven miles away. They were close to one another. The hike would take them through the heart of the jungle and to the base of the mountains. Their destination, a residence this time. The platoon leader knew only the location of the house, and the last name of the target.

ARTICLE 35

July 30, 2005, 6:30 a.m.
U.S. Aircraft Carrier Eisenhower, *In the Pacific*

The six pilots sat patiently in the briefing room awaiting the arrival of the captain and executive officer. They had been instructed to meet in the briefing room due to a change in their original mission. The group of F-15 pilots were feeling exhilarated by their successful sorties of the day before. They were speaking among themselves when the captain and executive officer walked into the briefing room. When they saw them, they stood at attention.

"At ease, gentlemen," the captain said as he walked to the overhead projector in the center of the room.

The captain turned the overhead projector on, opened a file he carried and pulled out two overhead transparencies. He placed one of the transparencies on the screen, and the image was reflected on the wall behind him. It was a map of South America.

"We've had a slight change in our flight plan today, gentlemen. For reasons that I will not question, we've been ordered to another target this morning. The route of approach will be as it was yesterday. You will fly at low altitude into Colombia and straight to the target."

The captain changed the transparency. This time the image on the wall behind him was a satellite photograph of a residence. The residence was located in Colombia. He took a laser pointer from the table upon which the projector sat, and used it as he spoke to his pilots.

"This is an INTELSAT recon photograph of our target. It is a residence, gentlemen. I don't know who lives there, and I don't know why we are being sent to destroy it. I don't care and neither should you. Whoever it is must have really pissed somebody off. Friends of our government don't get this kind of attention. You get in and get out. We don't anticipate any resistance, and there won't be any friendlies on the ground to worry about this time. No fly-by. Just in and out. Any questions?"

The pilots had none. They did not need to ask questions. This is exactly what they were trained to do. They didn't question the fact that it was a residence, it didn't matter. They were being ordered to destroy a target. That's exactly what they would do. The reasons behind the orders they received were none of their business. Successfully completing their mission was all that they concerned themselves with.

"Good. Wheels up at O-eight-thirty, gentlemen. Good luck," the captain said.

ARTICLE 36

July 30, 2005, 7:25 a.m.
Rojas estate, Medillin, Colombia

Alberto Rojas exited the bathroom with a large white towel wrapped around his waist. He walked to his bed where one of his servants had laid out the outfit he would wear today. Rojas removed the towel and threw it at the servant who stood near the bed.

"Did you hear anything this morning? I was awakened by what I thought was an explosion of some kind. It was faint, yet it woke me. Did you hear anything like that?"

"No, señor, I am sorry."

"I must have been dreaming. Where are my underwear, you fool? How can I dress if I have no underwear?" Rojas screamed.

Clay had been working nonstop at the computer. He sat back in his chair and stretched his arms. When he was through stretching, he rubbed his tired eyes and looked over at Christine who lay sleeping on the couch. After many hours of tutoring her on the meaning and application of cryptanalysis, she was exhausted. He had convinced her to try to sleep finally at just after four in the morning. It didn't take her long to fall asleep once she closed her eyes. Before she did, she looked at him and told him that she loved him. She still wore the dress that Rojas had made her wear. It glowed against her tan arms and legs as the sunlight began to grow stronger inside the room.

Clay turned his attention back to the computer. He had even impressed himself this time with what he had accomplished during the night. Of course he knew that this time it wasn't a game. He was working to save his life and the life of the woman that he loved. It was that motivation that allowed him to accomplish so much in so little time.

He had prepared a program which would demonstrate to Rojas how the trading account would function. He then set up two interactive programs that he could key up on the screen after he had accessed both the Swiss and the Canadian systems. The fake Canadian screen he had created showed an account belonging to Otrebla Sajor. The account balance did not reflect a dollar amount. It was a number. The fake Swiss screen was structured in the same manner. The same name was on the account and a number was shown in place of a dollar amount in the opening balance. Clay reviewed both screens one last time. They had only taken him thirty minutes to program. It was the first thing he did after Rojas had left the room for the last time the night before. He had spent the rest of the night working on the escape and his plan for revenge against Rojas.

Clay was concentrating on the monitor when he heard the voice of Rojas outside the house as he approached. The armed guard stood from his chair across the room in preparation for Rojas's entry. Clay looked at Christine and whispered her name.

"Christine . . . Christine, wake up. Christine, Rojas is coming!" Clay said so she could hear him.

Upon hearing the man's name, she sat up quickly and adjusted her eyes to the light. She moved quickly to the chair beside Clay and looked at the monitor with him.

"Do you know what to do?" Clay asked.

"Yes. Do you?"

"Yes. Keep your fingers crossed. And remember, no matter what happens, no matter how this day ends, I love you with all of my heart."

"I know. I love you too, Clay," Christine said as she looked longingly at him.

Their moment together was interrupted abruptly by Rojas as he entered through the front door. He was looking quite chipper this morning in his all-white ensemble. He looked first at Christine and Clay who were in their places at the computer. Then he turned his attention to the guard in the corner of the room.

"Did they give you any trouble, Manuelle?"

"No, Alberto. They were no trouble."

"Good. You may go and get some sleep and something to eat. Tell Phillipa to send someone down to replace you."

"Yes, Alberto," the guard said as he left the house.

Rojas walked to the couch where Christine had been sleeping moments earlier and sat down. He crossed one leg over the other and looked at the pair sitting in front of him.

"Well? Do you have the account ready?"

"Yes. It's ready," Clay responded.

"Good. Now let me see it." Rojas demanded.

"It might be better if you sat here next to me while I show it to you," Clay said.

"I'll move so you can sit," Christine said as she stood.

Rojas stood from the couch and walked to Christine. When he reached her, he put his arm around her waist and pulled her toward him. He looked into her eyes as his hand moved from her side and down to her butt. He watched her reaction as he grabbed her rear end firmly in his hand and jerked her closer. Christine managed a smile.

"Did you miss me last night, my dear?" Rojas asked.

"Yes . . . yes, I missed you. But I think that you'll see that my efforts here were worthwhile. Why don't you see for yourself?"

Rojas moved his head very close to her face. Then he stuck out his tongue and licked her face from her jaw to her temple. Christine tried not to show how repulsed she was by this. She swallowed noticeably and again managed a smile.

"I will see for myself. Show me what you have done, Clay Peterson," Rojas said as he turned lose of Christine and sat in the chair next to Clay.

Clay took a deep breath, looked at the monitor and began his presentation. Christine wiped Rojas's saliva from her face and sat on the couch to observe.

"Okay, first we access the Royal Canadian Banking system. To do that, we dial into the system from our location."

Clay keyed in the phone number and waited for the computer to acknowledge entry into the Canadian bank's system. Rojas watched the monitor intently. Nothing was happening. Rojas grew impatient after a few moments.

"What is going on? Why is there nothing happening?" He asked.

"It takes a few moments after the modems connect. The screen will change in a minute," Clay responded.

Rojas looked at Clay sarcastically and shook his head. Then he turned back to the monitor and was surprised to see the screen change. The new screen read THE ROYAL CANADIAN BANK.

"You are in? You are in the system just like that?" Rojas asked excitedly.

"Not quite. We had to break the primary and secondary security codes to enter the system. The primary codes I can handle myself. It was the secondary encrypted codes that Lisa was able to break that allows us access to the entire system."

Rojas looked at Christine and smiled at her.

"Very impressive, my dear. Very, very impressive. You have beauty and you have a brain. That is something that I believe is rare in women," Rojas said.

Christine returned Rojas's smile as she thought about what a degenerate ignorant pig he was. Rojas returned his attention to the monitor. During the brief moment that Rojas turned away, Clay keyed up the fake account screen. When Rojas looked at the monitor again he saw the new screen.

"Now what is this?" he asked.

"This is the collateral account that I have set up for you. I opened the account under the name of Otrebla Sajor, which is simply your name spelled backward."

"Otrebla Sajor . . . how very clever of you, Clay Peterson. Continue," Rojas demanded.

"The number shown where there should be an account balance corresponds with the number of the collateral account I deposited your ten million dollars into. I can't get that money out until the end of the trading period because the account is locked. However, I can direct the trading profits from that account into this one. Each time there is a trade made and profits are deposited, they will be automatically wired into this account."

"So, I will then have access to the money?"

"Not yet," Clay responded.

"Why not? It is my money!" Rojas shouted.

"Let me show you what happens to the money. Let's access the Swiss account now."

Clay exited the fake screen which showed the Canadian bank account information and keyed in the information necessary to access the Swiss account. This time Rojas sat patiently until the screen indicated SWISS WORLD BANK OPERATING SYSTEM. Rojas shook his head when he read the message on the monitor.

"This is truly amazing. Truly amazing, Clay Peterson," Rojas said sincerely.

"The hard part is really breaking the secondary encrypted security code. Lisa can explain that to you. Can't you, Lisa?"

Rojas looked at Christine seriously this time. He watched her intently as she spoke. It was exactly what Clay wanted him to do as he keyed instructions into the computer.

"Well, as Clay said, most computer systems have primary and secondary codes which must be deciphered before the system will allow access to certain files. Primary codes will usually allow access to an operating system, and they comprise plain text elements and code groups that run simultaneously in alphabetic or numerical order. Secondary codes allow access to specific file sections within a system and are structured with encrypted elements in alphabetic order and the code groups in random order. These are the more difficult codes to break," Christine concluded.

"And you are able to break these secondary codes?"

"Usually, yes."

"If they are encrypted, the more difficult of the two codes to break, then why can you not break the primary codes as well? Why do you need Clay Peterson for that?"

"Because my expertise is in cryptanalysis, the analytic solution of cryptographic systems without knowledge of the key. Clay isn't versed in cryptanalysis. He is good with numerical-based codes. That is why we complement each other."

Rojas didn't have any idea what Christine had just explained to him. He nodded as though he understood then turned his attention back to the monitor.

"What are we looking at now?" Rojas asked.

"This is the Swiss account. It is the trading account. I have programmed the account specifications so that when the locked Canadian account has trading profits equal to or greater than one hundred million dollars, the funds are automatically wired into the second Canadian account I set up in your name. When that money is wired, it automatically triggers the acquisition of a trading account purchase order. The purchaser order will control one billion dollars worth of Swiss World Bank prime bank notes or PBNs. The day the money is transferred from one Canadian account to the other is the day you start trading."

"How long will it take to have the one hundred million in the first account?" Rojas asked.

"At the discount rate and guaranteed minimum twice weekly trade, the account should generate ten million per week. So you would have one hundred million in ten weeks."

"And what will the new account produce in profits?"

"If we use the same discount rate of 4.842 percent, the minimum twice weekly trade, and the trading period of fifteen months? I estimate that you will have around three billion dollars in the bank. At that time you could take two billion in profits, and keep the one billion in the trading program. The numbers would be astronomical if you elected to do that."

Rojas sat and studied the monitor. He was thinking about how that amount of liquid capital translated into power. He could literally become one of, if not the most, powerful man in the world. He looked at Clay with a serious look on his face.

"This is done? I will be trading in ten weeks and see these profits?" Rojas asked.

"It's done."

Rojas turned to Christine who was watching him anxiously from where she sat on the couch. He smiled at her then spoke.

"Go and shower. Clean yourself up for me," Rojas ordered.

"But . . . we're not finished are—"

"Go! Go now!" Rojas shouted.

Christine jumped, startled by the loudness Rojas's voice. She stood slowly from the couch and looked at Clay. He gave her a reassuring nod, letting her know that he would be all right. Rojas watched her as she left the room. Rojas turned back to Clay after Christine was gone.

"Ah . . . She is a fine-looking woman. Don't you agree?"

"Yes, she is beautiful."

"It will be a shame to kill her," Rojas said bluntly.

"Kill her? Why would you kill her?" Clay asked in surprise.

"I don't need you both. She has given you these codes. You have them now, and we have no use for her. You will stay here with me; this will be your home for the next fifteen months. We will watch the trading account profits grow together and celebrate when it is done. How does that sound to you, Clay Peterson?"

Clay thought for a moment. He had to think of something that would buy some time. He had to be alone with Christine. He had to get her alone with him, and away from Rojas. Then he had an idea.

"It sounds like an excellent idea. But I would like to ask you a favor. I would like to ask you to grant me a wish."

"A wish?" Rojas laughed. "I am not a genie, Clay Peterson, but if it is within my power, and within reason, yes, I will grant your wish. What is it?"

"The girl."

"Lisa? What about her?"

"I would like to be with her before you kill her. Please, Mr. Rojas, it has been a dream of mine since I met her. If you could find it in your heart to grant me that wish, I would be forever grateful to you."

"You want to be with the girl?" Rojas asked in mild surprise.

Rojas thought about the request. Clay sat anxiously awaiting Rojas's response.

"Why not? I grant you your wish, Clay Peterson. You know of course that you will have to do whatever it is you want to do with her in front of one of my guards. I can not afford to leave you alone. You are too valuable to me now."

"In front of your guard?"

"Do not worry; I have done it many times. They are used to it. Sometimes if the girl did not please me, I let the guard have her when I finished. The guard will wait and probably hope that she does not satisfy you so that he will have a turn!" Rojas said as he started laughing at his comment.

Rojas stood from his chair and slapped Clay on the back as he continued to laugh. He moved away from Clay and walked toward the front door. He stopped and yelled down the hallway.

"Lisa! Lisa, come in here for a moment!"

Moments later Christine appeared at the end of the hallway wrapped in a towel. She had not completely undressed as she still wore the white silk stockings Rojas had provided for her. Rojas admired her for a moment then spoke.

"Come closer, my dear."

Christine walked slowly toward Rojas. She began to tremble with fear. When she was standing within arm's length of Rojas, he reached out and jerked away the towel exposing her half-naked body. Christine covered herself with her hands and closed her eyes in anticipation of the worst. Rojas looked at Clay.

"I grant your wish, Clay Peterson. You may have her for two hours to do with as you please. Then I will send for her."

Rojas opened the front door and summoned one of the two guards into the house. The guard walked in and Rojas closed the door.

"Our guest, Mr. Peterson, is going to take this woman. You are not to let them out of your sight. I have told Mr. Peterson that if she does not please him, he might consider giving her to you. I don't think that will happen, but you never know," Rojas said as he laughed again.

Rojas opened the door again and before he left, turned back to look at Clay. He smiled broadly as he spoke. "Enjoy, my friend. I will be thinking of you and the time you are having! It is truly a joyous ride."

Rojas closed the door. Christine stood not far from the guard who blocked the doorway. The guard motioned her to move in the direction of Clay. She obeyed and began slowly walking toward him. The guard admired her from behind as she moved. Clay looked at her anxiously. He watched her eyes for any sign that she may be about to make her move. Then she stopped. She closed her eyes briefly then opened them and looked at Clay. She winked at him then turned around and faced the guard that was standing a few feet behind her. The guard took a step back, surprised at the fact that Christine had turned toward him. The guard held his machine gun, but it wasn't pointed at Christine. He held it to his chest with both hands, the barrel of the gun pointing to the ceiling. Christine continued toward him and the guard looked beyond her to Clay. The guard looked confused and wanted direction from Clay. Clay responded to the guard's look with a shrug of his shoulders. Christine drew closer to him and the guard seemed to begin to relax a bit as she took her hands away from her breasts and placed them on either side of the guard's face. She stroked his face and the guard relaxed a bit more, Christine was exciting him now. She slowly moved her left arm up around his shoulder and began running her fingers through the hair on the back of his head. She moved her right hand down the left side of his face gently stroking his cheek with her fingers as her hand descended.

The guard was not tense any longer. He was taken with her beauty and by her touch. As her right hand reached the guard's chin, he slowly moved his head toward her lips. Christine had him now and she knew it. Suddenly she grabbed the hair in the back of his head with her left hand and pulled as she pushed his chin with all of her might. Her feet left the ground when she pushed his chin toward the ceiling with her right hand. Clay could hear the crack of the guard's neck from where he was sitting in his chair. The guard's body became limp and the air in his lungs could be heard escaping from his mouth. As he fell forward, Christine attempted to hold him up, but she could not support his weight. Clay dashed from his chair and caught them both before the body could hit the floor. The noise would have alerted the guard outside the door.

Christine scrambled to get out from underneath of the guard. When she was free, she grabbed the towel lying on the floor in front of the door and wrapped it around her again. Clay dragged the guard down the hallway and into one of the bedrooms. Christine followed. Once they were in the bedroom, they closed the door and stood over the dead guard looking at one another.

"Okay . . . okay, now what do we do?" Clay asked nervously.

"I'm thinking."

"God, where'd you learn to do that?"

"The academy. I didn't know it really worked but it does."

"I'd say it works pretty well. Did they teach you anything that will get us out of here? It's eight twenty-five. We need to be on our way pretty soon."

"First I have to get dressed. Take off the guard's clothes, I'll wear them."

Clay stripped the guard as Christine requested, and she put on articles of clothing as he handed them to her. The outfit was too big for her, but it was better than walking around the jungle in a silk dress and lace underwear. When she was dressed, she picked up the guard's machine gun and they went back into the living room. Christine pulled the edge of the drapes back just enough to see that there was one guard standing on the porch in front of the house. She surveyed the rest of the yard and saw no one.

She took her hand away from the curtain and motioned Clay away from the door. They walked quietly back to the middle of the room. Christine whispered to Clay, "We'll go out the back of the house. We can go over the wall and make our way down the mountain. Rojas said he would send someone for me in two hours. That gives us an hour and a half to get as far away from here as we can. I don't know if it's enough time, but it's all we've got. Let's go."

They walked to the kitchen. Christine signaled for Clay to get down on the floor with her so that they would not be seen through the windows in the kitchen. As they started crawling toward the back door, Clay remembered his disks. He had to have his computer disks.

"Wait," he whispered.

Christine turned and looked at him. She was irritated that he had stopped.

"What?"

"My disks, I have to get my file disks."

"Leave them, Clay, we have to get out of here. Rojas could come back any time. Now is our chance and we have to take it."

"I'll be right back," Clay whispered as he backed out of the room.

Once he was outside the kitchen and in the hallway, he stood and walked carefully and quietly back to the living room. He saw the disk holder on the table and walked over to pick it up. As he reached the table, he was startled. The front door opened and another guard entered. Clay was able to maintain his composure on the outside, however his heart felt as though it was going to beat right through his chest.

"Hello," Clay said as it was the first thing that came to mind.

The guard frowned and surveyed the room. He looked down the hallway, then pointed his gun at Clay and spoke.

"Where is Manuelle?" he demanded.

"Ah . . . Manuelle. Well, you see Manuelle is—"

Clay did not finish his sentence as sounds began coming from the direction of the kitchen. Both men stood and listened as the sounds grew louder and more intense.

"Oh . . . oh . . . oh . . . yes . . . yes . . . yes . . . Oh god . . . oh god . . . oh god! Uh . . . uh . . . Mmmm . . . that's it . . . yes . . . just like that . . . Oh Manuelle . . . Yes Manuelle! Yes! Yes! Yes!"

Clay turned back to the guard and smiled at him. He shrugged his shoulders as he spoke.

"He's with the girl. Alberto said I could give her to him if she didn't satisfy me. She didn't so . . . I did."

The sounds continued from the kitchen and the guard concentrated in that direction with a look of curiosity on his face. He took two steps forward and Clay spoke quickly.

"Ah-Ah-Ah. One at a time. I told Manuelle he could have her for one hour. That gives him about fifty-five more minutes with her. When he comes out, I'll tell him to come and get you. Understand."

"Yes . . . I understand. I will be waiting at the front door for him."

"I'll let him know."

The guard listened to the sound coming from the kitchen for a few more moments before turning and exiting the house. Clay followed the guard to the front door and depressed the lock as it closed. He walked back, grabbed the disks from the table and stuffed them in his pants. He turned and quickly walked to the kitchen where Christine continued to act out an orgasm. She stood against a wall with her eyes closed as she breathed heavily and spoke.

"Oh . . . oh . . . yes . . . god, yesssss! Don't stop—"

Clay tapped her on the shoulder startling her.

"Ahhhh!" Christine screamed.

"He's gone. Do you need a cigarette or can we get out of here now?" Clay said sarcastically.

"Let's just get out of here," Christine snapped back.

They crawled along the kitchen floor together again. When they reached the back door, Christine squatted and looked out of the window in the back door. She could see clearly in all directions and saw no one present. She opened the door slowly and signaled for Clay to follow her. She eased out the door and pointed the gun as she looked quickly around her. It was clear. Christine walked down the patio and peered around the side of the house. She jerked back quickly. She signaled Clay to move back and they both quickly went back into the house.

"What? Why did we come back in?"

"It's your friend. I think he's coming around back for a free shot. You take the gun and do exactly what I tell you or we're both dead."

The guard skulked down the side of the house rising to look into windows as he went. He reached the back of the house and quickly looked around the corner to see if anyone was there. He saw nothing and crept quietly along the back wall of the house. When he reached the back door, he looked curiously at it. The door was ajar. He peered in the door and saw nothing in the kitchen. He waited for a moment to see if he could hear anything. He didn't. The guard moved cautiously into the house. As he entered the kitchen, he was startled by the sudden appearance of Christine who walked from the hallway and into the kitchen. The guard stared at her as she came into the room. She wasn't wearing a top and he was taken by the sight of her round supple breasts.

"Oh, there you are! Manuelle went to the front door to find you and you weren't there. He's in the bedroom. We're getting ready to have a little orgy. Don't you want to come?" Christine said as she walked over and extended her hand to the guard.

"An orgy?" the guard asked.

"Yes, it will be fun. Come on," Christine prodded.

The guard could not keep his eyes off Christine's chest. He walked with her willingly out of the kitchen and down the hallway. When they exited the hallway and entered the living room, Clay who was hiding against the wall, hit the guard with all his might in the back of the neck with the butt of the gun. The guard fell to the ground as a result of the blow. He was not unconscious, however, and as he attempted to get up, Christine lifted her foot in the air and brought the heel of her boot down on the back of his neck again. This time the guard did not move.

Clay looked at Christine. "Is he dead?"

"I don't know, better him than us, though. Now let's go."

Christine picked up the guard's gun and they left him lying there. This time they ran to the kitchen and out the back door. Once outside, they looked to see if they could see anyone. When they didn't, they ran to the four-foot stucco wall approximately thirty yards from the back of the house. They both scaled the low wall without any difficulty. On the other side of the wall, they stopped and couched down. They found themselves looking over a large green valley from atop a steep hill.

"Which way's north?" Clay asked.

Christine looked at the position of the sun and guessed that it was to her right. She pointed that direction and spoke.

"I'm not sure, but I would guess it's that way."

"Good enough for me, let's go that way."

"Wait, why do we have to go to Medillin."

"Because it's where I made our reservations. Now let's go."

Christine did not argue with Clay although she did not understand what he was talking about. She trusted him and knew that she would probably not be alive right now if it were not for him. They started off to their right which also happened to be to the north. They both felt a slight sense of relief now that they were out of the confines of the Rojas estate. However, although neither one of them said it, they knew that if Rojas captured them now he would surely kill them both.

ARTICLE 37

Brian Whitfield sat inside the Citation's main cabin as it taxied onto the runway. He was on his cell phone. He had been talking on the telephone for most of the night. His attempts to get some cooperation had been futile. The bureau was spread too thin because of operation Second wave. He had tried to reach Associate Director Stafford but he would not take the call. The DEA couldn't help him even though they already had people in Colombia. They were all committed to and involved in their operation with the Colombian government troops down there. Brian was on his own at that moment, but he wasn't giving up just yet. He had some friends with the agency who owed him a few favors. He was about to collect on their debts.

Brian held the phone tightly to his ear as the engines roared and the jet sped down the runway for takeoff. He was waiting for someone to answer the phone at the other end of the line. Finally he heard a female voice.

"Foreign Affairs Division, how may I direct your call?"

"Steve Hart please," Brian said loudly, attempting to be heard over the roar of the jet engines.

He waited for Steve Hart to answer the phone. Brian remembered when he and Hart were partners at the bureau thirteen years ago. They had attended the academy together and both worked out of the Bethesda, Maryland field office. They were partners for eleven years before Steve decided he wanted to move on. He chose to go to work for the CIA, and when he left, Brian became disenchanted with the field and decided to go through the FBI version of graduate school. He went to career development, and from there became a field supervisor. Steve went to work for the CIA in their intelligence department. He worked his way up in the ranks of the agency and now headed foreign affairs intelligence.

Brian and Steve had been the best of friends while they worked together at the bureau. The fact that they chose different career paths had not had an adverse effect on their friendship. They saw one another whenever travel schedules permitted, always attended children's graduations and birthdays. Brian Whitfield and Steve Hart were the brothers neither had ever had.

"Director Hart's office, may I help you," the female voice asked.

"Yes, this is Brian Whitfield. I would like to speak to Director Hart, please."

"One moment please, Mr. Whitfield."

"What's up, Bud?" the familiar voice asked.

"How are you, Steve?" Brian said somberly.

"Uh-oh . . . you don't sound so good, my friend. What's wrong?"

"I need some help, Steve, and I need it in a hurry. I don't know if you can do anything and if you can't, I'll understand."

"God, Brian, what is it?"

"One of my agents has been abducted. She's been taken to Colombia, just outside of Medillin. The cartel has her, Steve, and I have to get her out."

"How do you know the cartel has her?"

"I got a message from her last night. She's being held by Alberto Rojas."

"Rojas! Son, you do have a problem. Hell, he reportedly controls over half of the drugs produced by the cartel. No one has been able to get close to the guy."

"Well, we got close and I've lost an agent. I'm supposed to meet her today in Medillin. Her plan was to escape from Rojas and somehow get there. I'm supposed to check the hotels for the name Rekcah. That's R-E-K-C-A-H, Rekcah. If I find the name, I'll find her. If I don't . . . well if I don't she's probably dead."

"What do you want me to do, Brian? I'll help you if I can."

"I'm en route to Colombia right now. We just took off from Dallas and I'm calling you from the plane. I won't arrive in Medillin until later this afternoon. I need to know if you have any contacts, friendly contacts, you can trust in Medillin. If you do, or you know of another agency that does, we need to locate Rekcah and keep her safe until I arrive and can get her out of the country."

"Brian, I don't have anyone down there. There may be another division here that does, but I don't."

"I just need some help until I can get down there and get her out. Do whatever you can for me, Steve. Just try, that's all I ask."

"You got it. How do I reach you if I find someone?"

"Call my office. Don't talk to anyone except communications. I'm having problems with Stafford right now and I don't want him to know what I'm doing."

"The bureau doesn't know you're headed to Colombia? Goddammit, Brian, you can't do that! You might end up getting yourself killed. Think about this for a minute, man!"

"I've been up all night thinking about it. I'm the reason this agent is in this situation. If she's not already dead, she will be if I don't find her. She's a rookie, Steve, and she's probably scared to death. I'm gonna get her out. Are you with me on this?"

"You don't even need to ask that question, Brian. Just don't get yourself killed in the process. Do you understand me?"

"Never happen, partner, never happen."

"I'll call your office in the next two hours. If I can't locate someone by then, chances are I can't help you."

"Understood. Thanks, Steve."

"Hey, this is going to work out, man. Don't get down there and lose your head. I'll figure something out on this end. Just be careful."

"All right, buddy. Talk to you in two hours," Brian said.

When he hung up the phone, the realization of the words Steve had spoken to him began to set in. The bureau didn't know he was going to Medillin. If Steve couldn't help him, he wouldn't have any backup. He would be on his own, and neither he nor Agent Hendrix may make it out of Colombia alive.

CHAPTER ELEVEN

ARTICLE 38

July 30, 2005, 8:40 a.m.
Medillin, Colombia

They arrived just before dawn and moved without being detected around the residence. They had placed their explosives where they would do the most damage to both property and human life. The guards who stood at the gated driveway when they arrived were now dead. The four guards who patrolled the perimeter of the estate were also dead. The platoon leader watched as the owner of the house walked out onto a second-floor balcony. He stood there for a moment taking in the beautiful view he had of the valley below.

The platoon leader was patiently waiting for one of his men to return to the cover of the jungle and get into position. As the owner of the house went back through the doorway and into the house, the platoon leader observed his man as he ran into the jungle and assumed his position with the others.

The routine was the same. The platoon leader raised his arm so that the demolitions specialist could see it clearly. He waited a moment then brought his arm down quickly. The demolitions specialist pressed the button on the transmitter. The ground shook violently indicating the force of the explosions. Debris was sent flying high in all directions and fell to the ground around the soldiers who lay with their heads down in the jungle two hundred yards from the residence. The magnificent mansion was hidden by the smoke and flames caused by the blasts. The soldiers held their positions.

As the dust and smoke from the initial blasts began to clear, the platoon leader could see that there was nothing but a pile of burning rubble where the drug lord's mansion had stood moments earlier. The platoon leader surveyed the site with his binoculars for any sign of life. This time the explosions had killed everyone. There was nothing left for them to do. The platoon leader raised his arm and signaled the men to move out and away from the target. Once again they had done their job thoroughly. The residence of Pedro Bevearo lay in ruin. Pedro Bevearo and his family lay dead and buried beneath it.

They had one more target that day. It too was a residence. It was a short hike just across the valley. They would be there at approximately nine-forty, and hoped to destroy the target and be gone by eleven. They had been briefed about this house. It was heavily guarded. The drug lord who owned it was a powerful and ruthless man. His name, they were told, was Alberto Rojas.

ARTICLE 39

Rojas estate, Medillin, Colombia

Alberto ran out of his house and onto the veranda. He stopped when he got to the ornate concrete sculptured railing bordering the edge of the veranda. Rojas surveyed the valley as did three of his armed guards.

"That was an explosion. Do not tell me that wasn't an explosion!"

"Look, Alberto!" the guard standing at the south end of the veranda shouted.

Rojas and the others walked quickly to the opposite end of the deck. They looked out over the lush green valley again. Their view of the valley was partially obstructed by a portion of the mountain upon which Rojas's estate was built. That is where they saw the smoke. A plume of black and grey smoke was rising into the sky above the mountain in front of them.

"Pedro," Rojas said in a whisper to himself.

It had to be Pedro Bevearo. He was the only one who lived on the back side of the valley. His was the only residence there. Rojas stood looking at the smoke as it rose higher into the air. He couldn't imagine what could have caused such an explosion.

"Bring me a phone!" Rojas demanded.

Rojas began to think and grow concerned about the fact that Diego and Santiago had not bothered to call him yesterday. They were to have had a meeting together late in the afternoon when they returned from the valley. Neither of them had called. Now an explosion. It could only be Pedro's house. Either that or a plane crash.

"Did any of you see or hear anything before the explosion?"

All of the guards looked at him and shook their heads no. Rojas returned his gaze to the smoke plume. It grew higher and more intense as time passed. Rojas knew that based on the power generated by the blast and the smoke now rising in the air that it had to be a scene of destruction if it was Pedro's house. The guard interrupted Rojas's thoughts as he brought him a cordless phone. Rojas quickly dialed Pedro's number, it rang but there was no answer. This concerned Rojas. Even if Pedro was not in, one of the servants would answer the phone. He continued to let the phone ring for a few moments then disengaged the call. Rojas then dialed Diego's phone number. Again the telephone rang and Rojas waited for an answer.

"Yes?" the female voice answered.

"This is Rojas, is Roberto there?"

"No, Señor Rojas, Señor Diego has not yet returned from his trip."

"He did not return last night?"

"No, Señor Rojas."

Rojas disengaged the call. Now he was concerned and paranoid. He used the phone again. This time he dialed Joseffe Pinilla's number.

"Hello," the male voice answered.

"Let me speak to Joseffe. This is Alberto Rojas."

"Uno momento, Señor Rojas."

Rojas waited for the Joseffe to come to the phone.

"Alberto, how are you this morning?" Joseffe said finally.

"Not well, my friend, I believe that we have some trouble."

"What kind of trouble?"

"Have you heard from Diego or Santiago?"

"No."

"I haven't either. They did not call last night. Diego's maid said he did not return yesterday. And now this morning, I heard an explosion and now see smoke coming from the direction of Pedro's home. You had better—"

Alberto stopped speaking because he heard an explosion on the other end of the line. He heard the phone drop to the ground then the phone went dead. He stood there for a moment with the phone pressed to his ear. He still heard nothing. He slowly lowered the phone from his ear and looked at the men around him. He began to boil with rage.

"We must leave! We will go into the jungle! We will stay for a while in the foothills camp! Get my things together! We leave in fifteen minutes!" Rojas shouted.

As he stood there seething with anger, he looked toward the pool and the pool house. He suddenly remembered his two guests. He frowned when he did not see either of the guards in front of the house.

"Two of you come with me!" He ordered to the guards.

Two of the guards followed Rojas as he walked quickly to the pool house. He attempted to walk right in the front door, but it was locked.

"Break it in! Now!" Rojas shouted.

One of the guards took two steps back from the door and kicked it with all his strength. The door broke away from the jamb and the three men entered the house. They immediately saw one of the guards lying face down just outside the hallway in the living room.

Rojas scanned the room for his prisoners. When he did not see or hear them, he screamed. "Search the house for them!"

The guards went looking through the house while Rojas stayed at the front door. Moments later the guards returned, shaking their heads.

"Manuelle is in the bedroom dead, Alberto. The Americans are gone."

Rojas stood with a possessed look on his face. He did not care about the money, he wasn't thinking about that at all. This was now about his power and his honor. Clay had betrayed his generosity by escaping and taking the girl, after Rojas had given him his life. Rojas surveyed the room in anger and noticed movement from the guard near the hallway. He grabbed the gun from the guard standing next to him and walked quickly to the injured man. Rojas kicked the man in the side and then rolled him with his foot. Rojas glared down at the guard. He was bleeding from his nose and mouth. Rojas screamed at the half conscious man. "Where are they? Where did they go?"

The guard, although semiconscious, realized that he was in very deep trouble with Rojas. In an attempt to beg Rojas for forgiveness, the guard raised his hands slowly above his body and placed them together in a praying position. He was hoping that Rojas would take pity on him. It had the opposite affect. Rojas kicked the guard's hands away from his chest and opened fire with the machinegun at the man's head. Rojas did not just shoot the guard once or twice, he fired the weapon until the clip was empty. Blood sprayed the room and bullets ricocheted off the floor, hitting the walls on all sides of the room. The others in the living room either dove to the floor for cover or ran back out of the front door. When the gun did not fire anymore and the guard now lay unrecognizable in a pool of brain matter, blood, bone, and torn flesh, Rojas paused. He looked at what he had done to the man's face. It was not enough. Rojas used the gun then as a club and began pounding what was left of the man's head. Again, as the gun hit the bloody mass, pieces of it flew throughout the room. When Rojas had beaten away most of what remained, he stopped. He looked at the guard's headless body. He was breathing heavily. He turned quickly to the others who remained. He was covered in the guard's blood, and pieces of the man's head hung on his pants. The guards were terrified at the sight of him and at the fact that he now had turned his attention to them.

"I want half of you! Half of the guard to find the Americans! The other half will come with me to the foothill camp! Now go! We leave in ten minutes! Go!" Rojas ordered.

The guards left the pool house quickly and ran to the main house to decide who would go with Rojas and who would go after the Americans. Rojas started walking toward the door of the pool house. He glanced to his right as he walked by the computer in the living room. He stopped and brought the gun which still dripped with the guard's blood high over his head and hit the computer monitor. The monitor sparked and the screen exploded due to the force of the blow. Rojas glared at the damaged computer for a moment then dropped the gun and walked out of the house.

Rojas did not bother going back to the main house to change this time. He was too angry. Instead, he walked up the long flight of steps leading from the pool to the main house. He walked across the veranda, down a set of steps and the walk which led to the four-car garage. Rojas chose the black Range Rover for his trip to the foothill camp. He entered the vehicle, spreading blood across the grey leather driver's seat as he positioned himself to drive away. Rojas started the vehicle and sat there for a moment. He reached for the microphone on his CB radio, put it to his mouth and spoke,

"Tito, this is Rojas. Can you hear me?" Rojas waited for an answer. When none came, he shouted into the microphone.

"Tito! This is Rojas . . . pick up the radio, you fool!"

"This is Tito . . . go ahead, Alberto."

"Two Americans, a man and a young woman have escaped from the house. They must be in the jungle right now. How many men do you have with you?"

"Twelve, Alberto."

"Take them all! Go find these Americans and bring them to me! I will be at the foothill camp. It has become necessary for me to hide there for a while. When you find them, do not kill them. I will do that myself. Do you understand?"

"Yes, Alberto."

"I want you to contact our people in Medellin, Pereira, and Manizales. I do not know which way they went, but if they get out of the jungle and into one of the cities, I do not want them to escape the country. Have our people watch for them in the city and have them send more people to the jungle. We will surround them, Tito. Tell them all not to kill them. I want them alive when they are brought to me. I will make these Americans wish they had never been born before they die. Do you understand, Tito?"

"Yes, Alberto, I understand. I will call Medellin, Pereia, and Manizales immediately. We will begin our search from here after that."

"Good. Contact me by radio and let me know what's going on. I should be in the foothill camp in two hours. Now go, and do not fail me, Tito!" Rojas shouted into the microphone.

Rojas paused for a moment then placed the microphone back into its clip on the dashboard. He put the vehicle in drive and drove it out of the garage, down the circular driveway and out the front gate.

"Tito is a good man, he will find the Americans. When he finds them, I will cut them apart, and I will eat their hearts for my dinner tonight!" Rojas shouted to himself.

Rojas was obsessed with them. He also had other things on his mind. He could not figure out who was attacking the cartel. He would not allow himself to believe that it was someone within the cartel. That would be unthinkable. He thought it may be the Colombian government yielding under the pressure of the American government to come down harder on the cartel. If this were the case, there would be assassinations. Rojas had been through something similar six years prior. He had had to kill several leading members within the Colombian government and in the military before he got the attention of the government. Then he put people he paid in positions of power. He got to them anyway he could. He would blackmail them, threaten family members, he had even kidnapped and raped the daughter of the defense minister. He did not have any more trouble from the army after that incident. If these attacks had been committed by his government, they would pay; and he would see to it that they paid with their lives.

Rojas was about halfway down the side of the mountain when he saw them. They were flying in formation. There were three, moving very quickly toward his position. Rojas stopped the vehicle and got out to get a better look at them. He stood by the Range Rover with the door open. Suddenly one of them began firing at him. The rounds were hitting the road below him and moving toward his direction quickly. Rojas dove into the ditch against the side of the mountain. The machinegun rounds hit the Range Rover, causing it to explode and burst into flames. Rojas felt a sharp pain in his arm and leg, and the initial blast from the Range Rover sent a surge of heat across his back. Rojas kept his head down. Then he heard huge violent explosions coming from the top of the hill—two, four, then several more in rapid succession. The ground shook, small rocks and chunks of earth began breaking free from the side of the mountain and hitting Rojas in the back. He put his head down and clasped his hands over the back of his head in an effort to protect himself. Rojas lay in the ditch trembling, his left arm and leg were throbbing with pain, and both of his arms and the back of his head felt as though they were burned.

After a few minutes, Rojas lifted his head from the ground and listened. He could hear the Range Rover burning on the road next to him. He could feel the heat against his face and smell the burning rubber. Small rocks and pieces of earth still fell periodically from the side of the mountain above him. He did not hear any more jets and he did not hear any more explosions. He remained still on the ground for several more minutes before working up enough courage to stand.

As he stood, he noticed that all of the hair had been singed off his arms; so too had the hair been burned away from the back of his head. All that remained was a bright red bald spot that pulsated with heat and pain. He had been wounded in the left arm by flying debris from the Range Rover, and he looked to see how bad it was. When he did, he noticed a piece of silver metal protruding out of his pants in the middle of his thigh. He studied the object then realized that it was one of the door handles from the Range Rover. The explosion had sent the handle through the air like a dagger into Rojas's leg. Rojas was surprised by the fact that the wound was not more painful. He was able to put pressure on the leg, and that allowed him to begin walking slowly back up the hill toward his house. He did not know what he would find when he reached the top of the hill, but he had to see for himself how bad it was.

ARTICLE 40

They had been making their way though the dense jungle as fast as they could. Their clothes were already showing signs of the unforgiving thorns and branches that hindered their progress. Both of them had cuts on their arms and faces. They were not about to stop and they were not going to allow themselves to be captured again by Rojas. Nothing the jungle could do to them compared to the fate they would face if Rojas captured them.

Clay and Christine stopped walking and crouched down when they heard the explosions behind them in the distance. They turned to see where it was coming from, but the thick jungle overgrowth coupled with the trees blocked the view behind them. Clay glanced down at his watch and nodded in approval.

Christine watched him then spoke, "Why did you do that?"

"What?"

"Look at your watch and nod, like you knew something was supposed to happen."

"I didn't know anything was going to happen, I was hoping, but I didn't know."

"What were you hoping for?"

"I was hoping that we would both be alive right now. All we have to do is get to Medellin and then we should be all right."

"How far are we from Medellin?"

"About ten miles, maybe . . . eight now, I don't know."

"Are you sure we're headed in the right direction?"

"I'm not sure. But let's keep moving. The farther away we get from Rojas, the better off we're going to be."

Clay turned and started walking through the thick vines and plant life which covered the trees and the jungle floor. He used the machinegun to move vines and branches to clear the path as they walked. They had continued on about one hundred yards when Clay heard something. He held up his hand and Christine stopped behind him.

"What?" she whispered.

"Shhhhh," Clay sounded as he listened.

The sound he heard was the river. He motioned to his right and Christine followed him. As they walked, the jungle undergrowth grew thicker and harder to maneuver through. Just as Clay was about to turn and go back, he could see that the undergrowth and the trees began to thin out in front of them. They continued on and crouched at the edge of the tree line. Clay surveyed their surroundings. They had reached the bank of a very large river. Clay was relieved; he knew then where they were.

"It's the Cavaca River," he whispered.

"How do you know that?" Christine asked.

"I saw it last night on the computer. I pulled up the GPS map in the Pentagon computer system. This river starts at the Caribbean Sea and runs south through the country. It runs right through Medellin on its way south. If we follow it, we should walk right into Medellin."

Clay turned and looked at Christine. She had a surprised look on her face as she looked back at him.

"What?" Clay asked.

"You, that's what. What all did you do last night on that computer?"

"Let's just say I left a lot of messages and probably pissed a lot of people off. Now, what do you say we go to Medellin?" Clay said with a confident smile.

ARTICLE 41

The jet had been refueled and now sat, again awaiting clearance for takeoff. Their destination was Medellin, Colombia. Brian Whitfield sat in his seat and looked out his window as the large passenger jets passed by on their way to the terminal buildings. He was thinking about what he would do when he got to Medellin. If Steve was unable to assist him, he would be on his own. He believed that on the one hand this would benefit him. No one would know he was there and no one would know who he was. It was widely known that the Colombian government and its law enforcement agencies were riddled with corruption. If the wrong people found out he was in the country looking for a missing agent, he might never get Christine out alive. On the other hand, lack of backup support could get them both killed. He didn't know what to expect when he got there, he only knew that he had to go. The telephone on the table in front of him rang. He looked at it for a moment before answering. The phone rang a second time and he picked up the receiver.

"Whitfield," he answered.

"Goddammit, Whitfield, where the hell are you?" Stafford screamed.

"Associate Director Stafford, and how are you today?" Brian asked sarcastically.

"Cut the bullshit, Whitfield, I asked you a question!"

"Well, I'm in Miami right now, following up on a lead on the Hendrix investigation."

"I've talked to Dallas, Whitfield. I know about the message from Peterson and I know that Rojas may have Hendrix. Now you get your ass back here, and I mean now!"

"I . . . can't do that, sir."

"What the fuck do you mean you can't do it? You better damn well do it, or I swear to god, I'll have your ass hanging from the flagpole in front of this building!"

"That doesn't sound very comfortable, sir."

"I don't think you're taking me seriously, Agent Whitfield! Now, I'm commanding you to get your ass back to Washington. I'm ordering you to do it right now! I'll bring you up on charges if you don't, Whitfield, you know I'll do it."

"Director Stafford, you do whatever the fuck you think you have to do. I have an agent that has been kidnapped by one of the Colombian cartel drug lords. He's going to kill her, if he hasn't already. I've called everyone I know to try to get someone down there to help get her out and I'm not getting any cooperation. I called you on three different occasions last night and you were too busy to take my calls."

"Whitfield, you son-of-"

"I'm not finished, Stafford! I'm going to Colombia and I'm going to do whatever I can to help that young woman get out of that situation. Now if you don't want to support me in that effort, if you want to bring me up on charges, you go ahead. I have a job to do and I don't have time to spend arguing with you on the phone. Good day, Director Stafford."

"Whitfield, if you hang up—"

Brian hung up the phone. Stafford didn't bother him. He had almost twenty-five years in. He would retire when he got back, if he got back alive. Stafford could kick and scream all he wanted, but Brian knew that what he was doing was right. He knew that if it were he being held, someone would at least make the attempt to get him out. Whether it was the

FBI, where he had many friends, or one of the other Washington agencies, he knew that someone would at least make the attempt. Brian's thoughts were interrupted by the ringing of the telephone once again.

"What!" Brian shouted into the receiver.

"Jesus, Brian, settle down, man," Steve Hart said.

"I'm sorry, Steve, I thought you were Stafford calling me back again."

"You talked to him?"

"I guess you could say that I did all of the talking, yeah."

"Man, I don't know if you know what's going on in Colombia right now, but your agent Hendrix is right in the middle of all of it."

"What do you mean?"

"Hell, man, everyone has people down there right now: the agency, the bureau, NSA; and the air force, marines, and army have operations in the area right now as well. And I'll tell you this, the guys aren't down there on maneuvers either. They're down there on serious business, Brian."

"Did you find anyone who could help me?"

"I found a guy. Now I don't know anything about him, all I know is that he does us favors every once and a while. He's on our special operations payroll."

"What kind of favors does this guy do for you, Steve?"

"Let's just say he makes people disappear, Brian."

"What? The guy's a specialist?"

"He's good, Brian, and I was lucky to get him for you. Look, he knows Medellin, he knows who to trust and who not to trust in that city and country, and that's no one. If your agent is still alive and gets to Medellin, he'll find her and he will protect her."

"What does he know about the situation?"

"I told Ops that your agent was going to check into one of the hotels under the name you gave me. This Rekcah name. They told him to check the hotels, if he found her he was to contact us and stay with her until you got to them. He is then supposed to help you get her back to the airport and out of the country."

"What's his name?"

"Raven."

"Raven? That's it?"

"That's it. They didn't tell me any more and I didn't ask. If your girl is alive, she'll be in very capable hands until you get to her, Brian."

"Listen, Steve, I really appreciate this, and—"

"Shut up, man. You owe me a beer, that's it. You just do me a favor and make it back here in one piece. If you don't, I know a guy here that I can fix up with Marlene and you know I'd do it."

"Thanks, man. It's good to know that you would look after my interests if something were to happen to me."

"Just don't let that happen, buddy. Get in and get out of there as soon as you can. If you don't find your girl, don't wait around to find out why. You know as well as I do that she could already be dead. Go down and do your thing, then get out."

"Okay, Steve. I'll call you when I'm safely out of the country."

"Good enough."

Brian hung up the telephone just as the jet engines started roaring. The jet began speeding down the runway and the wheels left the ground seconds later. Brian watched the coast line disappear as the plane flew with incredible speed over the Atlantic. Brian thought about the fact that he might never see the United States coast line again.

ARTICLE 42

Christine and Clay were both tiring. They had walked another hour and a half. Walking along the river was much easier than trying to make their way through the middle of the jungle. They had quickened their pace and were now making good time, Clay believed. But the quickened pace had taken its toll on their bodies. Both had had little sleep the night before and neither had eaten since before their abduction in Dallas. They were tired, weak, and out of breath. Clay had to stop and rest.

"Wait . . . let's stop here for a minute," Clay gasped as he fell to the ground.

"We can't stop, Clay, we have to keep going," Christine insisted.

"But . . . you look really . . . really tired. Really tired, Christine."

Christine looked at him and smiled. He was gasping for breath, he looked beaten up and exhausted. And, she thought, he had been the one up all night working on the computer and teaching her about cryptanalysis.

"You're right, I do feel tired. We'll rest for a few minutes, but then we have to go."

"Okay . . . just until you get your breath."

"Right," Christine said smiling as she slowly sat down.

Once she was sitting next to him on the ground, she did have a chance to catch her breath. She looked at Clay who was lying on his back with his eyes closed. His cheek was swollen and his lip had a nasty-looking cut, visible evidence of Rojas's treatment of him. Her wounds weren't as visible. She remembered how he had humiliated her. She remembered what he had made her do. Christine had been made to feel cheep, like a piece of expendable meat. She remembered his touch and grimaced at the thought of it. She remembered how he smelled and her stomach began to churn. Then she remembered how the man lying next to her on the ground had treated her when she returned to his side after being with Rojas. She remembered his understanding words and the look of compassion he had given her. Christine reached over and brushed some jungle moss from his hair.

She smiled at him and spoke. "You and your stupid Fibonacci Sequence," she said quietly.

"Huh? What does the Fibonacci Sequence have to do with anything?" Clay asked as he raised his head off the ground and looked at her.

"Well without it, you wouldn't have been able to access the computer systems that got us into this mess."

"Yeah, that's true enough I guess. But we probably wouldn't have been able to get away from Rojas either, ya know."

"I know, and I probably would never have met you."

"Is that good or bad? I guess that's not a good question to ask you sitting in the middle of the Colombian jungle, is it?"

Christine leaned over so that her head was just above his. She looked at him lovingly and smiled. She brushed some hair away from his forehead and spoke softly. "You are an amazing man, Clay Peterson. And I'm glad that Mr. Fibonacci, wherever he is, came up with that crazy number theory. I love you."

Clay looked up at her. He had never loved anyone like he loved Christine. He placed the palm of his hand gently against her cheek and began to speak. "I know that you do . . . and I love—"

Clay's sentence was interrupted by the sound of an engine. Christine put her head down next to Clay and he rolled to his stomach. Both of them watched and listened. Then they saw the vehicle pull into a clearing near the river a few hundred feet in front of them. Four men carrying automatic weapons got out of the jeep after it stopped. One of them shouted orders to the others. They spread out and began slowly walking toward Clay and Christine.

"What do we do?" Clay whispered.

"Stay very still. Do you know how to use that thing?" Christine asked referring to the machinegun he had in his hands.

"No," he whispered back.

"Cock it and pull the trigger when I tell you to. Just point and pull the trigger. Try not to hit me."

"Great," Clay said anxiously.

They watched as the four men walked toward them and closed in slowly on their position in the grass.

Christine whispered to Clay again, "I'll take the two on the left; you try for the ones on the right. Follow my lead."

"Okay," Clay whispered back.

The men continued to draw closer to them. They all wore dark clothing and had blue bandannas around their heads. Christine thought they must be part of Rojas's armed guards. Christine positioned her gun on her shoulder and took aim at the guard on the far left. Clay watched her intently and mimicked her movements. As the men walked to within less than fifty feet of them, Christine suddenly opened fire with her weapon. She killed the first man immediately then began spraying rounds back and forth in the direction of the second guard. Clay tried to fire his weapon, but when he pulled the trigger, it didn't move.

The guards dropped to the ground and began returning fire. Bullets and tracer rounds were passing just above their heads. Clay tried to get his gun to work, but couldn't. Christine continued to fire her weapon until she no longer had any rounds in the clip. She reached into her shirt pocket and pulled out another full clip and put it quickly into the chamber. She looked at Clay to see what he was doing.

"Are you out of rounds?"

"I haven't even fired the gun yet!"

"Here, take this," she said as she handed her weapon to him.

The gunfire continued from the direction of the guards. They had not stopped firing. As she looked at the weapon Clay had given her, she immediately saw the problem.

"The safety is on!" she snapped.

"Sorry!"

Christine waited before firing again. She watched the jungle in front of her to see if she could see where the gunfire was coming from. As far as she could tell, there were only two of them. Christine patiently waited. Clay looked at her with panic on his face.

"What are we waiting for?"

"Shhh. Let's see if we can get them to show themselves."

After a few moments, the gunfire ceased. The jungle was quiet. The smell of gun powder and smoke filled the air in the immediate area. Christine watched the jungle ahead of her for any sign of movement. She did not move. Then suddenly in front of her the two guards on the right both jumped up out of the grass and began running toward their position firing their weapons wildly. Tracers and bullets flew past them again. Christine calmly took aim at first one and then the other guard. She killed them both. Clay was lying on the ground covering his head. When the firing stopped, he looked up to see what was going on.

"What happened?" he asked.

Christine did not look away from the jungle in front of her. She watched for any sign of movement. She answered Clay without looking at him.

"I think we got 'em all."

"We? Christ, I still haven't fired a bullet," Clay said as he rolled onto his back and started to sit up.

"Stay down, they may—"

Just then machine gun rounds started peppering the ground all around them. Christine ducked her head this time. Clay looked behind them and saw a guard moving toward them as he fired his weapon. Clay was on his back and pointed his gun at the approaching assailant. Clay pulled the trigger, and this time the gun began firing rapidly in the direction of the oncoming guard. Clay's aim was good enough to hit the guard in the legs. As he fell, Clay continued to fire and hit the guard in the stomach and neck as he collapsed to the ground twenty-five feet from them. Clay stopped firing his gun and looked wildly in the direction he had been shooting. He was breathing rapidly and his pulse was racing.

"I think I got him, Christine. I think he's dead," Clay said still looking in the direction of the dead guard.

"Christine? Christine!" Clay shouted when he finally turned to look at her.

Christine lay on the ground bleeding from a wound to her head. A round had creased her temple and rendered her unconscious. Upon further examination, Clay could see that she had also sustained a direct hit in her shoulder. The bullet had hit her in the shoulder blade and gone completely through her body. Clay was frantic. He rolled her onto her back and held her head in his arms. He began to cry as he looked down upon her pale face and spoke to her in an angry broken voice.

"You listen to me, Christine . . . You . . . listen to me. You are not going to die. I will not let you die on me. Do you hear? We have too much to do together."

Clay's tears fell upon Christine's face as he pleaded for her to live. Then he looked to the sky and spoke. "God! Don't you take her from me now! Please, God, not now!" he screamed.

Clay looked back down at her again. He composed himself and realized that the only way she would live is if he got her to Medellin and got her there in a hurry. He looked toward the clearing and saw the Jeep sitting there. He then gently placed Christine's head back down on the ground. Clay rose to his knees and took off his belt. Then he removed his shirt. He worked his belt behind Christine and brought it up under her armpits. He ripped his shirt in half and wadded the torn halves up in a ball. Clay put one piece of the shirt on against the wound in her back and the other on the much larger exit wound just above her right breast. Then he pulled the belt as tightly as he could and secured it in place. He picked up both machineguns and put the straps over his shoulders. Clay then knelt down and picked Christine up in his arms. He walked with her quickly to the jeep. When he reached the Jeep, he placed her limp body in the backseat as gently as he could. Clay ran quickly to the driver's side and found the keys were still in the ignition. He started the vehicle and dirt flew from under the rear wheels as he depressed the accelerator. Something happened to Clay Peterson in the Colombian jungle. He had an angry determined look on his face as he drove the jeep down the path and toward the dirt road. He wasn't a computer nerd from Dallas any longer. He was a soldier in a war, and his mission was to get Christine to Medellin alive. He would do that no matter what the consequences, and he vowed to kill anyone who tried to stop him now.

ARTICLE 43

July 30, 2005, 11:15 a.m.
Rojas estate, Medellin, Colombia

The platoon leader held his fist in the air. The soldiers stopped and crouched low in the grass with their eyes fixed on the platoon leader. They looked at the carnage in front of them. The platoon leader did not like it. He signaled for his communications specialist to move toward him. Once the communications specialist reached the platoon leader, he handed him the radio headset.

The platoon leader spoke quietly into the headset. "Red Dog leader . . . this is Red Dog . . . do you copy? Red Dog leader . . . this is Red Dog . . . we have a situation here . . . do you read?"

"Red Dog . . . this is Red Dog leader . . . I read. What is your situation?"

"We've reached the fourth target. It looks like someone beat us to it."

"What is the target status, Red Dog . . . copy?"

"Destroyed, sir. There's nothin' left . . . no sign of life . . . from the looks of it, sir, I would guess this had two birds."

"That's not possible, Red Dog . . . We didn't call birds down on that target."

"Well, sir, I could be wrong, but that's what it looks like to me."

"Very well. Hold your position. Make sure that the destruction was complete. After you have confirmed that status, proceed with your mission."

"Roger Red Dog leader . . . Red Dog out."

The platoon leader handed the headset back to the communications specialist. He looked back at the burning rubble in front of them. He picked up his binoculars and looked closer at the scene. As he panned the property, he could plainly see the mutilated bodies of those who had once occupied the residence. He did not see any movement which would indicate that there were any survivors. He turned to his communications specialist and spoke.

"Dammed if I see anyone alive. Whoever did this knew what the fuck they were doing."

The platoon leader was satisfied that the site had been destroyed and that there were no survivors. He raised his arm and was just about to signal the men to begin moving out when his communications specialist spoke.

"Sir?"

The platoon leader turned to look at the communications specialist. He pointed toward the burning rubble. The platoon leader turned toward the target and squinted to try to get a better look. Then he used his binoculars. He panned the area until he found what he was looking for. It was a man. From the looks of him, he had been severely wounded. He had blood all over his clothes, he was limping, and the platoon leader could see something protruding from the man's thigh as he slowly walked through the rubble. He watched the man for a moment. He seemed as though he was in shock as he walked along aimlessly, shaking his head from side to side. Then the man suddenly stopped, looked to the sky and began screaming. The platoon leader signaled to one of his soldiers then turned to watch the man again.

"Those who did this will die! They will die by my hand! Do you hear me? They will die by my hand! I will kill them all . . . I will kill them all slowly . . . They will wish they had never been born when I am through! I am god in Colombia! No one does this to me! I am Alberto Ro—"

Rojas never even heard the shot. The snipers bullet was amazingly accurate. It entered Rojas's mouth before he could finish screaming his name. The bullet exited through the back of Rojas's head and the platoon leader watched through his binoculars as it burst open in the back due to the impact of the shot. Rojas's eyes were wide and his mouth remained open as his lifeless body fell to the ground.

The platoon leader looked back at the sniper who was observing his target through the scope on his long range rifle. The sniper looked toward the platoon leader and smiled; the platoon leader responded with a thumbs-up to the soldier. The platoon leader turned back to the devastation and surveyed the area one last time for any more sign of life. This time he was satisfied. He held up his arm and signaled the men to move out. Their work was finished as far as this target was concerned.

Rojas lay dead on what was left of the veranda in the back of the house. His head lay on its side in a crimson pool, his mouth wide and his eyes open. He was looking over the valley. A valley he had terrorized and ruled over for many years. A valley where many innocent people had been brutally killed by Rojas, or as a result of orders given by him. There was an eerie peace that hung over the valley now. It was very quiet. Not a bird or animal could be heard. Perhaps it was the bombs from the F-15s, or the sniper's gunfire that had silenced them. Or perhaps the jungle knew that there was going to be peace for a while now. There would be peace until another Alberto Rojas came to power in the region.

CHAPTER TWELVE

ARTICLE 44

July 30, 2005, 11:20 a.m.
Valley Road, Medillin, Colombia

Clay was speeding northward on the winding valley road that led into the city of Medillin. He would glance back every few minutes to look at Christine who was still unconscious in the back of the jeep. She was pale and he was concerned that if he did not hurry, he would lose her.

Clay was speeding down an unusually long straight section of the winding road. He looked back at Christine then back to the road in front of him. When he looked ahead, he saw another vehicle moving toward him in the southbound lane. Clay watched anxiously as the vehicle quickly approached then sped by him. It was another jeep and it had four armed men riding in it. When the jeep sped by him he waited a moment then turned to look behind him. His heart sank when he saw that the jeep had slowed and was turning around. They were coming after him. As the other jeep began its turn, one of the guards in the back of the vehicle began firing his weapon in the direction of Clay.

Clay pressed the accelerator down as far as it would go. The straight stretch in the road lasted about one hundred more yards. Clay thought, "Stay calm. Just stay calm and think. There's four of them, all armed, and it's just a matter of time before they get lucky and blow out a tire or wound me. I have to do something or both of us will die."

The straight portion of the road ended just ahead of Clay. As he rounded the bend and slid around the sharp left curve, he applied the brakes. The jeep began to skid sideways then stopped. Clay drove the jeep into the southbound lane then off onto the shoulder. He picked up both machineguns, made sure the safeties were off, cocked the weapons and waited for the armed men to come around the bend.

Clay heard them before he saw them. The men were shouting over the sound of the jeep engine as it rounded the bend. They were not prepared at all for what greeted them as they made their way around the sharp curve in the road. When Clay saw the jeep, he began firing both machine guns. He watched the surprised faces of the men as he fired. Clay peppered the jeep and the men with bullets. The driver was hit immediately; the two in the back were also wounded. The passenger in the front seat started to stand and return fire, but the jeep was out of control at that point. The driver was dead and slumped over the steering wheel, the jeep suddenly jerked hard to the left, and flipped over. The jeep rolled over twice, throwing two of the passengers high into the air. The driver and passenger in the front seat were both crushed by the jeep the first time it flipped over. The four men lay dead in the middle of the valley road.

Clay did not waste any time. He placed the machineguns in the passenger seat and sent dirt flying as he turned the jeep around and sped away. He glanced back at Christine to make sure she was all right. She was still unconscious and bleeding from the wound in her shoulder. Clay had to get her to a hospital. He would take her to Medillin and get her into a hospital.

Steam or smoke was coming out from under the hood of the jeep. Clay did not know which and he did not stop to investigate. He just kept his foot pressed hard on the accelerator. He drove around another sharp left curve and another curve to the right. Then he saw it. Medillin, Colombia was less than two miles straight in front of him. He had made it. Now he had to find a hospital.

He did not slow down as he drove toward the city. There wasn't any traffic in front of him in the north- or southbound lanes. Medillin was situated in a valley surrounded by lush green mountains. A thin layer of smog hung over the city and the skyline, though there wasn't much of one. Clay guessed that the tallest building he could see was perhaps six or seven stories high. As he entered the city, he drove by lean-to houses with corrugated tin roofs where children played in piles of garbage and old tires. Undernourished dogs played with them. Farm animals roamed free among the shacks. He saw cows, donkeys, horses, chickens, and goats, most of which were not in a pen or tied to anything. As he drove farther into the city, the development grew more commercial. First he drove through what he assumed was a kind of farmer's market. Fruit and vegetable stands were abundant. Then he stopped the jeep. To his right sat a white car with a blue stripe down the side. It had two blue lights on top and the word "POLICIA" in bold black print above the blue stripe.

Clay left the jeep running in the middle of the road as he jumped out and ran to the police car. The two officers inside the vehicle were eating what looked to Clay like burritos. Clay crouched down and spoke to the officer that sat behind the steering wheel.

"I need a hospital. I have a girl that has been injured and I need to get her to a hospital. Can you help me, please?"

The officer looked at Clay. The obese man had pieces of food stuck in his mustache and strands of whatever kind of meat that was in the tortilla hanging out of his mouth. He had a look of irritation on his face as he spoke back to Clay.

"Do you not see that I am eating?"

"Look, all I need is directions. Just tell me how to get my friend to a hospital."

"What happened to your friend?"

"She . . . She was shot. We were climbing a mountain in the jungle and we were attacked by some armed men. She's hurt very bad and needs a doctor. Will you help me . . . please?"

The officer looked to his partner and shrugged. Then he took a bite of his burrito and turned back to Clay. A truck carrying crated live chickens pulled up behind Clay's jeep. It sat for a moment then began honking its horn.

"I am not going anywhere until I have finished my lunch. Is that your jeep blocking the road?"

Clay turned to look at the jeep. Then he had an idea. It would either get them to a hospital quickly or it would get them thrown in jail. Either way, Christine would get to see a doctor. Clay turned back and looked at the officer with a very serious look on his face.

"No, it's not my jeep. The friend we are staying with loaned it to us this morning when we left his house. Perhaps you know him? His name is Alberto Rojas."

The guard almost choked on his food when he heard the name. Half chewed food flew out of his mouth and landed on to the steering wheel and windshield in front of him. Both of the officers looked at Clay in a panic. The driver spoke, still with a mouth full of food.

"Rojas? You are friends of Alberto Rojas's?"

"Yes, very good friends."

"Why did you not say so, señor? We will escort you to the hospital. Please . . . Please follow us," the officer said apologetically.

Clay ran back to the jeep as the police car siren began to sound and its lights began to flash. When Clay was in the jeep, the police car pulled away from the curb and drove quickly down the main road. They drove approximately two miles through traffic that included bicycles, motorcycles, automobiles, carts being drawn by horses, mules, and cows. It was an eclectic city, Clay thought, as he followed close behind the police car. The police car did not slow down for anything or anyone in its path. The people and even animals seemed to know this as they moved out of the street upon hearing and seeing the speeding vehicle. The police car made an abrupt left and Clay could see a relatively new modern-looking building straight ahead of them. He followed the police car into the parking lot and pulled up behind it as it came to a stop under a canopy. The officer on the passenger side of the police car jumped out of the car and ran into the hospital. The officer driving the car struggled to shift his weight out of the vehicle. Clay got out of the jeep and attended to Christine. Moments later, two women and three men wearing white jackets came running out of the sliding glass doors from the hospital. They ran to the jeep where Clay was standing holding Christine's hand. Two more white-clad men came out of the hospital with a gurney and went to the jeep as well.

One of the women studied Christine as she lay in the back of the jeep. "What happened to her?"

"She was shot," Clay responded.

"Get her inside. I want her in the trauma room. Now! Move!"

The two men with the gurney lifted Christine out of the jeep gently and laid her on the gurney. They wheeled her into the hospital as the other doctors and nurses followed. Clay started into the hospital as well until the over weight officer spoke to him.

"Señor! Wait!"

Clay stopped abruptly and slowly turned to see what the officer wanted. The large man waddled over to Clay. He was really a repulsive individual, Clay was thinking as the man approached. The food he had been eating was spattered down the front of his shirt, in his mustache, and all over his chin. In addition to his appearance, he smelled as though he had not bathed in quite some time. He moved very close to Clay and spoke quietly to him. Clay tried not to become ill as the man spoke.

"I hope that your friend will be all right, señor."

"I hope so too. Thank you for showing us the way and getting us here."

"It was my pleasure and my duty, señor. You know that my brother works for Alberto Rojas?"

Clay was surprised by this revelation. He attempted not to show the officer that he was uncomfortable by the remark.

"No . . . no, I didn't know that."

"Yes, he has worked for him now almost six years. His name is Tito. Tito Cortez. He is one of the guards in charge. Have you met him?

"Ah . . . yes . . . yes, as a matter of fact, I think I had breakfast with him this morning."

"Excellent, then you have met him. I wonder if you could tell Señor Rojas that I was of assistance to you in your time of need today?"

"Oh yes, I will. I'm sure that Alberto will be very appreciative of your helping us. He will be very pleased with you."

"Do you think he will show me his gratitude?"

"As soon as he finds out it was you, I'm sure you will be hearing from him. And I would imagine that he will show his gratitude as only Alberto can."

"Excellent. Excellent, señor. Thank you, and again I hope that your friend is all right."

"Thanks again for your help," Clay said as he turned and walked into the hospital.

The rotund officer was smiling widely when his partner came out of the hospital. They both walked back to the police car. The smaller officer spoke as they stood at the door of their car.

"The girl, she is in bad shape."

"No matter, my friend. Even if she dies, we helped them get to the hospital. They are friends of Rojas's. He will be very appreciative to both of us. The American said he would tell him what we did. Rojas will be appreciative if the girl lives or dies. Let's go get something to eat. We should celebrate."

The two men got into the police car and drove away from the hospital, unaware that they may have saved the life of one of the Americans Rojas's men had searched the jungle and three cities to find.

ARTICLE 45

July 30, 2005, 12:30 p.m.
Belisario Airport, Medillin, Colombia

The FBI Citation touched down and the reverse thrusters slowed the speeding jet, allowing it to turn off the runway and proceed to the terminal. Brian picked up the phone and dialed as the plane made its turn toward the terminal.

"Director Hart's office, how may I help you?"

"Director Hart, please, this is Brian Whitfield."

"Yes, Mr. Whitfield, one moment, please."

Brian waited for Steve to answer. He watched out of his window as the plane approached the small terminal building.

"Brian?"

"Yeah, I just touched down in Medillin. Have you heard anything?"

"Just a call. He wants you to go to the El Presidente hotel. Rekcah has a reservation there."

"A reservation?"

"That's what he said. When you get to the hotel, call the operator and ask for Rekcah's room. If they haven't checked in yet. Wait in the lobby. If you are not met in the lobby within fifteen minutes after you make the call, go to the front desk and check in as Reckah. Then go to the room and wait. Raven will call you. Got it?"

"Yeah, I got it. He didn't say anything else?"

"No, that's it. Be careful, Brian. These guys don't give a shit what credentials you hide behind. They'll kill you if you give them reason, and they won't think twice about it."

"I know, Steve. I'll watch my back. Do you have the number to the hotel?"

"Not on my desk, but I'll get it. I'll call if anything changes."

"Good. Thanks again."

"Just get your ass back here and buy me that beer, buddy."

"You got it."

Brian hung up the phone and the jet came to a stop at one end of the terminal building. Brian gathered his things, checked to make sure that he had his gun then walked toward the front of the cabin. He knocked on the cockpit door and the copilot opened the door from the inside.

"Listen, I want to get the hell out of here today. I don't know how long I'll be in the city, but I want you guys to stay with the plane and be ready to go. I mean you have to be ready immediately when I get back to the plane."

"We'll be ready, sir. We'll have the plane fueled and pointed toward the States when you get back."

"Thanks, Captain," Brian said as he backed away from the cockpit door.

Brian stood now at the cabin door. He watched and listened as the hydraulic steps lowered to the ground. When he could see the steps had reached the ground, he opened the door. The hot humid tropical air flooded inside the air-conditioned cabin. Brian felt perspiration pop out of his body immediately. The heat was horrific. He exited the plane, walked down the steps and stood on the tarmac for a moment to survey his surroundings. It was a small airport with just a single runway. The terminal building looked as if it had been constructed in the fifties and was in need of repair. As Brian looked toward the terminal building, he saw two men approaching him. They both had caps on, wore white shirts and blue pants, and had silver badges which reflected in the bright sunlight. Brian walked in the direction of the two men he assumed were customs officials.

"Passport, señor?" one of the men asked.

Brian reached into his inside jacket pocket and pulled out his passport along with his FBI credentials. Upon seeing the FBI identification, the two customs officers looked at one another.

"What is the purpose of your visit, Señor Whitfield?"

"It's a government matter," Brian said coldly.

"A government matter?"

"Yes."

"Why were we not informed that you were coming if it was a government matter, Señor Whitfield?"

"Probably because it is . . . a government matter," Brian snapped.

The officers looked at one another. They found it difficult to argue with the logic of Brian's response. One of the officers stamped Brian's passport and handed his credentials back to him.

"Please give me your attaché case."

"I'm afraid I can't do that."

"I must insist, Señor Whitfield. It is policy that all luggage brought into the country be searched."

"Tell you what, let's go inside the terminal. I'll get either the defense minister or the president of Colombia on the phone and you can explain to them why I'm going to be late to my meeting this afternoon. Which one of you wants to talk to one of them?"

The officers looked at one another. Neither of them wanted to be responsible for anything that had to do with government business. They both knew better. They looked back at Brian who stood in front of them, perspiring, and with a very serious and angry look on his face.

"Please proceed, Señor Whitfield. Have a pleasant stay in our country."

"Thanks," Brian said as he walked away from the officers.

Brian walked quickly into the terminal, down the single corridor where the gates were located and out the front of the building. He stood in the sweltering heat and looked around for a cab that could take him into the city. Out of nowhere a beat up purple Plymouth duster pulled up to the curb where Brian stood. Spanish music was thundering out of the car. The interior was bright multicolored shades of blue, orange, yellow, and green. Dice hung from the rearview mirror and small puffy balls bordered the windshield and rear window.

The driver leaned toward the passenger side window and spoke to Brian. "Transportation, señor? Reliable transportation?" he yelled over the music.

Brian studied the driver and then the outrageous vehicle. He shook his head then spoke back to the driver. "El Presidente hotel, do you know where it is?" Brian asked.

"Ah . . . *si*, señor, it is like my second home. A very nice place. I will take you there."

Brian reluctantly got into the backseat of the vehicle. The volume of the music was still as high as Brian thought it could possibly go, and as they drove away from the airport, he shouted at the driver. "Can you turn the music down?"

"What? I'm sorry, señor, what did you say?"

"I said turn the music down!" Brian shouted.

The driver reached for the knob on the radio and turned the volume down. Brian sat back in the seat and sighed in relief. The driver looked at Brian in his ornately decorated rear view mirror and spoke to him.

"How long will you be in Colombia, señor?"

"Not long."

"That is a shame. The fiesta will begin next week. It is a very big party. You will miss it?"

"I hope so," Brian said.

The driver frowned at Brian's response. He reached back to the radio and turned up the volume again. He looked in his rearview mirror and saw that Brian was looking back at him with an angry glare. The driver smiled and defiantly nodded once, letting Brian know who owned the car he was riding in.

The drive to the El Presidente took about twenty minutes. Brian got out of the cab and walked to the driver's side window. The driver was dancing in his seat as he listened to his music.

Brian shouted at him. "How much?"

"Thirty dollars . . . American," the driver said with a smile.

Brian stood and looked at the driver in shock over the amount he had quoted. He thought about protesting the fare then decided it was worth the price not to have to hear the man or his music any longer. He reached into his pocket and pulled out a folded wad of green bills. He counted out thirty dollars and handed it to the driver.

"I don't need a receipt," Brian said sarcastically as he handed the man the money.

The driver smiled as he took the money and continued to dance around. Brian gave him a look of disgust then turned and went into the hotel. Brian was surprised to see that the lobby of the hotel was plush, almost elegant. It was decorated in dark woods, red carpeting, and had two very large and very beautiful chandeliers hanging from the ceiling. The check-in desk was a dark hardwood bordered in brass; and the large winding staircase leading to the upper floors was the centerpiece in the lobby. Brian surveyed the lobby and spotted a bank of phones toward his right on the far wall. He walked through the lobby and picked up the receiver on one of the generic-looking telephones.

"Operator."

"Yes, Operator, could you connect me to a Miss Rekcah's room, please?"

"Uno momento."

"Thank you."

"I am sorry, señor, Miss Rekcah has not checked in to the hotel. Would you like to leave her a message?"

"No . . . no, thank you."

Brian hung up the phone and looked around the lobby. There were many people milling about. He looked for any sign that one of them may attempt to get his attention. When no one did, he looked at his watch and saw that it was one-twenty. He looked around the lobby once again. He remembered his instructions. Steve told him to attempt to call the room first then, if no one was in, he was to wait fifteen minutes. If no one approached him, he was to check into the hotel under the name of Rekcah. He went over the instructions again in his mind then walked to an empty chair in the lobby. He studied the people around him one last time before sitting down. Now he watched the door. He would watch the door for fifteen minutes; if nothing happened and no one approached him, he would check into the hotel. He sat in the chair hoping that all of this was going to end the way it should. At any moment, Raven would walk through the door with Christine Hendrix by his side. They would load up immediately and go to the airport where the plane would take them back safely to the United States. Then he sighed. He remembered where he was and he knew that Colombia was not known for happy endings in situations like this.

ARTICLE 46

July 30, 2005, 1:25 p.m.
St. Mary's Hospital, Medillin, Colombia

The doctors had worked feverishly on Christine in the trauma room for over an hour. Their first priority was to stabilize her. She had lost a large quantity of blood. They were successful in stopping the bleeding from the shoulder wound. After they had determined her blood type, they immediately began a transfusion. Her head wound was not severe. The bullet had only grazed her, but the impact of the projectile had been enough to render her unconscious. Clay stood outside the room and watched the doctors and nurses work on the woman he loved. One of the doctors stepped away from the table and removed her rubber surgical gloves. She looked at Christine for a few moments then turned to the door where Clay was standing just outside. He watched her anxiously through the window in the door as she walked toward him. The doctor walked out of the trauma room and pulled off the mask which covered her mouth down below her chin. Her smock and shoes were covered with Christine's blood and her face reflected concern as she spoke to Clay.

"We stopped the bleeding for now. She's lost a great deal of blood. The wound to her shoulder is a bad one, although it was a clean wound. The bullet passed through without damaging any vital organs. She was lucky in that sense. I am going to keep her here until we are sure she is stabilized then we will take her into surgery and repair the damage to the shoulder. The head wound was superficial; however, we will x-ray to make sure there is no hemorrhaging internally."

"So will she be all right?" Clay asked nervously.

"She is critical right now, but as I said, she is stable. I think she will be all right. We just need to keep her calm and resting until surgery. She is awake if you would like to speak with her. Stay only a minute or two, though. She must rest."

"Thank you, Doctor. Thank you for helping her."

"It was you who saved her. If she hadn't arrived when she did, it would have been too late to do anything for her."

The doctor walked away and Clay looked through the glass in the door. He watched the nurses clean up around Christine's bed. He walked through the door slowly and went to her side. She was starting to get her color back and smiled when she saw him standing over her. Christine raised her hand slowly for Clay to hold. He grasped her hand and looked at her as tears filled his eyes. They did not speak to each other for several moments.

Then Clay swallowed and began the conversation. "I'd ask you how you feel, but I'm afraid I'd get slapped."

"I feel like I've been run over by a truck."

"The doctor says you're gonna be okay if you rest."

"Yeah . . . she told me. She also said I was lucky."

"Lucky?"

"Lucky to have you. She said that if I hadn't made it to the hospital when I did, I wouldn't have made it. How'd you get me here?"

"I know how to read maps and I stopped to ask directions. I'm not the stereotypical male, you know?"

"That's for sure," Christine said as she grimaced in pain.

"You want me to call someone?"

"No . . . no, it goes away. It's a pain in my shoulder. It goes away after a minute."

"Well, they're going to take care of that after you are stable. God, you look so much better already."

"You don't. You look like shit."

"Thanks," Clay said smiling.

"You really look tired. You should get some sleep. You're no good to me half awake."

"I'll take a nap when they take you into surgery. Now, you had better rest and get ready for that now. I'll be right outside the door if you need me."

"Clay . . . thank you. Thank you for saving my life. You really are my knight it shinning armor," Christine said as a tear fell from her eye and rolled down the side of her cheek.

"Hey, let's get something straight. I didn't do it for you. I'm a very selfish person and I want to spend the rest of my life with you. I did it for me. And now you're stuck with me."

"I like that. I like being stuck with you."

"Good, cause you don't have a choice. Now you rest."

Clay watched her as she smiled and closed her eyes. He squeezed her hand once firmly before placing it gently back down on the bed. He turned from her and walked out of the trauma room into the hall. Once he was in the hallway, he leaned against the wall, put his head in his hands and broke down crying. The events of the past two days hit him all at once, and emotionally he couldn't handle it. He'd been kidnapped, beaten, humiliated, and had feared for his life. He'd watched as the woman he loved was abused and nearly killed. He had killed five human beings with his own hands. He let the flow of emotions out all at once. He was glad they were alive. He was relieved it was over. He didn't know how wrong he was.

ARTICLE 47

The jeep drove slowly down the road as the five armed men scanned the store fronts and people around them. They had been on their way in from the jungle when they came across the remains of their fellow guards lying in the middle of the valley road four miles back. When they saw that all of them had been killed, they drove directly to the city in search of their prey. Tito Cortez sat in the passenger seat in front of the jeep. He held his machinegun in his lap and scanned the area for the Americans. He wasn't looking ahead when he heard the horn the first time. He heard the horn again, only this time, someone was calling his name. He looked in front of the vehicle and saw his large brother standing next to his police car. Tito signaled the driver to proceed over to him.

As they drew close to the police car, the large man greeted Tito loudly. "Tito! My brother, how are you this fine day?"

"I am fine. We are looking—"

"I have some good news for you, Tito! Alberto Rojas will be very proud and grateful to both of us! I took his American friends to the hospital."

"What!"

"Yes! They drove into town and I saw that the girl was injured. I was of course very concerned and asked if we could help them. I escorted them to the hospital. I even used the lights and the siren on the way! Are you not proud of me, my brother?"

"You fool! To the hospital! Go! Go!" Tito ordered his driver.

The large man stood in the street as he watched the jeep speed away in the direction of the hospital. He had a look of confusion on his face as he turned to his partner and spoke. "What did I say?"

The jeep full of armed Rojas guards sped to the hospital. Tito looked angry and determined as the vehicle drew nearer to their targets. When they rounded the corner and could see the hospital in front of them, Tito spoke. "Stop here!"

The driver obeyed and brought the jeep to a stop at the curb. Tito studied the hospital for a moment.

"We will watch for a moment," Tito snapped.

"How are we supposed to get them out, Tito?" the driver asked.

"Let's just go in and start shooting. We will find them," one of the guards in the backseat suggested.

"All of you, shut up. Let me think. If there is a way to get them out without causing a disturbance, then I will think of it."

He was planning the assault in his mind. They had to have a way to get the Americans out without causing panic in the hospital. He wanted to go in, get them out and leave the premises without anyone knowing that he was ever there. A smile slowly appeared on his face as he watched an ambulance pass by the jeep and drive up to the hospital emergency room entrance. The drivers got out and opened the back doors of the vehicle then walked slowly into the building. They weren't delivering an emergency patient to the hospital they were there to pick someone up. As it happened, so was Tito Cortez.

ARTICLE 48

Brian walked down the long dimly lit hallway to room 367. He had waited for fifteen minutes in accordance with the instructions he had been given by Steve Hart, then he checked into the hotel. He had given the desk clerk the name Rekcah upon check-in, paid for one night in cash and walked up three flights of steps to the third floor. He inserted the key and went inside the room. He looked to his right as he entered the room and flipped the light switch. It was a nice room by any standards. It was spacious, decorated tastefully, and was furnished with a king-sized bed, couch, coffee table, a small round table with four chairs in one corner, and a bureau for storing clothes. Brian placed his briefcase on the bed and removed his sport coat. His shirt evidenced the heat of the day as it was covered with dark perspiration stains. He tossed his coat on the bed, loosened his tie and unbuttoned the top button of his shirt. Once he was comfortable, he opened his briefcase and looked through the files. He was searching for the file on Peterson when the telephone rang. Brian dropped the files he was holding back into his briefcase and dashed to the phone. Before it could ring a second time, he answered it.

"Hello?"

"Mr. Rekcah?"

"Who is this?"

"Raven, Mr. Rekcah."

"Where the hell are you?"

"Settle down, Mr. Rekcah. Everything is under control for now. I've located your missing agent."

"Where? Is she all right?"

"Let's just say she's alive. I don't know how she got away from Rojas alive, but she did."

"Where is she?"

"I am where she is and you can't help me here. If you want to get her out of Colombia alive, you do exactly what I tell you."

"I'm listening."

"You leave the hotel now. You go directly to the airport. Tell customs that you have a patient en route from the hospital, and do whatever you have to do to get us clearance. Get the plane ready for take off. If I'm not at the airport by 3:15, assume that I'm dead, which means your agent is dead also."

"How will I know when you arrive at the airport?"

"You just be on the plane and ready to leave. You'll know when I arrive."

"Okay, I'm leaving the hotel right now."

"I'll see you at the airport, Mr. Rekcah."

The phone went dead at the other end. Brian sat a moment and thought about what he would do when he reached the airport. He knew that the plane would be ready, but he did not know what he would say to customs. He'd already made enemies of them when he arrived. Brian thought about what he would tell them. What could he say that would allow Hendrix access to the plane without benefit of a passport and possibly with no identification? Then he had a thought. He needed Steve Hart for one last favor. If he would agree, Brian thought he had the answer to his problem. He gathered up his belongings, put the files back into the briefcase, put his jacket on and left the room. Brian ran down the three flights of stair to the lobby then walked quickly to the hotel front exit. He looked for a cab and then heard some familiar music. Brian closed his eyes and turned his head in the direction of the music. When he looked, he saw a familiar purple vehicle and a driver bouncing around in the front seat waving at him.

ARTICLE 49

July 30, 2005, 2:35 p.m.
St. Mary's Hospital, Medillin, Colombia

The nurses had left the trauma room and Clay sat in a chair next to Christine's bed. She was resting quietly. The doctor had examined her x-rays and found that she did not have a hemorrhage. They had given her a sedative so that she would continue to rest soundly until they took her to surgery. Clay's head rested on the chair. He too was sound asleep. He was startled by two orderlies who entered the room abruptly. Clay sat up and tried to focus his tired eyes on the men. The two men seemed a bit nervous as they surveyed the room after they entered.

"Is everything all right? Is it time for her to go to surgery?"

The men didn't answer. Instead, one of them walked quickly to Clay, pulled a knife from under his white jacket and jammed it against Clay's throat.

"Yes . . . it is time for surgery and I am the surgeon. I will split you like a pig if you do anything foolish. Do you understand me, American?"

Clay's eyes were wide and blood appeared on his neck where the blade was cutting through the first layer of skin. He nodded in response to the man's question.

"What do you think, Edwardo, should I let him live or kill him now and tell Rojas that he was too much trouble?"

"Kill him now, Tito. It is one less we have to worry about. Go ahead and kill him now!"

Tito looked at Clay. Tears were forming in Clay's eyes. Finally, as if to give in to his fate, Clay closed his eyes and waited for the blade to open his throat. Tito grabbed the hair on the back of Clay's head and jerked it back. He glared at the terrified victim.

"Good bye, American pig!"

Clay heard two muffled sounds and grimaced. He felt a warmth on his face and Tito had loosened his grip on the back of his head. When Clay did not feel the blade at his throat any longer, he opened his eyes. It was difficult to see, there was some kind of liquid all over his face and now in his eyes. Clay wiped his eyes with his arms, and when he could finally see, he could tell that he was covered with blood. He saw the man who had been holding the knife at his throat lying at his feet. The front of his face had been blown away. Clay looked toward the door and saw a man he had never seen before. He was holding a handgun and it was pointed now at Clay. The other orderly lay on the floor at the strangers' feet, his body quivering and his head partially blown away as well.

"Who are you?" the man asked.

"Clay Peterson."

"Tell me why I shouldn't kill you too, Clay Peterson."

"Look, I don't give a shit anymore what happens to me, just don't kill Christine. Kill me, but don't kill her."

"You want to help get her out of here alive?"

"I'll do anything."

"Then let's move."

The stranger closed the blinds on the door, put his gun away and grabbed two white jackets off the wall rack. He put one on and lay the other on the gurney next to Christine. Clay was wiping the blood from his face and arms with a sheet he had taken from a shelf in the room. When he was finished cleaning up, he turned and spoke to the stranger. "What do you want me to do?"

"Put that jacket on."

"How are we going to get her out?" Clay said as he walked to the bed and put the jacket on as the man ordered.

"The same way she came in. Right through the front door."

Clay watched as the man took the IV bags of blood and medication that were stabilizing Christine off their stands and arranged them neatly next to her.

"I have to ask you something," Clay said.

"What?"

"Do you work for Rojas?"

"Shit no, son. Now do you want to get this girl back to the States in one piece?"

"Yes."

"All right then. Shut the fuck up and listen," the stranger said as he reached into his pants pocket and pulled out a set of car keys. "These keys belong to the red Jeep Cherokee parked out in front of the hospital next to the ambulance. We're going to walk through the hospital with her on this gurney and put her in the back of the ambulance. I'll get into the ambulance and drive, you get into the Cherokee and drive. But before you go, you have to let the friends of these guys know who you are and that you are escaping."

"How do I do that?"

"They're sitting out front in a Jeep waiting for these two to come out. They are far enough away that I don't think they'll be able to tell we're not them right away. After we get her in the ambulance, you walk around to the side and wait a few seconds until I get behind the wheel. Take off the jacket and run to the Cherokee. Do whatever you have to do to get their attention. Then you take off. Hopefully, they'll follow you, and I can get her to the airport."

"And how do I get to the airport?"

"You're on your own, boss. I can't help you there. My priority is this girl. I don't give a shit what happens to you.

Don't mean to be an ass about it but that's how things are. Now are you ready?"

Clay took a deep breath and looked at the stranger. He did not have an option. He knew it was the only way to get her out of there and the bodies on the floor were evidence enough for Clay that as long as she was in Colombia, she wouldn't be safe. He moved toward Christine who was sleeping and oblivious to everything that was going on around her. Clay bent over and gave her a gentle kiss on the forehead. He stood back up straight and looked at the stranger.

"I'm ready," Clay said reluctantly.

"Then let's do it."

The two of them took their positions on either end of the gurney. Clay nodded at the stranger, reassuring him that he was ready to go and knew what he was supposed to do. The stranger stood at the foot of the bed and opened the door behind him. They rolled the gurney out of the room. Clay grabbed the doorknob on his way past and closed the door behind him. As he did, he glanced at the gruesome sight of the two men lying in large pools of blood in the floor. Then Clay noticed that the man lying closest to the door had a handgun sticking out of the back of his pants. Clay quickly knelt down, took the gun and put it behind him in his pants under his jacket. The stranger gave Clay an irritated look.

They walked down the corridor of the hospital rolling the gurney along with them. They were only a few feet from the door now and Clay could see the back of the ambulance. The back doors of the ambulance were open. Clay looked beyond the ambulance and could see a dark green Jeep parked off the hospital grounds. He could see three men in the Jeep and could tell that they were watching the front of the hospital intently.

As the stranger backed onto the floor pad that triggered the glass doors to open, Clay's heart jumped as he heard the piercing scream of a woman behind him. He started to turn his head, but the stranger jerked the gurney and Clay with it.

"Don't turn around, let's get her in the ambulance!" he shouted at Clay.

Clay obeyed, and they moved out the doors and to the back of the ambulance with the gurney. Clay glanced to his left and could see that two of the men in the Jeep were standing watching them. The stranger folded the front legs of the gurney under and set the head of the bed inside the ambulance. He moved quickly to the rear of the bed and helped Clay fold the back legs under. Then they both pushed the gurney into the ambulance. The stranger closed the back doors and went to the driver's side of the vehicle. Clay went to the passenger side and took his jacket off. He stood for a few seconds as he had been instructed. Then he heard the hospital door open again. A security guard exited the hospital, and upon seeing Clay, reached for his holstered gun. Clay quickly took the gun out from behind his back and fired over the guard's head. The guard ducked and retreated back inside the hospital.

"Go! Go! Go!" the stranger shouted.

Clay ran out in front of the ambulance and toward the Jeep Cherokee. He glanced again toward the direction of the green Jeep and saw that it was now moving slowly toward the hospital. Clay got into the Cherokee and started the engine. Then he got out of the vehicle and pointed the gun toward the three men and the Jeep. He fired three rounds, missing them each time. The stranger in the ambulance shook his head from side to side as he watched Clay. Clay jumped back into the Cherokee and sped away. The men in the Jeep paused for a moment. The driver looked at the hospital where the ambulance was still sitting then looked back at the Cherokee as it sped away. The stranger put his arm out the window of the ambulance and signaled the men in the Jeep to follow the Cherokee. The driver assumed that it was Tito signaling to them and he squealed the tires of his vehicle as he drove after the Cherokee. When the stranger saw that the men in the Jeep had committed to the Cherokee, he drove the ambulance slowly and calmly away from the hospital. Christine Hendrix lay in the back, still sleeping soundly. She would awaken later not knowing how she had gotten out of the hospital, or anything about the bravery that Clay Peterson and the man known only as Raven had displayed in getting her safely away.

ARTICLE 50

July 30, 2005, 3:10 p.m.
Belisario Airport, Medillin, Colombia

Special-Agent-in-Charge Brian Whitfield paced nervously in the customs office. The two officers watched him as he walked back and forth in front of them. He looked at his watch and grew concerned about the late hour. He looked anxiously at the phone and hoped it would ring in time. Brian walked to the office window and looked at the Citation that was fueled and ready for departure. He stared at the fenced guarded gate which blocked outside access onto the tarmac. His pulse was racing and his stomach was churning. So much needed to go right in the next few minutes and there was so much that could go wrong. Both the odds and time were working against him in this situation. His thoughts were interrupted by the sound of the telephone ringing. Brian jerked his head around and looked at the telephone on the officer's desk. It rang again and the officer just sat there watching Brian. Brian clinched his teeth in an effort to control his temper. He was screaming in his mind, "Answer the phone, you pompous little fucker!"

The phone rang yet again and Brian this time moved toward the desk. The officer sat up in his chair quickly and slowly reached for the head set. He calmly placed the phone to his ear and smiled at Brian as he spoke. "Customs, this is Pedro," he said as he continued to look at Brian smugly.

Pedro listened for a moment and then his smug look disappeared. Pedro stood abruptly from his chair. He was suddenly standing at attention and saluting as he spoke. Brian watched the officer and his comical antics as he spoke.

"Yes, El Presidente . . . I will see to it myself, El Presidente . . . Yes . . . Yes, El Presidente it will be done . . . Yes, El Presidente . . . he is right here," the officer said as he handed the phone to Brian with a look of panic on his face.

"Brian Whitfield here."

Pedro and the other officer watched Brian intently as he spoke to the president of Colombia on the other end of the line. They were now sorry that they had ever given this American a hard time. They should have known better.

"Is he shittin' in his pants?" Steve Hart asked.

"Yes, El Presidente, and I thank you for taking time to call and straighten this thing out," Brian responded.

"I think I scared the poor bastard to death," Steve said laughing.

"I agree, El Presidente, and I will inform you personally if I do not receive cooperation from them. Yes, El Presidente, I believe his name is Pedro."

"Man, you're bad, do you want me to talk to him again?" Steve asked.

"No, El Presidente, I don't think that will be necessary."

"Very well then, carry on, Agent Whitfield. I have urgent business that requires my immediate attention. Get your ass out of there now!"

"I will, sir, and thank you again," Brian concluded.

Brian looked sternly at the officers. They were visibly shaken and disturbed by the fact that the president himself had to call. Brian spoke to them sternly, "Am I going to have any more trouble out of either one of you?"

Both of the officers shook their heads no.

"Good. Then when this patient arrives at the airport, I don't want any further delays. She is very ill and I want her on that plane and out of here no less than five minutes after she gets here. Do I make myself clear, gentlemen?"

"Yes . . . Yes, Señor Whitfield. We will do everything we can to make sure that she is on the plane and gone quickly," Pedro responded.

Brian was about to continue his scolding when he heard the siren of an ambulance. He dashed to the window and saw the ambulance parked outside the fence. He looked back at the two officers and shouted. "Open the goddamn gate! She's here, now go open the gate and let her in!"

The officers jumped at Brian's command. They both rushed out of the door and ran to the gate. They instructed the guards to open the gate and allow the ambulance to enter onto the tarmac. The guards did as they were instructed. One of them unlocked the primitive padlock on the gate and the other opened it, allowing the ambulance to drive on to the tarmac and out to the waiting jet. Brian ran from the customs office to the steps of the plane as the ambulance drove up. He looked back and saw the two customs officers walking quickly to the plane. Brian yelled at them. "I am through with you! We don't need your help!"

The officers stopped and turned back toward their office. They walked slowly and dejectedly back inside the building where they watched the ambulance pull up to the plane and the ambulance driver exit the emergency vehicle. Brian stood at the nose of the plane and yelled at the pilot who had his side window open. "I want immediate clearance for take off. Tell the tower that we want to take off as soon as we have her on the plane!"

As the jet engines started and began to roar, Brian ran to the back of the ambulance where the driver was opening the doors. When he reached him, Brian extended his hand. "Mr. Raven I presume?"

"Yes, and you must be Mr. Rekcah. We'll shake hands once she's on the plane. Help me get her out."

Both of the men pulled the back of the gurney out of the ambulance. Raven let the back legs down and locked them in place. They then pulled the front end of the gurney out and Raven let the front legs down and locked them into place. Brian looked at his wounded agent. She was still sleeping.

"Is she all right?"

"She was alive when we left the hospital. I think they gave her a sedative. You just need to get her on that plane and out of here now!" Raven yelled

They rolled the gurney to the steps leading into the airplane, and stopped there.

"We'll have to carry her on!" Brian yelled above the noise of the jet engines.

"I'll carry her, you get the IVs!" Raven yelled back.

Brian nodded, signaling to Raven that he understood. Raven gently picked Christine up in his arms and held her for a moment while Brian tried to handle all of the IVs without getting them tangled up. When Brian signaled that he was ready, Raven began walking up the steps backward with Christine in his arms. He walked slowly and carefully so as not to pull away from Brian who held the IVs. He took his time with the fragile girl and admired her as he made his way to the top of the stairs. He had been very gentle with her and he hoped that she would be all right. That was an unusual thought for Raven to have. He was in the killing business, he was used to death. But somehow he felt differently about the young woman he held in his arms.

Raven had to prop her back up as he entered the airplane cabin door. Christine moaned in pain although she did not awaken as they entered the cabin. Raven continued to walk backward until he reached the leather couch in the back of the cabin. He waited for Brian to ready the IVs, and then gently laid her down. He slid his arms out from under her body and stood over her for a moment. Brian laid the two IVs on the back of the couch above her head. Then he stood and faced Raven.

"We couldn't have done this without you. I can't really tell you how much I appreciate it and how thankful the bureau is for your help."

"Hey, Mr. Rekcah . . . it's what I do," Raven smiled as he took Brian's extended hand.

"Whitfield," Brian said.

"What?"

"The name . . . it's Brian Whitfield."

Raven nodded at Brian and smiled.

"Raven . . . Mr. Whitfield. Nice to meet you. Now you guys better get the hell outta here. I'm gonna split myself. Look kinda conspicuous driving around town in that meat wagon. Gotta dump it and get a good ride," Raven said as he walked back to the front of the plane.

"Thanks again. Christine thanks you too," Brian said as they reached the cabin door.

"All I did was get her out of the hospital, man. The guy that was with her saved her life. I don't know how they got away from Rojas and out of the jungle, but that guy saved her ass."

"Peterson," Brian said to himself.

"What?"

"What happened to him, where is he?"

"Don't know. He used a Cherokee I stole to decoy Rojas's people at the hospital. He drove off, they followed him. I told him I was coming here. Guess they got him."

"He acted as a decoy so you could get Christine away from the hospital?"

"Yeah—"

Raven was about to respond to Brian when he looked out the cabin door toward the gate leading onto the tarmac. There was a green Jeep with three armed men. They were arguing with the gate guards.

"Give me your gun."

"What? You can't go down there by yourself, man."

"Just give me your fucking gun and get this plane off the ground."

Brian didn't argue with the man. There was a look on his face he had never seen before. He reached into his holster and pulled out his gun. He handed it to Raven. Raven admired the gun.

"Nice piece. I shoulda been a feebee. See ya on the flip side, Brian!" he said with a cocky smile.

Raven ran down the steps of the plane and crouched down in front of the ambulance where the men in the Jeep could not see him.

Brian closed the cabin door and pressed the button which activated the airplanes hydraulic steps. He then went to the cockpit door and yelled at the captain. "Move this plane, captain!"

"Sir, the steps aren't up. We can't move until—"

"Fuck the steps, Captain, if you don't move this plane now, we're going to be dodging bullets inside this cabin. Now go!"

The captain obeyed and the plane began moving forward. Brian watched anxiously out the cabin door window. The men in the Jeep saw the plane begin to move and opened fire on the gate guards killing both of them. They drove the Jeep through the gate and onto the tarmac. Then they encountered Raven as their vehicle approached the ambulance. His aim was precise three rounds, three dead. It was just that quick and he was just that deadly. The three men never had a chance. After he had killed the last man, he ran from his position behind the ambulance and caught up with the Jeep which was beginning to steer out of control. He ran beside it for several steps, then reached up with his right hand, grabbed the driver by the hair and pulled him out of the Jeep. His lifeless body hit and rolled several times on the tarmac. Raven then jumped in behind the wheel of the moving vehicle and took control of it. He turned and waved triumphantly at the

FBI plane as it continued toward the take-off runway. Raven turned the vehicle toward the exit gate and sped away in his new ride. Brian shook his head in disbelief at what he had just witnessed the man do. He had read about men like Raven, but he had never witnessed one of them in action.

Brian left the cabin door window and walked back to Christine. She was still sleeping peacefully. He looked at her wounds and her face. She looked very comfortable, almost at peace as she lay there. Brian sat on the floor next to her. He reached up and placed his hand upon hers. Brian was exhausted; he hadn't had any sleep himself for the past two days. He lay his head down beside her on the couch and closed his eyes. That is where he would stay during the entire three-and-a-half-hour flight back to Miami International Airport.

CHAPTER THIRTEEN

ARTICLE 51

The Federal Reserve System is the Central Bank of the United States. The Federal Reserve is divided into twelve privately controlled separate central banks located in Atlanta, Boston, Chicago, Cleveland, Dallas, Kansas City, Minneapolis, New York City, Philadelphia, Richmond, St. Louis, and San Francisco. Each bank serves a designated district in the United States. The system was organized this way to diffuse the power of the Central Bank. The First Bank of Boston is a Federal Reserve Bank.

Edward D. Rathsmuson III was preparing to leave his palatial office after a very long six-hour day at the bank. Edward was the fifty-year-old president of First Bank. He had a tee time at four thirty. Edward was anxious to get to the club early as he had some major concerns about his short game that he wanted to address on the practice tee before the round. He placed a stack of files in his briefcase, surveyed his large mahogany desk to make sure that everything was in its place, and started toward the rear exit door of his office. He stopped when he heard the intercom.

"Mr. Rathsmuson . . . Mr. Rohlfing is here to see you," the secretary screeched.

Edward's shoulders slumped and his head fell forward so that his chin rested on his chest. He turned, irritated by this delay, and walked back to his desk. Delbert Rohlfing was the CFO of First Bank. Edward didn't like Delbert. He was a very bright and very capable man, but Edward never really knew what his agenda was. Delbert had come to First Bank with an extensive and successful corporate background. He was proficient at his job as well as in corporate games and manipulation tactics. Delbert was everybody's friend so long as it served his purpose.

Edward pressed the intercom button and spoke to his secretary with an irritated tone. He did not want to be late for his golf game. "Send him in."

Edward sat back down in his chair and watched the door as Delbert entered. Delbert was not his usual jovial, plastic self as he approached Edward's desk and sat down.

"Edward . . . data processing was posting the wires and something came up that I think you should take a look at. I can't explain it and frankly don't know what to do about it."

"What, Delbert? Get to it, man, I'm late for a meeting," Edward demanded.

"We received a wire transfer this afternoon. The originating bank was Colonial in the British Virgin Islands. The amount of the transfer was staggering."

"Why is that unusual? We have large deposits come in from all over the world. We're a reserve bank for christ's sake. Two-, three-, even ten-million-dollar wires come in all the time."

"I know, Edward, but this one . . . this one is unusual."

"Just let me look at the print out, Delbert," Edward snapped.

Delbert gave the wire print out to Edward. As Edward began reading the transaction report, he sat back in his chair and his mouth fell open.

Transaction Report

Transaction:	Wire Transfer	Originating Bank:	COL-BVI-5436
Receiving Bank:	FBB-BMS-7330	Originating Acct:	458930754

```
                                         458845963
Receiving Acct:    733882975             458737843
                                         458375021
Transfer Amount:  $ 2,783,654,963.00     458883954
```

Special Instructions: Compliments of Agent Christine Hendrix, Federal Bureau of Investigation

Edward read the transaction report three times. He could not believe the amount of money that was reflected on the paper he was looking at. He slowly raised his head and looked at Delbert.

"Have you already verified this with BVI?"

"Twice. They weren't happy about the transfer, but they said it was real."

"Almost $2.8 billion? What is this note all about? Who is Christine Hendrix?"

"I don't know. I didn't do anything but verify the funds with BVI. I thought that you would want to call someone about the instructions."

Edward thought for a moment then pressed the intercom button on his desk so he could speak to his secretary. "Get me Chairman Stephens. Tell him it's urgent if he's in a meeting," Edward ordered.

"You're calling the chairman?"

"Who would you suggest I call, Delbert?"

"I don't know, but I would call the FBI first. Find out about Christine Hendrix and what this is all about."

"I don't want to deal with the FBI, Delbert. I'm calling the chairman of the Federal Reserve. I'm going to tell him that the FBI just wired my bank $2.8 billion. He can deal with Washington if he so chooses. That's what he's good at. Now instead of worrying about who I'm talking to and why, you get your ass down to securities and place those funds. Knowing Washington, my guess is we have about six days until that money is transferred somewhere else. I want to generate as much residual profit as we can from those funds while they're in my bank."

"Yes, sir," Delbert responded quickly.

As Delbert stood and left the room, Edward looked back at the transaction report he held in his hands. He shook his head from side to side and spoke to himself. "Where in the hell would the FBI get $2.8 billion? And why did they send it to my bank?"

ARTICLE 52

July 30, 2005, 4:17 p.m.
Joint Chiefs' war room, Arlington, Virginia

The Pentagon is a five-story five-sided building that is headquarters for the department of defense and of the army, the navy, and the air force. The building sits across the Potomac River from Washington, D.C. The Pentagon consists of five pentagon-shaped buildings that form concentric rings joined by corridors. It has approximately 3,700,000 square feet of office space, its own fire department, police force, radio and television station, and phone exchange. The building also serves as the base of operation when the Department of Defense or one of the armed forces is involved in any type of strategic operation.

The strategic planning room, or "war" room as it was nicknamed by officials, was full. All the Joint Chiefs were there, the secretary of defense, the head of the DEA, and the assistant director of the CIA were also present.

General Robert T. Siegal was addressing the group in an angry tone. "I don't know who is responsible for this thing, Mr. Secretary, but I had men on the ground out there, and they could have all been blown to hell if they had reached that target thirty minutes earlier. Now we have to get this thing coordinated before it becomes one big cluster fuck and we all look like idiots!"

Admiral Theodore Taggert listened to General Siegal intently as did all of those present at the meeting. He was next to speak. "Mr. Secretary, I have spoken with Admiral

341

Franklin on the *Eisenhower*. Now he tells me that he got an ETM from the Pentagon late in the evening on July 29. The executive officer on the *Eisenhower* confirmed the transmission with communications and he presented the orders to Admiral Franklin. The orders were specific: the target was identified with exact coordinates and an INTELSAT visual verification. Admiral Franklin and his men carried out those orders. Now I don't know who gave the orders or who is responsible in this matter. All I know is that Admiral Franklin followed procedure."

Frank Paterson, assistant director of the CIA was next to speak to the secretary. "Mr. Secretary, it has been suggested by some in this room that the agency may have had something to do with this. I would like to go on record as saying that we had nothing to do with this, nor do we have any knowledge of it."

"Isn't that what your agency handbook directs you to say whether you're involved or not?" General Siegal said sarcastically.

"Mr. Secretary, I object to the general's tone and unwarranted attack on the integrity of the agency."

"Integrity, my ass! You guys are looking for things to fuck up because you don't have anything to do now that the cold war is—"

"Gentlemen . . . Gentlemen . . . Please!" the secretary shouted.

The room quieted, and instead of shouting at one another, the general and associate director gave one another dirty looks. The secretary of defense, Bob Talbot, was a man that not everyone in the room always agreed with; however, all of them respected him. He was fair in his decision making, always hearing every side of an issue. Talbot had been secretary since this administration had won the election three years prior. During his tenure, the United States had completed four widely publicized peacekeeping missions in association with the United Nations and five not so widely publicized missions described internally as vital to the security of the United States. In each situation, the United States had been successful in large part due to Secretary Talbot's ability to act as arbitrator between the Department of Defense and the Joint Chiefs.

Secretary Talbot cleared his throat, then stood and addressed the room. "Gentlemen, I believe I may be able to shed some light on this whole situation. What I am about to tell you will no doubt disturb you. It disturbs me. No one outside this room except the president and the National Security Agency knows what I am about to tell you. It is critical to the security of this nation that we keep it that way.

"The Defense Department did not change the *Eisenhower*'s orders, nor did any one of the armed forces, the CIA, or the DEA. We frankly don't know who changed the orders, gentlemen, we only know how they did it and where they were when they perpetrated the act."

"What do you mean they? Who is they, Mr. Secretary?" General Siegal asked.

"I don't know, General, and neither does the NSA. The orders were changed through the SCN or Strategic Communications Network. Someone accessed the communications computer, ordered an air strike on the target, gave the exact GPS coordinates, and the order was sent. Whoever did this did not know that the orders would be sent to the *Eisenhower*. The computer selects the most expedient and effective way to carry out the order based on information given. The *Eisenhower* was in the vicinity of the target, had in fact completed several sorties in Colombia recently, and therefore was the logical choice for the computer to make. The orders were sent, origination was authenticated, and Admiral Franklin did exactly what he should have done. He carried out those orders."

"Are you telling me that someone outside the loop, a group or an individual, accessed the Pentagon's computer system, asked it to blow up a house in Colombia, and the computer did it? Hell they could have asked the computer to nuke Washington!" Admiral Taggert shouted.

"No, they could not program or request a nuclear attack through the Pentagon system. The use of nuclear weapons must have authorization manually keyed into the SAC system. Those authorization codes are under lock and key, gentlemen. We all know who has the combinations to the safes where those codes are kept.

"But the general is correct. Someone outside of the loop did access the computer system and did order the attack on this target," Secretary Talbot concluded.

"Who could have done it?" Admiral Taggert asked.

"We don't know who did it, but we do know from where the orders originated. The NSA traced the security breach to the residence in Colombia. The target, gentlemen."

"You mean the silly bastards blew themselves up?" General Siegal asked.

"It appears so. We don't know who did it, or why it was done. However, there is a bright side to this situation, gentlemen. We know that the security codes that protect outside access into a number of highly confidential computer systems in the government need to be updated and changed. This situation has resulted in that need becoming a priority, not just for this administration, but also for the security and safety of the American people and future generations. The president will call a closed-door emergency session of Congress this afternoon. He will present them with a bill which will enable us to update the current government agency computer security systems immediately. In addition, the bill will call for an annual appropriation of the funds necessary to maintain the highest level of security possible within these systems. They will be changed and updated twice annually from now on.

"Fortunately this incident occurred on foreign soil, and although it resulted in the loss of human lives, it is my understanding in speaking with General Siegal that this residence was supposed to be destroyed anyway. The point being . . . human beings still fly our war planes. Human beings captain our ships and lead our troops into battle. Human beings pull the triggers and press the buttons, gentlemen. The computer does nothing more now than disseminate information that is programmed into it, and then it processes that information. The computer doesn't have what God gave human beings, gentlemen. The computer doesn't have common sense. I would hope that if an order was given to send war planes over an American city, or to fire nonnuclear missiles from one of our destroyers at an American target, that we would all stop. We would all stop and use that gift that God gave us and do the unthinkable. We would question that order."

ARTICLE 53

The National Gallery of Art was conceived, founded, and endowed in 1937 by the collector Andrew W. Mellon. The original neoclassic marble building was designed by the architect, John Russell Pope, and opened to the public in 1941. The collection focuses on the major schools of European and American painting, sculpture, graphic arts, and decorative arts from the twelfth through the twentieth centuries. Cleo Armstrong, curator of the historic gallery, was preparing to leave her office. The gallery had finally made the decision to relocate the portrait of Ginevra dei Benci to a more visible location within the gallery. The portrait had been painted by Leonardo da Vinci in 1475 and is the only painting of his in the Western Hemisphere. Cleo had been fighting for several years with the gallery trustees to relocate the painting. She had finally won the battle.

As Cleo stood from her desk and started to walk toward her open door, a young man entered her office carrying a document. He was one of the office staffers she had recently hired.

"Mrs. Armstrong, I have a fax here that you should probably look at. We all think it's probably a joke, but you never know, do you?" the young man spoke in a very effeminate manner.

"No, you never know. Thank you," Cleo replied.

The young man turned a swayed out of Cleo's office. Cleo's reading glasses were on a gold chain around her neck.

She picked them up and placed them on the end of her nose and began reading the facsimile. There was no heading on the document.

July 30, 2005

To: National Gallery of Art, Washington D.C.
From: A Friend

Please be advised that I have plans to ship my complete collection of original works of art to your Gallery. If I am able, I will have the art delivered to you from Switzerland by the end of August.

The collection is valued at a little over $ 275,000,000.

Thanks.

Cleo read the facsimile with interest until she got to the last line. When she saw the value the sender had placed on the mysterious collection, she chuckled.

"That would be some kind of 'friend,'" she said as she wadded the document up and threw it in the wastebasket on her way out of the door.

CHAPTER FOURTEEN

ARTICLE 54

Brian had the captain radio Miami en route and request medical assistance at the airport when they landed. The doctors had examined Christine and found her to be stable. The doctor told Brian that she would be all right if he elected to take her on to Maryland; however, he strongly recommended that he allow them to take her to the hospital in Miami. Brian left the decision up to Christine. She insisted on going back to Maryland. The physicians replaced the IVs and changed the bandages on her shoulder and head. They gave her some pain medication so that she would be comfortable during the one-hour-and-forty-minute flight to Maryland.

The plane left Miami and flew to Washington National Airport. Brian made sure there was an ambulance waiting for them on the tarmac when they arrived. The paramedics were able to get Christine off the plane on their gurney. They had her in the ambulance and on her way to the hospital within minutes after the jet came to a stop at the executive terminal. Brian rode with Christine to the hospital, and when they arrived, the doctors took her straight into surgery. The surgery lasted two hours as the surgeons had to perform some major reconstructive work on Christine's shoulder. She came out of surgery and they sent her to recovery. Her prognosis was excellent.

Brian had made calls to his wife first to let her know that he was fine. Then he called Steve Hart and thanked him again for his assistance in getting Christine out of Colombia alive. He attempted to call the office and speak to Stafford, but he was out and they did not have a number where he could be reached. Brian just left a message that he had called. When he finished his calls, he went to the waiting room and stayed until the doctor notified him that Christine was out of surgery and in the recovery room. Brian was relieved when the doctor told him that Christine would be all right. He asked the doctor if he could wait in the recovery room with Christine and she agreed. It had been a slow night and she was the only patient in the room. Brian walked in and studied her for a few minutes then sat in a chair next to the hospital bed. Brian was exhausted. He lay his head back, and within a few minutes, he was asleep. Brain was awakened when he heard someone calling his name. He sat up and was disoriented for a moment. He did not know how long he had been sleeping, and initially, he wasn't sure where he was. As his eyes adjusted to the light, he saw the hospital bed in front of him. He stood and approached the bed. He looked at Christine who was now awake and coherent. He held her hand as he spoke to her.

"Hey, lady, you gave me quite a scare."

"I'm sorry. Really, I'm so sorry."

"Don't be sorry, Christine. Don't even think about anything right now except your recovery. That was a pretty bad wound to your shoulder."

"I don't remember getting shot. I was watching the jungle in front of me then the next thing I knew, Clay started firing at something behind us. Then I went blank."

"You had a head wound too. Probably a graze. That's what probably knocked you out. But you're gonna be all right now."

"What about Clay? How is he?"

Brian looked down at the bed and away from Christine. He did not know what to tell her about Clay Peterson. He did not know what happened between them in Dallas or in

Colombia. He continued to look at the bed in the hope that she would forget about the question. He was wrong.

"Is he all right, sir?"

"Christine . . . Peterson didn't make it to the plane in Colombia."

"What do you mean?"

"You were in the hospital in Medillin."

"The hospital?"

"Yes. Apparently Peterson got you out of the jungle where you were wounded, then somehow . . . nobody knows how . . . he got you to Medillin and into the hospital. The guy saved your life."

"So where is he now?"

"I really don't know. There was a man in Medillin that helped get you out of the hospital there. Apparently Rojas found out where you were and his men were outside the hospital. Peterson acted as a decoy, Rojas's men followed him, and our man drove you to the airport. We didn't have time to wait around for him, Christine. Rojas's men showed up at the airport and we had to get out of there. You were my priority. I had to get you out."

"You left him there?"

"I had to. I didn't know if he was alive or dead. I had you on the plane, you were wounded and you were alive, you were my priority. You were the reason I went to Medillin. I didn't go down there to get Peterson."

"I know. But he saved my life more than once when we were down there. And I fell in love with him. I know that's wrong and I know that you could never understand. You'll probably kick me out of the bureau, but it happened . . . I fell in love with Clay Peterson."

Christine turned her head away from Brian and began sobbing quietly. Brian knew that what she was telling him about her feelings toward Peterson was wrong. He knew that he should reprimand her. But he wouldn't, at least not right now. She had been through enough. He squeezed her hand and then let it lie back on the bed beside her. Brian left the side of the bed and walked out of the recovery room. He stood just outside the door and looked at the ceiling as if to ask a higher force what he should do. He looked back down to the floor and walked slowly to the elevator.

Christine lay in her bed, now all by herself in the room. She continued to sob. She didn't care about her job or SAC Brian Whitfield at that moment. All she could think about was the man she had given her heart and body and committed her soul to. There would never be anyone like him in her life again. He was gone, gone forever. And she knew there was no way that such a loss could ever be forgotten or replaced.

ARTICLE 55

July 31, 2005, 8:00 a.m.
Hoover Building, Washington, D.C.

Special Agent Brian Whitfield had just walked into his office when his phone rang. Brian set his briefcase on the floor and walked to his desk to answer the phone.

"Whitfield."

"Agent Whitfield, Associate Director Stafford would like to see you, sir."

"Great. I'll be right down, Margaret, thanks."

"Oh and, Agent Whitfield . . ."

"Yes?"

"The director is in with Mr. Stafford, sir. Just thought you might want to know."

"The director?"

"Yes, sir."

"I guess I've really screwed up this time, Margaret. I'll see you in a few minutes."

Brian hung up the phone and sat at his desk. He took a deep breath and looked around his office. He would miss it. He would miss the excitement of the work and the satisfaction that went along with it. Brian looked at the dozens of plaques that hung on his wall. They were accolades given to him by his superiors—commendations, recognition for achievements he had accomplished during his distinguished career. They would leave with him. The plaques and the memories would be all that he would have.

Brian took another deep breath, stood from his chair, composed himself and walked out of his office. He made up his mind during the walk to Stafford's office that he wasn't going to allow Stafford to belittle him or his career in front of the director. He had done what any other special-agent-in-charge would have or should have done if faced with the same situation. He was proud of what he had done, and he wasn't about to apologize for his actions in the matter.

Brian walked into Stafford's waiting area and confronted Margaret.

"Does he know I'm coming?"

"Yes, sir."

"Shall I wait?"

"Not today, Agent Whitfield. He told me to send you right in when you arrived."

"It's gonna be quite a show, Margaret, wish you could be there to see it," Brian said as he proceeded to Stafford's office.

Brian opened the door and went into the office where Stafford and the Director were waiting for him. Brian had not spent a great deal of time with Director Phelps, but he had heard many people who knew him speak highly of him. He was supposed to be a fair man, with a feel and an understanding for the field. Phelps came from the field, just like Brian. He had been with the bureau almost thirty years. He'd seen a lot of changes; and when he became director, he had made a lot of changes. The bureau was a much better and more efficient arm of the United States law enforcement community largely because of Director Phelps.

When Brian entered the room, Stafford immediately jumped up from his desk and greeted Agent Whitfield. "Brian, how are you? Did you have a difficult trip back?" Stafford said as he extended his hand.

"Huh . . . no, no it was an uneventful trip home," Brian responded, confused by Stafford's jovial demeanor.

Brian took Stafford's extended hand and looked curiously at Director Phelps as both of them started back to Stafford's desk. Director Phelps still stood waiting.

"Good, Good. And how about Agent Hendrix? I trust that she is recovering nicely."

"Yes . . . yes, she is. I called the hospital before I left the house this morning. She's stable and doing well."

As Brian approached the desk, Director Phelps extended his hand to Brian. He looked at him with a broad smile as he spoke. "Agent Whitfield, it is a pleasure to see you again. We are all quite proud of you, as you might imagine."

"Proud of me, sir?" Brian said as he shook the Director's hand.

"Yes, Brian. A stroke of genius, a true stroke of genius," Stafford quickly said.

All of the men sat down at the same time. Brian was totally confused as to what was going on. He had been prepared to tell Stafford and the Director if necessary that they could both go to hell. Now he was receiving praise from both of them. He decided to sit, keep his mouth shut and listen until he understood what was going on.

"I was just explaining to Director Phelps that you and I had been planning this operation for quite some time. Then when Agent Hendrix was abducted, we moved up our schedule. We had to if we were going to get her out of Colombia alive," Stafford continued.

"I am amazed at your tenacity, Agent Whitfield. It was a daring and brave thing you did. I don't know how you got the money out along with Agent Hendrix, but that certainly is quite a bonus to the trip."

Brian looked to Stafford and waited for him to enlighten him. Stafford was watching Brian intently and spoke as soon as he had an opening. "It is a bonus, sir. Obviously our priority was Agent Hendrix, but we took advantage of the situation and got the money out as well—almost three billion dollars.

And a portion of the credit certainly belongs to Agent Whitfield here," Stafford said as he looked at Brian.

Brian nodded and smiled at Stafford. Stafford was smiling back at him because he knew that Brian was in sync. Stafford knew this would do enormous things for his career and he had counted Brian catching on soon after he entered the office.

Brian did catch on, and spoke to Director Phelps. "Three billion dollars. Three billion dollars?" Brian asked as he stood and began walking around Stafford's office.

"What?" Director Phelps asked.

"Brian doesn't like a great deal of praise, Director. I'm sure that he is just embarrassed by the fact that you took the time to come over here and congratulate both of us."

"No . . . Oh no, I like praise, Director Phelps . . . really, I like praise as much as the next guy. It's something that I haven't received much of from this office."

"Brian, I don't think that the director—"

"Let me talk, Stafford! You've obviously been telling the director what you wanted him to hear. Now Director Phelps how would you like to hear the truth?"

"Agent Whitfield! This is outrage—"

"Excuse me . . . Director Stafford, I would like to hear what Agent Whitfield has to say to me. That is, unless you object?"

"Thank you, Director Phelps. I don't know anything about any money. I don't know about three billion dollars. I walked into this office after I found out that I had an agent missing and told Director Stafford that I was going to find her."

"You barged into my office after I specifically instructed you to wait outside."

"That's true. That's very true. And when I did come in I found you standing in the corner with a putter in your hand. Director Phelps, I told Director Stafford that I was going to Dallas to find Agent Hendrix. I told him that she was my responsibility and I wasn't going to sit around here on my ass.

He told me I couldn't go. In fact, Director Phelps, he ordered me not to go. I chose to ignore his orders and I went to Dallas."

"Is this true, Director Stafford? Did Agent Whitfield disobey a direct order?"

Stafford looked reassured. The director was on his side in this matter. Now was the opportunity he had been waiting for. He could bury Whitfield and he could do it in front of the director.

"Yes . . . yes, he did, sir. I wasn't going to report the incident, but that's exactly what happened."

"Please continue, Agent Whitfield."

"As I was leaving Director Stafford's office, he indicated that he would have my job. I think that his exact words were 'I'll have you're job anyway, you stupid black asshole.'"

"You're lying, Whitfield!" Stafford shouted as he stood from his chair and pointed his finger at Brian.

"Sit down, Director Stafford," Director Phelps ordered.

Stafford took his chair and glared at Brian. Brian continued to walk around the office as he continued. "Margaret will verify what I'm telling you, Director, if you choose to ask."

"Don't take an attitude with me, Agent Whitfield," Director Phelps cautioned.

"I'm sorry, sir. After I left and went to Dallas, we received information that Agent Hendrix had been abducted and taken to Colombia. I made a lot of calls, sir. I couldn't get any cooperation. I couldn't get anyone to help me in Colombia. So, I made the decision to go down there myself. I flew to Miami and called Director Stafford when I got there. I told him what I was going to do. Again, he ordered me not to go, and I ignored him."

"Is this true, Director Stafford?" Director Phelps asked.

"Yes," Stafford snapped.

"I left Miami and went to Medillin. I got some help down there from a friend. He got Agent Hendrix out of the hospital and brought her to the airport. He was a brave man and Agent

Hendrix and I both owe him our lives. He killed three men armed with machineguns at the airport in Medillin which enabled us to escape."

"Who was this man?" Director Phelps asked.

"I don't know, sir, he preferred it that way."

"How did you find him?"

"Friends, sir. People who owed me favors."

"That's a pretty big favor, Agent Whitfield," Director Phelps commented.

"Bigger than I thought it would be, sir. Anyway, we got Agent Hendrix on the plane and got the hell out of there. That's exactly what happened. The first I heard about three billion dollars was in this office when I walked in this morning."

"Then how do you explain the wire?"

"The wire, sir?"

"One of the Federal Reserve banks received a wire late yesterday afternoon. The wire amounting to over $2.7 billion. It was wired from five separate accounts in the British Virgin Islands. There was a note on the wire. It said compliments of Agent Christine Hendrix, Federal Bureau of Investigation. How do you explain that, Agent Whitfield?"

"Peterson," Brian said softly as he realized what must have happened.

"Who is Peterson, Agent Whitfield?" Director Phelps asked.

"He's the reason Agent Hendrix was abducted. We were investigating him because he broke the security and entered the computer systems at the Pentagon and the U.S. Treasury. He and Agent Hendrix must have somehow accessed the account information of the cartel while they were holding them down there and wired the money out."

"Where is this Peterson now?" Phelps asked.

"Dead, sir. He did not make it back to the airport in Colombia. We are assuming that he is dead."

"Is that it?"

"That's it, sir. But I'll tell you something while I have the chance. I'm sure that you guys are gonna kick my ass out on the street because I didn't have anything to do with the money. I did what I did because I had a responsibility to my agent. She was in trouble, and I went to get her out. That is my responsibility as SAC. At least that's what I think my responsibility is. Director Stafford doesn't know about commitment to his people. All he cares about is seeing how far he can keep his nose up your ass, Director."

"That's it, Whitfield, your ass is mine now!" Stafford shouted.

"Shut the fuck up, Stafford! My ass is nobody's but mine. That's something you haven't understood since you took this job. I've lost my job now, but I'm going to tell both of you something that I think you should understand. You don't own people, Stafford, and I've seen the effect you're having on the people here and in the field. Morale is down. People feel like pawns, not professionals. You need to start worrying about your people instead of your own ass, Stafford, or you won't have a soul out there that will back you up when you really need it."

"Whitfield, I've heard all I want from you!" Stafford shouted.

"Not yet!" Brian said as he walked to within inches of Stafford.

"Not yet! There's one more thing that you're gonna hear from me. You are an arrogant, ass-kissing, bigoted, paranoid, little prick who has no business sitting in this office. I've got a rookie agent in the hospital who deserves to sit in that chair more than you do. Now do you have anything that you want to say to my black ass before I walk out of this office for the last fucking time, Stafford?" Brian said as he got right in Stafford's face.

Stafford said nothing. He backed away from Brian and sat at his desk. He did not look at Brian, nor did he look at Director Phelps who had remained seated during the exchange.

Brian looked at Stafford and shook his head in disgust as he spoke. "You're one hell of a poor excuse for an FBI agent, much less the associate director of the bureau."

Brian turned away from both of the men and started out of the office. He pulled his identification out of his back pocket and held it in the air as he walked.

"I'll have my resignation on your desk this afternoon, Director Phelps. It's been quite a ride," he said as he reached for the door.

"I'm afraid the ride isn't over, Agent Whitfield," Director Phelps said.

Brian stopped and turned to look at Director Phelps who was standing now, facing him. Stafford was still sitting at his desk looking at Phelps with surprise on his face.

"I don't understand, sir. I don't want to work here anymore. I'm leaving."

"No, Agent Whitfield, you don't like working for Director Stafford here. Isn't that what you mean?"

"Yes, sir, that's exactly what I mean. But you obviously condone the way he runs this place, and—"

"You're wrong, Agent Whitfield, I don't condone anything. I don't condone being lied to. I don't condone treating people unprofessionally and I don't condone racism."

"Whitfield lied about that, sir, he out and out lied—"

"Shut up, Stafford. I got a memorandum from your secretary several days ago. She complained about your treatment of your people and referred to Agent Whitfield specifically. Her version of what happened in this office verifies what Agent Whitfield said here today. No, Agent Whitfield, there is only one resignation I will accept this afternoon, and that is Director Stafford's."

"What? No! This is an outrage! I will not resign! I won't do it!" Stafford shouted.

"That is your option, Director Stafford. I'll fire you if you don't and I'll fire you this afternoon."

"You wouldn't fire me, I've—"

"Yes you have, Stafford. You have served this bureau well. And you'll be recognized for that when you retire. Unless of course you want a very public hearing on the matter. I can certainly arrange that. As a matter of fact, I could arrange to have a congressional investigation of racism within the FBI. They would love that and I would hand you to them on a platter. It's up to you. Now I have a meeting at the White House. I have to explain the money that was wired into the reserve. I would like you to brief me further on that subject, Agent Whitfield. Will you accompany me, please?"

"To the White House, sir?" Brian asked in surprise.

"To the White House, Agent Whitfield," Phelps said with a smile.

"Yes, sir, I'd be happy to accompany you."

Director Phelps walked to the door and stood next to Brian. He winked at him then turned back to a dejected-looking associate director. "I want you out of this office by the time I get back here, Mr. Stafford. If you are not, I will have security escort you out of the building."

Brian opened the door when Director Phelps was finished speaking. They walked out of Stafford's office together. As they passed by Margaret's desk, Brian looked back and winked at her. She smiled at him and watched at they walked down the hall toward the elevator.

CHAPTER FIFTEEN

ARTICLE 56

Fifteen Months Later
October 27, 1996, 7:45 a.m.
Hoover Building, Washington, D.C.

Agent Christine Hendrix arrived to work early as she always did. She walked into her office, set her briefcase on the floor, took off her overcoat, and hung it on the hook behind the door. She went to her desk, sat down and looked at her computer to see if she had E-mail then turned her attention to the files lying on the desk in front of her. Christine had been confined to investigative backup work and research ever since her field injury fifteen months prior. Although she hadn't been disabled by the gunshot wound to her shoulder, she did have the limited ability to lift her arm any higher than her shoulder. Christine did not mind the work she did for the bureau from her Washington desk. Her one field experience was enough to last her entire career as far as she was concerned. Christine was just getting into the file on her desk when her phone rang.

"Christine Hendrix," she answered.

"Agent Hendrix, Associate Director Whitfield would like to see you if you have a minute."

"Sure, I'll be right up."

Christine stood from her desk, closed the file she had been reviewing and walked out of her office. Associate Director Whitfield's office was a floor above hers and she always took the stairs in lieu of standing and waiting for the elevator as many of her peers did. As she walked up the stairs to the fourth floor, Christine thought about Director Whitfield. He had assumed the position of director not long after Christine got out of the hospital where she had been recuperating from her shoulder wound. Director Whitfield had been selected by Director Phelps after the sudden and unexpected resignation of Associate Director Stafford. Director Stafford told the press that personal health and the fact that he wanted to spend more time with his family were the reasons he was choosing to retire from the bureau so suddenly. Christine thought that he must be a very kind and caring man to give up such a prestigious position so he could spend time with his family.

Christine reached the top of the stairs and turned left toward Director Whitfield's door. She walked into the reception area and was greeted by Margaret.

"And how are you today, Agent Hendrix?"

"Fine thanks, Margaret, and how are you?"

"Wonderful. You can go right in, Agent Hendrix."

"Thanks, Margaret."

Christine could see Director Whitfield sitting at his desk. The door to his office was only shut when he was having a SAC staff meeting. Other than those brief meetings, his door was always open to anyone. Brian looked up from the document he was reading as Christine entered his office.

"Christine! Come in. How's everything going in research?"

Christine walked to the desk and sat in one of the two chairs in front of it. Brian took his seat and watched her as she spoke.

"It's going fine, sir."

"Good . . . Good, how's the shoulder?"

"I still go to therapy twice a month; I won't be playing any golf or tennis for a while, but it's getting better."

"Great, that's really good news"

Christine had spent enough time around Director Whitfield to know that he was taking the long way around trying to get to the subject of their meeting. She could see that he was uncomfortable and decided to press the issue.

"Is everything all right, sir? Have I done something wrong?"

"Oh no, no it's nothing like that, Christine, really. It's just that I have something to discuss with you and I know that it will bring back some very painful memories for you."

"Colombia?"

"No, not Colombia. It's about Clay Peterson."

"What? What about Clay? Is he alive?" Christine asked excitedly as she moved to the edge of her chair.

"No, Christine, he's not."

Christine sank back down in her chair, and looked at Brian with sadness and disappointment in her eyes.

"The Federal Reserve Bank in Boston received another wire last night. This time it was from the Royal Bank of Canada. The amount was far less this time, ten million dollars exactly. The same note was on this wire that was on the first one. 'Compliments of Agent Christine Hendrix.' I just need to know how to explain this to the director, Christine. Can you help me out?"

"Yes, sir, I think I know where the money came from. That was the money that Clay had taken out of the cartel account when everything started. He was just going to use the money long enough to figure out how the account worked. Then he was going to put it back. The account was locked, though. He couldn't get the money out and he tried all night to do it. I was there, I saw him try. What is today?"

"The twenty-seventh."

"My guess is that if you count back fifteen months it would fall on July 27, 2005. That's the day he transferred the money and the trading account was supposed to start. The account was locked for fifteen months."

"I see."

"Is that all the money that was wired?"

"Yes, as far as I know. Why?"

"Because the trading account was supposed to have made hundreds of millions of dollars. I guess Clay was wrong. He did it for nothing. Everything happened for nothing," Christine said as she looked down in her chair.

"Well listen, that's all I wanted. Are you gonna be okay?"

Christine stood up which prompted Brian to stand as well. Christine looked at Brian, her eyes were filled with tears. She maintained her composure, nodded yes in response to his question, then turned and left his office. Brian watched her walk away. He knew that the young woman was in pain. He'd never asked her what had gone on in that house in Dallas. He never questioned her about the semen stains. He also never asked her what had gone on in Colombia. He knew that if she wanted to tell him she would when she was ready.

Christine walked back down the stairs and went back to her office. She sat down at her desk and swiveled her chair around so she could look out the window. She looked at the Washington, D.C. skyline and took a deep breath as a single tear fell from her eye and rolled slowly down her cheek. She didn't know how long she had been staring out the window when the beep of her computer startled her. It was the E-mail alarm and the monitor was notifying her that she had received some correspondence. Christine rolled her chair to the computer and placed her fingers on the keyboard. She entered the command which prompted the computer to display her new mail. She waited as the computer searched her file. The screen changed and she began reading the correspondence.

Christine,

I've always had a dream. A dream of meeting this really special girl. A beautiful girl. We would live on an island where the weather was always perfect, and the sunrise and sunsets were always beautiful and even intense. In my dream, we would hold each other as we watched the sun rise and set each day. We would make love on the beach, or wherever and whenever the mood struck us. We would swim naked in the moonlit sea and dance together slowly in the gentle rain. I would write her poems; she would greet me with a beautiful smile each morning. I would send her flowers and she would give me her heart. And I would love her with a passion she had never known before. I would make sure that each day we were together she knew, she understood what a special woman she was, and how lucky I felt that she had chosen me to spend the rest of her life with.

If this dream sounds familiar to you, it is. If you would like to meet a guy who has dreams like these, you have. If you would like to live this dream, then go to your window and blow me a kiss.

I love you.

Christine sat in shock at what she had just read. She could not move. She did not believe. It had to be a cruel hoax. Who could be so heartless as to play on her emotions like this? She clinched her teeth and grasped the arms of her chair with such force that her knuckles turned white. She did not want to look toward the window. Christine knew that he wouldn't be there. Clay was dead, he had to be. But who else knew about his dream. They had been alone together when he described it to her the first time in Dallas. It was after the first time they had made love. The only time they had made love.

Christine's pulse was racing, her breathing quickened. She had to look. She forced herself to stand from the chair. Her head was spinning and her knees trembled as she moved toward the window. She walked to the sill and placed her perspiring palms down upon it. She felt as though the windowsill was all that was holding her up. She closed her eyes tightly then lowered her head until it rested against the glass. She forced herself to slowly open her eyes. She had held them closed so tightly that it took a moment for her blurred vision to focus. Her eyes opened then as far as they could possibly go as she gazed at what could only be a vision from her mind. Her mouth dropped open and she attempted to scream, but she could not.

Clay Peterson stood on the street directly below her window. He wore a black tuxedo, held one dozen red roses, and stood next to a black stretch limousine. Christine stood in shock for a moment at the sight of him. Clay watched her intently, knowing how she was feeling. Christine watched him as he placed his open hand over his mouth and blew her a kiss. Christine could not control the tears of joy that now streamed down her face. Her hands covered her mouth as she stood shaking her head in disbelief. She slowly took her quivering hands away from her mouth and attempted to compose herself.

She focused on him, placed her open palm to her lips, returned the kiss, then dashed out of her office to be with him.